POE IN NORTHLIGHT

POE IN NORTHLIGHT

THE SCANDINAVIAN RESPONSE TO
HIS LIFE AND WORK

CARL L. ANDERSON

1973

DUKE UNIVERSITY PRESS

DURHAM, N.C.

© 1973, Duke University Press

L.C.C. card no. 72–88734

I.S.B.N. 0–8223–0275–6

PRINTED IN THE UNITED STATES OF
AMERICA BY HERITAGE PRINTERS, INC.

CONTENTS

v

ACKNOWLEDGMENTS

I record with pleasure my thanks for help of various kinds generously extended in the years during which this book was in the making.

I am grateful for financial aid granted by the Penrose Fund of the American Philosophical Society, the Duke Endowment, the Committee on International Studies at Duke University, the American Institute at Oslo University, and The American-Scandinavian Foundation;

—for the use of the facilities and services of Det kongelige Bibliotek in Copenhagen, Kungliga biblioteket in Stockholm, Universitetsbiblioteket in Oslo, the Alderman Library of the University of Virginia, and particularly the William R. Perkins Library of Duke University;

—for the kind assistance of Dr. Harry Järv at Kungliga biblioteket, of Miss Marete Licht at Det kongelige Bibliotek, of Mr. Carl Bergstrøm-Nielsen at Gyldendal Nordisk Forlag; and not least, for their careful attention to my numerous requests over the years for the purchase or loan of books, I am thankful to Miss Gertrude Merritt and Mr. Emerson Ford at the William R. Perkins Library;

—finally, for placing its *nihil obstat* on my request to include in this volume an English translation of Ola Hansson's essay on Edgar Allan Poe, I wish also to express my thanks to Tidens förlag, Stockholm.

Friends and colleagues who took precious time from their own concerns to abet me in one of mine deserve special thanks. I have drawn gratefully on the advice and suggestions of Professors Arlin

Turner, Sigmund Skard, and William H. Irving. In fairness to them I should add that they read my manuscript at an intermediary stage of its preparation.

The translations in the text, notes, and appendix are mine unless otherwise noted. Scandinavian titles are supplied at their first appearance with a literal English translation. For details of published translations of these works, some of them under several different English titles, the reader is referred to the lists included in Elias Bredsdorff, *Danish Literature in English Translation: A Bibliography* (Copenhagen, 1950); P. M. Mitchell, *A History of Danish Literature* (Copenhagen, 1957); Harald Beyer, *A History of Norwegian Literature* (New York, 1956); and Alrik Gustafson, *A History of Swedish Literature* (Minneapolis, 1961). Since the publication of these guides, some additional works pertinent to the discussion in the following pages have appeared or reappeared in English translation: Knut Hamsun's *Sult* (*Hunger* [New York, 1967]) and *Fra det moderne Amerikas Aandsliv* (*The Cultural Life of Modern America* [Cambridge, Mass., 1969]); J. P. Jacobsen's *Niels Lyhne* is again available in English under the same title (New York, 1967); essays and plays by Pär Lagerkvist have been collected in *Modern Theatre* (Lincoln, Nebraska, 1966); selected plays and letters by Ibsen and Strindberg and selected essays and prose fiction by Strindberg have been newly translated by several hands chiefly for the Oxford Ibsen, the New American Library, and Doubleday Anchor. Not included among these translations are several tales by Strindberg of present interest (*Tschandala, I havsbandet*, and "Hjärnornas kamp"), but they have been described in the text.

C. L. A.

POE IN NORTHLIGHT

CHAPTER 1

INTRODUCTION

Edgar Allan Poe has appealed to tastes as various no doubt in Scandinavia as they are elsewhere. His broadest appeal in Scandinavia has probably been as the writer of "horror stories" and murder mysteries. The first of Poe's work that was translated into a Scandinavian tongue, a Danish collection of "Tales" (*Fortællinger*) published in 1855, included fiction of this sort. Ever since then, Danish, Norwegian, and Swedish publishers have issued and reissued similar collections of "strange tales" and "fantastic stories." A Pan-Scandinavian society dedicated to conviviality and the study and practice of the art of the murder mystery calls itself the Poe Club and publishes in Copenhagen an annual, *Poe-Klubbens Årbog*, devoted to the genre.[1] Book reviewers use Poe's fiction as a touchstone for Gothic or romantic terror. Whether called "Rædselsromantik" (Danish), "redselsromantik" (Norwegian), or "skräckromantik" (Swedish), its association with Poe seems to be taken for granted.

---

1. *Årbog* 1970, ed. Tage la Cour, Harald Mogensen, and Åke Runnquist (Copenhagen, 1970), contains articles on "the crime novel in the 'seventies," "the saga and crime," "Dr. Watson and Subclavia Arteria," etc.

Professor Paul Rubow discusses Poe as the author of detective stories in "A. Conan Doyle," in *Epigonerne: Afhandlinger og Portrætter* (Copenhagen, 1956), pp. 124–130. Conan Doyle's stories, though indebted to Poe's, are said to take a brighter view of life, to repeat themselves (whereas each Poe story is essentially new), to go slack toward the end, and above all to allow the detective to become increasingly a comic figure (whereas Poe's Dupin is a kind of superman).

Historians of Scandinavian literature have for their part found Poe to be a convenient point of reference when commenting on their own writers' works of "strange beauty" or "strange horror." There are several such references to Poe in Vilhelm Andersen's history of Danish literature of the late nineteenth century. He finds, for example, "Edgar Poe's terrors" in a melodrama by Gustav Wied performed in 1892 about a woman's efforts to seek revenge by murdering her grandchild. And an obscure historical novel from 1903 by Laurids Bruun is said to tell of the fall of a family "as in Edgar Poe." Similarly, in a Swedish survey of that part of Strindberg's fiction which is set in Stockholm and its skerries, one of Strindberg's last tales is described as being "a real ghost story in the style of Edgar Allan Poe."[2]

No doubt such references serve their purpose, but they obscure the impress actually left by Poe's works on Scandinavian letters, especially in the last decade of the nineteenth century. It was then that Scandinavian interest in Poe reached its height in the "neoromantic" and symbolist reaction to naturalism. Writers suddenly found compelling reasons to know about Poe and to seek in his work implications for their own. They mentioned Poe in their letters, and they wrote essays about him; their poetry and fiction bore traces of his influence. French interest in Poe had inspired this enthusiasm, which at times plainly carried the mark of its derivation, yet Scandinavian interest in Poe had strong indigenous support and often followed paths of its own.

In tracing this interest, we face certain difficulties. Although the three Scandinavian countries are closely related geographically and culturally, they are nevertheless three distinct countries each with its own language and not simply a dialect, and each with its own

2. Carl S. Petersen and Vilhelm Andersen, eds., *Illustreret Dansk Litteraturhistorie* (Copenhagen, 1924–1934), vol. 4, Vilhelm Anderson, *Det nittende Aarhundredes anden Halvdel* (1925), pp. 646, 695; Walter Berendsohn, *August Strindbergs skärgårds- och Stockholmsskildringar* (Stockholm, 1962), p. 200.

literature, not merely a branch of one. These facts have obliged me to shift the reader's attention in the next two chapters from country to country and to bid him follow for each country a chronology beginning with the earliest notices and culminating in the enthusiasm for Poe shown in the early 1890s. It will then be in order in the two succeeding chapters to linger over the special interest taken in Poe by two Swedish writers, Ola Hansson and August Strindberg, before we proceed to a final chapter on the scattered interest shown in Poe after the 1890s.

An additional complication arises in consequence of the state of knowledge about Poe prevailing in Europe around 1890. Charles Baudelaire's biographical accounts and critical judgments of the 1850s were commonly still as persuasive as ever and found their way into Scandinavian criticism in many variations.[3] To be sure, other sources of information were becoming known, notably John H. Ingram's memoirs prefacing the editions of Poe's works that he began publishing in Edinburgh in 1874. George E. Woodberry's scholarly though negative biography of 1885 became known on the whole too late to supply some needed corrections of fact. Facts were, however, in no very great demand. The Reverend Griswold's perfidy in tampering with the facts of Poe's biography was often noted, but most writers on Poe were content to accept Baudelaire's anguished account of Poe's life and to place their own emphasis on the unfathomable and obscure qualities of both his life and work.

Here yet another complication arises. Interest in Poe was often interest rather in a current image of Poe. By the nature of the role

---

3. An extreme version of the Baudelairean concept of Poe appeared as late as 1928 in a Danish review of Régis Michaud's survey of American literature. Remarking that the level of writing achieved by such "neorealists" as Sinclair Lewis and Theodore Dreiser had been reached in the past only by a very few Americans, such as Henry James and Edgar Poe, Kai Friis-Møller added, "Poe was punished for his arrogance by being totally ignored in his lifetime." *Skribenter og Bøger* (Copenhagen, 1942), p. 307.

assigned to him in the symbolist movement, he was made out to be an elusive and tantalizingly mysterious figure. It is perhaps not too fanciful to liken Poe in this role to the famous nicker or nix of Scandinavian folklore, or rather to a contemporary romanticized version. In the first years of the 1880s the Swedish painter Ernst Josephson adopted the nicker as a subject for a series of paintings, one of which now hangs in the National Museum in Stockholm, a striking though somewhat labored impressionistic depiction of this spirit of the waters, half-demon and half-divine, a fallen Israfel, it may be, coaxing from the fiddle held to his breast the tunes that if found acceptable will win his return to heaven. Poe of the 1890s is an urbanized, displaced version of Ernst Josephson's nicker, an anguished spirit from another world condemned to suffer the horrors of "la cité fourmillante." An obscure being, he is yet strangely, hauntingly real. Again and again the realness of the "unreal," of the irrational element in Poe's fiction and poetry, is insisted upon in the references made in this time. He was the poet of the soul, attuned to all the hidden currents in the spirit of man. Mere facts were of little importance in support of such a representation.

Given these difficulties in defining Poe's role in the literature of perhaps the most heterogeneous decade of the nineteenth century, it has seemed prudent, if not altogether just, to suggest in the following pages the possibility of influence only when definite evidence could be adduced. Any other course would have been unworkable.

Although Scandinavian interest in Poe was, like the French, rooted in Poe's genius for rational analysis of the irrational, we will do well to realize from the outset that it did not produce the profound effects on Scandinavian literature that have been claimed for Poe's influence on French literature. In France, the symbolist poet Charles Morice was able in 1889 to look back in his book *La Littérature de tout à l'heure* on the growth of half a century of

French commentary on Poe and argue that Poe's sense of "the grotesque and the horrible" had actuated a complete reordering of French romanticism: "V. Hugo saw [these qualities] only from the outside. Quasimodo is merely a vulgar monster, his one claim to our interest the hump on his back. It is within the soul, the heart, and above all within the mind of man that Poe sees the grotesque; and it is to our souls, and not our eyes, that he appeals." Patrick F. Quinn, quoting this passage in *The French Face of Edgar Poe*, qualifies the claim but believes that it nevertheless points directly to the reason one might go even further: "It was the discovery of Poe by Baudelaire that finally brought France into the mainstream of modern literature. For here was a writer who combined . . . a sense of form and a respect for the intellect with . . . the ability to move as in dreams through the depths of the mind and to illuminate the kind of verities the reason knows not of."[4] Poe's influence in Scandinavia came at least a decade too late to produce any such effect as this, and it was felt only in concert with numerous other influences. Although not so diffuse nor so varied as in France, it has to be sought in a tangle of new and old, native and foreign currents of literary history.

The 1890s, as diversified and turbulent a period in Scandinavia as it was elsewhere, concluded a century of social, political, and economic upheaval that left a deep mark on literature. The processes of democratization, though not yet complete, had accelerated rapidly during the century until through a series of parliamentary acts monarchy in the three countries had been left at the last with little more than nominal power. Free access to education and culture for everyone had become an established principle if not yet a reality. One of the most urgent issues, given the rapid rise of industry, especially in Sweden, was the equitable redistribution of

4. *The French Face of Edgar Poe* (Carbondale, Ill., 1957), pp. 44–45. The quotation from Morice's book appears on pp. 40–41.

wealth and income; labor had begun aggressively organizing its newly discovered powers, socialism was a new and highly inflammatory economic and political topic, and the women's rights movement, much advanced in Norway and Sweden, was turning ever more militant. The inevitable conservative reaction to all this change was both stubborn and harsh, and controversy was at times bitter and deeply divisive. Science and industry, abetted by revolutionary ideas of social and political reform, were well on the way to transforming bleak, straitened, isolated Scandinavia into prosperous and increasingly cosmopolitan welfare states. It was inevitable that provincialism in taste and manners would come under heavy attack. Scandinavian writers of the 1870s and 1880s soon discovered two particularly fertile subjects: the hypocritical complacency of conventional mores and the bankruptcy of conventional religion. They created with these and other subjects a whole new epoch in their literary history, the beginnings of modernism. When some of their work—most notably, the plays of Henrik Ibsen—became known outside Scandinavia, it exercised a similar influence there as well. By the late 1880s, however, this new literature was already showing signs of having spent much of its original energy. The rising generation of writers became increasingly restive and felt that a change was overdue. It was in their reaction to the preceding decades' dominance of naturalism and social realism that they became fascinated with new literary developments in France, including the election of "Edgar Poe," as the French insisted on naming him, to preside over the poetic activities of the *décadents* and *symbolistes*.

The winds of change blew first in the isles of Denmark. During much of the nineteenth century Copenhagen was one of the liveliest centers for the arts in all Europe. In "the Athens of the North" Thorvaldsen's sculpture and Bournonville's ballet could be seen, and there Grundtvig, Kierkegaard, H. C. Andersen, Oehlenschläger, J. L. Heiberg, and Georg Brandes lectured and wrote. Its theaters and publishing houses were the foremost in Scandinavia, and it was there that every Scandinavian writer—Danish, Swedish, and Norwegian alike—realized that he would do well to win approval if he wished for more than local fame. Publication and critical acclaim in Copenhagen were virtually prerequisite for publication in Germany, France, and the rest of Europe. In the 1870s and 1880s the most powerful literary personage in Copenhagen was Georg Brandes, internationally known as a critic, literary historian, and lecturer. His brother Edvard Brandes served as editor of the liberal newspaper *Politiken* (founded in 1884) and was an author and critic in his own right. Although *Politiken* was not the only publication to which new writers could look for sympathetic reviews, its approval carried with it the possibility of notice also from Georg Brandes. Georg Brandes had brought back to Denmark from lengthy tours of Germany, France, and England a broad acquaintance with the literature of those countries as well as strong democratic, anticlerical convictions. The first four volumes of his *Main Currents in Nineteenth Century Literature* (as the English translation was entitled) appeared during the 1870s and established his reputation as a polemical yet perceptive critic with a remarkable talent for appraising whole periods of literature. For at least two generations *Main Currents* introduced important fields of European literature to Scandinavian students and set a standard for writing fluent and energetic literary criticism of a liberal persuasion. After writing a series of book-length studies of individual authors, Brandes published in 1883 a landmark in Scandinavian literary history, *Det moderne Gjennembruds Mænd* [The men of the modern breakthrough]. This collection of lectures, given originally at the University of Copenhagen beginning in 1871, argued the presence in Scandinavia of a truly modern literature in the work of Bjørnstjerne Bjørnson, Henrik Ibsen, J. P. Jacobsen, and others. Brandes had developed his definition of modernism in literature from his reading of French naturalism and particularly of Zola's literary criticism. He had also adopted Taine's deterministic views of the influence of milieu and heredity on artistic creativity, and in essays on the novels of Balzac and Stendhal he traced the beginnings of social and psychological realism in modern fiction. The position he took in his book on "the modern breakthrough" in Scandinavia was a logical extension of his advocacy in these essays of "objective" narration and of his defense of the social value of literature. Indeed, in the earliest of his university lectures he had announced that the surest indication of modernism in literature was its willingness to place moral, social, and religious issues under debate.[5] Conservative critics and genteel idealists denounced "Brandesianism" and the work of the modern writers praised by Brandes as atheistic and immoral, but liberal critics and aspiring young writers followed Brandes in seeing in this literature the beginnings of a new era of social and cultural progress in Scandinavia. Strindberg tells in chapters 8 and 9 of *Jäsningstiden* [Time of ferment] (Stockholm, 1886), the second part of his autobiographical novel *Tjänstekvinnans son* [The son of a servant], of the impact that Bjørnson and Ibsen had made in Sweden and of the sensation caused by the publication of Brandes's essays in a Stockholm news-

5. Brandes succinctly restated this position in Kristiania in 1883 in an article in *Dagbladet*: "In our time in the North all literature that has vitality and strength will of necessity be critical of society" (quoted in Francis Bull et al., *Norsk litteraturhistorie* [Oslo, 1961], vol. 5, A. H. Winsnes, *Norges litteratur: Fra 1880-årene til første verdenskrig*, Ny utgave, p. 38). Also quoting this passage, Hans Lindström, *Hjärnornas kamp* (Uppsala, 1952), pp. 20–22, points out nevertheless that Brandes is often misinterpreted as having inflexibly insisted in the 1880s on the need for airing social issues in literature. Only occasionally did he do so to the exclusion of all else. In 1880 Strindberg criticized him for being too much the esthete and reactionary, and in 1883 Brandes found himself admonishing fru Leffler, a leading lady author of protest literature, to put "less controversy, more psychology" into her work. In the 1880s Brandes began moving toward the cults of genius and aristocratism that have parallels in Ola Hansson's Poe essay (see chapter 4) and that Brandes fully developed in his lectures on Nietzsche in the spring of 1888. See Karl-Erik Lundevall, *Från åttital till nittital* (Stockholm, 1953), p. 285.

paper in 1870 calling for the emancipation of Scandinavian literature from pallid "estheticism."[6] In place of estheticism had in fact
come social realism and naturalism, principally in fiction and drama.
Unlike French naturalism, however, Scandinavian naturalism took a
strongly moral, even at times theological, tone, and its standards of
exactness and objectivity were derived chiefly from *Madame Bovary*.
On the whole, Scandinavian naturalism did not follow the quasi-
scientific and deterministic example of late French naturalism.[7]

So convincing had Brandes been in arguing the modernity of his
Scandinavian contemporaries that when the inevitable reaction to
naturalism occurred, it was on his head that the coals were heaped.
"Brandesianism" became a term of opprobrium designating to the
rising generation of writers what seemed no longer new and modern
but limited and stale. Nor were these aspirants to literature, who
were to become the writers read and commented upon in the 1890s,
above disparaging and deploring the work of even the most distinguished of the Scandinavian naturalists, Ibsen. Their protest, however, was not exclusively negative; they were convinced that
naturalism and social protest literature had been obliged by definition to neglect utterly two subjects of supreme importance for
literature, the human soul and the ideal of beauty. Their own commitment to these two subjects led them into taking positions highly
characteristic of the 1890s. They learned, for one thing, that Ribot's
studies of the personality and Bernheim's and Charcot's studies of
hypnotism, in which the French naturalists had already found
much of interest, opened up for poetry as well as for science new
ways of probing the hidden, secret life of man. In the second place,
they discovered that *décadence* and *symbolisme*, which constituted
the principal French reaction to naturalism, suggested possibilities

6. August Strindberg, *Samlade skrifter* 18 (Stockholm, 1920): 354–355,
376–377.
7. Sten Linder, *Ernst Ahlgren i hennes romaner* (Stockholm, 1930), pp.
7–9; Torbjörn Nilsson, *Impressionisten Herman Bang* (Stockholm, 1965),
p. 29.

in poetry for transcendence and for self-fulfillment not limited, as in naturalism, to the gratification of the flesh or the survival of the species. In the third place, many were persuaded that the most subjective—and by their definition, therefore the most precious—impressions available to the human spirit could find their authentic expression best in lyric poetry. Finally, for a few, religion, particularly Roman Catholicism, offered late in the decade yet another sort of promise of possible transcendence and self-fulfillment, one that was sanctified in an ancient and richly textured faith.

In all but the last of these typical interests of the writers of the 1890s, Edgar Allan Poe's life and work supplied valuable insights and at times served as principal example. The Baudelairean exhibition of Poe's sensitivity and suffering was of no less interest to the new writers than the acuity and daring of the psychological insights of his fiction and the elaborate harmonies of his verse. "Out of space, out of time," they were fond of quoting, for Poe had written of nothing less than the longing of the soul for its proper habitation, a region where the ticking clock of naturalistic time could not be heard. In a lecture given in Sweden in 1913, the Danish poet and playwright Helge Rode, remembering Brandes's term "the modern breakthrough" to describe the 1870s, looked back on the 1890s and called it the period of "spiritual breakthrough." It was more than an era of lyricism, he said; it had at least given him something tantamount to a religious experience in William James's sense. Naming Strindberg, the Norwegians Arne Garborg and Sigbjørn Obstfelder, and the Dane Jakob Knudsen, he declared that in them and in many of their contemporaries "we find a craving for a new law of life or in any case for a new illumination of life, and what is common to them all is mysticism."[8] For Rode it was Nietzsche, in his view a great religious figure, who filled this need better than had any other. For others, the craving for a new law or a new illumina-

8. "Det sjælelige Gennembrud," in Det sjælelige Gennembrud: Udvalgte Kritiker II (Copenhagen, 1928), p. 23.

tion of life was usually of a more purely literary character; for them, Edgar Allan Poe's life and work held peculiar significance. They explored the mysteries of the unconscious self not only in a study of the new psychological literature but also in their reading of Poe's fiction and poetry. In both they discovered grounds for the new symbolism and the new lyricism of the 1890s.

CHAPTER 2

DENMARK

The beginning years of Danish interest in Poe gave little indication of the varied character of later interest either in Denmark
or in Norway and Sweden. Translations, for one thing, were slow
in coming. Baudelaire's energy and devotion as a translator of Poe
found no counterpart in Scandinavia. Indeed, beginning with the
publication in Copenhagen in 1855 of *Fortællinger* [Tales], a Danish translation of seven stories—"The Tell-Tale Heart," "The Cask
of Amontillado," "A Tale of the Ragged Mountains," " 'Thou Art
the Man,' " "The Black Cat," "The Oblong Box," and "The Pit
and the Pendulum"—most Scandinavian translation of Poe has
been limited to a small group of tales, a handful of poems, and
excerpts from the criticism.

The seven stories published in 1855 seem to have disappeared
from view almost at once. When a second volume of translated
tales appeared twelve years later, the translator supplied an introduction, chiefly biographical, in which he could recall only the
previous publication in Danish of "an odd story or two" as feuille-
tons unaccompanied by any notice of the author. It is therefore
wholly to be expected, he wrote, that Danish readers will ask, "Who
is Edgar Poe? . . . Is he a real person? Where is his home? What
does he do? etc., etc., and I candidly admit that it was not long ago
that I asked the same questions."[1] The translator was Robert Watt,

1. "Edgar Poe. Biografiske Notitser," in Edgar Allan Poe, *Phantastiske*

who was also to translate within the next few years several volumes of Bret Harte's stories, Mark Twain's sketches, and the work of other American humorists. In 1872–1873 he published a three-volume travel book on America, but he had had his first travel experiences in an English-speaking country as a youthful emigrant to Australia. On his return to Denmark he had got into publishing and in 1866 founded *Figaro*, a weekly paper which merged two years later with a daily newspaper, *Dagbladet*. In its brief lifetime *Figaro* published in Watt's translation three tales by Poe—"A Descent into the Maelström," "The Purloined Letter," and "The Tell-Tale Heart"—as well as the biographical notice that served as the introduction to his volume of Poe's fiction. The volume contained the three stories from *Figaro* and six others: "The Murders in the Rue Morgue," "The Black Cat," "The Oval Portrait," "The Oblong Box," "Eleonora," "The Gold Bug," and "The Tell-Tale Heart."

Robert Watt explained in his introduction that it was the expatriate Danish critic P. L. Møller who had first mentioned Poe's name to him one day in Paris and had urged him to read "the strange productions of America's most richly imaginative author."[2] Watt reported the attention recently paid to Poe in *Revue des deux mondes* and the numerous translations that had appeared in France, particularly those by William L. Hughes;

Fortællinger, trans. Robert Watt (Copenhagen, 1868), p. i. It is evident from Watt's reference to the previous translations that they were of "The Gold Bug" and "The Murders in the Rue Morgue." The three stories in his volume that had been previously published in *Figaro* were "I Malströmmen" (no. 66, 30 June 1867, and no. 67, 7 July), "Det stjaalne Brev" ["The Purloined Letter"] (no. 70, 28 July, and no. 71, 4 August), and "Et Hjertes Banken" ["The Tell-Tale Heart"] (no. 77, 15 September). The introduction, "Biografiske Notitser," appeared in *Figaro* (no. 65, 23 June).

2. "Edgar Poe. Biografiske Notitser," p. i. P. L. Møller, who had settled in Paris in 1851, died after several months' illness in Rouen on 6 December 1865. Watt would therefore have met Møller in Paris two or more years before writing his biographical notice for *Figaro*.

but perhaps [as Poe's translator] the French writer Charles Baudelaire has been the most successful. In any case no one has occupied himself with Poe with greater admiration and devotion, in witness whereof are the introductory remarks accompanying the first volume of tales he published. That his work has been appreciated by the public is attested by the numerous editions it has run to and the epoch-making effect which the young poet's work has had on French literature.[3]

Watt then reviewed the life of Poe as described by Baudelaire:

His whole life, Baudelaire says, was a long tragedy, and his death was horrible; for him America was nothing but an enormous prison through which he hastened frenetically as though he were a creature intended for a different and better world; and even his deplorable vices were only [the result of] a constant endeavour to escape the influence of this atmosphere, which was so antipathetic to him.[4]

Watt's book of Poe translations, although dated 1868, followed the common practice of appearing in the bookstalls in time for the previous Christmas season. It was reviewed anonymously in three newspapers in December. The critic at *Berlingske Tidende* considered the American author now being introduced "for the first time" to Danish readers to be "more an interesting figure than someone genuinely appealing. There are indications in the tales, at least in several of them, of a quite special talent, doomed, however, to extinction in the maelstrom of a wild and extremely unhappy life," an impression that was confirmed for the critic by the biographical information supplied in Watt's introduction. In *Dagbladet's* review Poe's stories—the product, it was said, of narrative powers unusual for their vividness—were described as examples nevertheless "of an

3. "Edgar Poe. Biografiske Notitser," p. ii.
4. "Edgar Poe. Biografiske Notitser," p. ii.

unlovely, crazed [uskjøn, delirerende] imagination, fortunately equally unusual, which feeds on horrible fears and is inflamed by a kind of drink that does not flow from Castaly's spring." The author's talents are so formidable that he remains of interest despite the esthetic revulsion that his work arouses; he appears, to judge from both the stories themselves and Hr. Watt's introduction, to be a man ruined by drink. "Alongside the demented, appalling fantasies there are traces in the stories of the often marvelous sagacity and instinct for association that the insane possess." The book has this much to recommend it, that it bears witness to "untamed powers and to a rich but damaged spiritual organism that mixes the beautiful with the hideous." The reviewer for *Dags-Telegrafen* was content to recommend Watt's translations of Poe to the newspaper's readers "as a work of interest in several respects."[5]

A few days before the appearance of these notices, a young student of natural history at the University of Copenhagen, soon to become the principal Danish translator and popularizer of Darwin and, as the author of important naturalistic novels, one of Georg Brandes's "men of the modern breakthrough," recorded in his diary: "Today wrote the poem 'det er dejligt at leve i Drømmenes Land' [It is lovely to live in the land of dreams]; read in *Phantastiske Fortællinger* by Edgard Poe," and the next day, 18 December, "Finished reading Edgard Poe . . . ."[6] J. P. Jacobsen made no further reference to Poe, but he adopted, evidently from Watt's mention of it in his introduction, Poe's term *arabesque*. He used it both as a title and as a common designation for a small number of poems that have sometimes been regarded as representing a new departure

5. *Berlingske politiske og Avertissements-Tidende*, no. 297, 20 December 1867; *Dagbladet*, no. 295, 19 December 1867; *Dags-Telegrafen*, no. 345, 20 December 1867. Publication of *Phantastiske Fortællinger* was announced for the week of 30 November–3 December (*Nordisk Boghandlertidende*, 2, no. 23 [4 December 1867]).

6. J. P. Jacobsen, "En begavet ung Mands Dagbog," in *Samlede Værker*, ed. Morten Borup (Copenhagen, 1927), 3: 11.

in Danish poetry. Georg Brandes praised Jacobsen's "En arabesk" as a poem "that strikes an entirely new tone in Danish poetry, with emotions expressed in the symbolism of plants and flowers, with something Shakespearean in the wildness of its passion, and with something of H. C. Andersen in its loving immersion in nature."[7] To a later critic, Oluf Friis, the arabesque poems seemed modern indeed but monstrously so in their disregard of form and therefore not to be compared with Jacobsen's poems written in the tradition of the folksong and of the hymn.[8] In any case, Jacobsen—unpublished, uncertain still of his talent and unsure of his technique, gradually abandoning the historical romance of his earliest poetry in favor of intense little monologues—read Poe at a critical moment in his search for a distinctive style. The evidence suggests that he profited from his reading. On the basis of linguistic evidence in the arabesque poems, Frederik Nielsen, a leading student of Jacobsen's work, conjectures that Jacobsen continued his study of Poe beyond his reading of Watt's translations, and he adds:

> Jacobsen's interest in Poe is not surprising. The world of decay, horror, and perversity which is often latent in Poe's poetic prose must have fascinated Jacobsen. He read Poe as he read Shakespeare's depictions of insanity, disintegration, and devotion, or as he read Swinburne's luxuriant, profuse poetry about Our Lady of Pain, or Oehlenschläger's sensuous tragedy of the revenge of a king and a queen. And connected with this is the fact that precisely at the close of the 1860's Jacobsen was preoccupied with the passions of madness; his tragic conception [in a long early poetic romance, "Hervert Sperring"] of Hervert's death by elfshot is in itself a Poe motif just as is his variation of the dead, doomed king's wild

7. Georg Brandes, *Det moderne Gjennembruds Mænd*, 2d ed. (Copenhagen, 1891), p. 153.
8. Oluf Friis, "J. P. Jacobsen i Belysning af hans efterladte Papirer," *Tilskueren*, 46, pt. 1 (1929): 149–164.

nightride. Of these experiences, literary and real, he writes in the poems he calls arabesques.[9]

Jacobsen's "En arabesk," tentatively dated 1868 by his editors, is a poem of fifty-six lines on the murderously passionate nature of love. It contains in the second section what may be two slight echoes from Poe, the first from "The Tell-Tale Heart," the other from "Ligeia":

Har du faret i dunkle Skove?
Kjender du Pan?
Jeg har følt ham,
Ikke i de dunkle Skove,
Medens alt Tiende talte,
Nej, den Pan har jeg aldrig kjent,
Men Kjærlighedens Pan har jeg følt,—
Da tav alt talende.

I solvarme Egne
Vokser en sælsom Urt,
Kun i dybeste Tavshed
Under tusinde Solstraalers Brand
Aabner den sin Blomst
I et flygtigt Sekund.
Den ser ud som en gal Mands Øje,
Som et Ligs røde Kinder:
Den har jeg set
I min Kjærlighed.[10]

9. Frederik Nielsen, *J. P. Jacobsen, Digteren og mennesket* (Copenhagen, 1953), pp. 306, 331–332. Although Jacobsen knew English and practiced writing and speaking it with his friend H. S. Vodskov, his adoption of "Edgard," common in France as the spelling of Poe's Christian name, suggests that he had already read of Poe in French sources before his Christmas purchase of the Danish translations, and that this is the "further" study of Poe conjectured by Nielsen.

10. *Samlede Værker*, 9th ed. (Copenhagen, 1923), 1: 330.

Have you roamed in deep forests?
Have you met Pan?
I have known him.
Not in the deep forests
Where all silence spoke.
No, that Pan I have never met.
But the Pan of Love I have known—
Then all speaking fell into silence.

In sunbathed regions
Grows a rare plant.
Only in the deepest silence
In the flame of a thousand sunbeams
Does its blossom open
In a fleeting second.
It looks like the eye of a madman,
Like the red cheeks of a corpse:
This I have seen
In my love.

Whether the horror expressed in this poem and others derives, however, by any direct route from Jacobsen's reading of Poe is impossible to say. Frederik Nielsen believes that in "Monomani," "Jacobsen learned from Poe to write with diffuse vagueness [uklar ubestemmelighed] that both conceals and reveals. For what passes here for monomania is in other places called disability," revelatory of the poet's own psychic situation; thus "madness is transformed into poetry."[11] Nielsen finds resemblances in the form and style of "Nævner min Tanke dig" [Should you enter my thoughts], a poem on the terrible transiency of love, to the visions of the beloved in Poe's "Berenice" and "Eleonora," but the resemblances, if granted, are not demonstrable.[12] A poem not mentioned by Nielsen as pos-

11. Nielsen, *J. P. Jacobsen*, p. 335.
12. Nielsen, *J. P. Jacobsen*, p. 338.

sibly bearing traces of Poe influence is "Det er Stævnemødets Time" [It is the trysting hour]. The rising hysteria of a woman waiting for her lover has as a subject no direct counterpart in Poe, and the poem as a whole reads like a ballad, only the essence of the story having been told; yet its heavy use, unusual for Jacobsen, of anaphora, repetition of lines, assonance, and alliteration is suggestive of devices characteristic of Poe's verse—but also, it must be added, of Swinburne's, with which Jacobsen was also familiar. A few lines from the second section of the poem may suffice as illustration:

> Og jeg glædes, og jeg ængstes,
> Bliver rød og bliver bleg.
> Ganske stille vil jeg sidde,
> Jeg vil nynne,
> Hvis jeg kunde!
> Men jeg mangler næsten Aande.
> Ganske stille vil jeg sidde,
> Jeg vil stirre paa hans Billed.
> Nu han kommer—kommer ikke,
> Nu han kommer—kommer ikke,
> Kommer ikke—kommer ikke.[13]

> And I rejoice, and I anguish,
> Blush and turn pale.
> I will sit quite still,
> I will hum,
> If I could!
> But I am almost breathless.
> I will sit quite still,
> I will gaze upon his picture.
> Now he comes—comes not,
> Now he comes—comes not,
> Comes not—comes not.

13. *Samlede Værker*, 9th ed., 1: 335–336.

Jacobsen received Georg Brandes's praise for his poetry only after having first published fiction. It was above all as a naturalistic novelist, the author of *Mogens* (1872), *Fru Marie Grubbe* (1876), and *Niels Lyhne* (1881), that he became one of Brandes's "men of the modern breakthrough." The novels benefited stylistically from Jacobsen's exercises in arabesque verse, but they seem otherwise to have carried over from the verse nothing attributable to Poe's influence. The evidence shown in Jacobsen's fiction of his studies in current psychology was perhaps linked with his reading of Poe, but anything more than this, though it has been suggested, can scarcely be demonstrated. Two of Jacobsen's short stories, "Et Skud i Taagen" [A shot in the fog] from 1875 and "To Verdener" [Two worlds] from 1879, are said, because of the pathological, compulsive behavior that they depict, to have been written with Poe's fiction in mind. Both stories, however, are narrated naturalistically, and quite apart from what they may owe in mood or style to the arabesque poems, they remain essentially objective in method and owe nothing in construction, motif, or diction to Poe.[14]

Herman Bang is another major writer closely associated in Dan-

14. Brita Tigerschiöld, *J. P. Jacobsen och hans roman Niels Lyhne* (Göteborg, 1945), suggests that Poe's influence, though slight in the novel *Niels Lyhne*, becomes "fully apparent" (pp. 82–83) in the two short stories. "Et Skud i Taagen," *Samlede Skrifter*, 9th ed. (Copenhagen, 1923), 2: 336–354, is a story of self-destructive revenge. A rejected lover kills his rival in the fog while they are seal-hunting. The girl marries a third man, who later falls into debt to the rejected lover and forges his name on promissory notes. He is apprehended; his wife, weak from recent childbirth, dies. The rejected lover has had full revenge, but with that his life is essentially finished, and he dies on the beach, also in the fog. "To Verdener" (pp. 357–363), takes as its theme the power of suggestion. A woman is cured of her illness by following the advice of an old crone to throw a bunch of twigs and flowers at the first healthy woman to pass by. But the cured woman is filled with remorse over having visited her illness on another and commits suicide. In a final scene the second woman passes by once more, now a bride and, mysteriously, not ill at all. Neither story seems even remotely derived from Poe.

ish literary history with "the modern breakthrough." Like Jacobsen, he acquainted himself with much of the new psychological literature that formed part of French naturalism. His novel *Haabløse Slægter* [Lost generations, 1880], a tale of the *décadent* William Høg and his alter ego Bernhard Hoff, preceded by four years the appearance of Huysmans's classic novel of *décadence, A Rebours*. But whereas Huysmans's hero Des Esseintes openly acknowledges Poe to be his model, Bang's sources lay within his own family experience. Many years later, Bang possibly had Poe's "fantastic tales" (as a group, rather than individual tales) in mind while writing two of the three stories published in 1907 in the volume *Sælsomme Fortællinger* [Strange tales]. Both stories, written when Bang was in poor health, seem contrived and are perhaps the least effective of his fiction. Only in the possible borrowing of a detail from "The Tell-Tale Heart" does one of them suggest any direct influence from Poe.[15]

J. P. Jacobsen's poetic prose and his and Herman Bang's use of ideas emanating chiefly from French psychological studies are early signs of trends that indirectly contributed to the reaction to naturalism in the late 1880s and early 1890s. In 1879 Bang had confidently advanced the premise (adopted from Taine) that since "one's emotional life is infinitely more complex than has previously

15. Harry Jacobsen, *Den tragiske Herman Bang* (Copenhagen, 1966), pp. 178–182. Bang's " 'Barchan er død'—" ['Barchan is dead'—], *Fortællinger* (Copenhagen, 1912), vol. 2, *Værker i Mindeudgave*, pp. 559–572, is an elaborate frame story of psychic murder. The psychological effect of the false report of a mutual acquaintance's death is to cause the death of the person to whom it has been reported when he finds his friend still alive. The bloodshot eye that stares accusingly in both the first and second inner story was perhaps borrowed from "The Tell-Tale Heart," but rather than acting as a point of psychic fixation, it is, like the symptoms in Strindberg's *Creditors*, an effect which by being duplicated turns into a cause. Psychic murder is also the subject of "Stærkest" [The strongest], pp. 584–626. Harry Jacobsen suggests that a "Poesque mood" is present in the story; no details of an influence are apparent.

been supposed," to truly know "the soul's anatomy" the writer must "collect observations with the zeal of a scientist,"[16] but this "scientific" method had begun within a decade to yield to intuitive studies of the psyche, supported or encouraged nevertheless by medical studies probing with increasing subtlety what was already being commonly denoted "the unconscious." A typical sign of the revolt in France against narrowly interpreted, second-rate naturalism was a long article in *La Nouvelle revue* in 1884 on the nature and history of naturalism. The article concluded that "le naturalisme pessimiste et matérialiste passera; il passe déjà"; the new literature to come would perceive in man "le corps et l'esprit, l'action du dehors et la réaction du dedans."[17] It was the latter—"la réalité intérieure," as another critic in the same journal put it[18]—that was now to receive major emphasis. The literary exploration in the following years of man's inner reality did little to relieve the gloom of naturalistic pessimism; often it deepened it in studies of the strange or morbid tastes and decadent behavior of a dying civilization or defied it in a cult of artificiality and in the search for "pure" art.

Over the French scene of these new activities the pale features of Edgar Poe floated constantly into view; his name was invoked almost ritualistically on all sides. Barbey d'Aurevilly, who since 1853 had been disposed to dismiss Poe as insincere or mad or as a literary curiosity, was obliged to acknowledge in 1889 that it was Poe and Baudelaire who "had become the most striking expression of modern poetry. They were the kings of that poetry which was enthroned on the tomb of the poetry of the Past—the poetry of serenity, idealism, luminosity! They were the poetry of *spleen*, of nerves, and of the *frisson* in an old materialistic and depraved civili-

16. "Litt om dansk Realisme," in *Realisme og Realister* (Copenhagen, 1879), p. 10.
17. George Renard, "Le Naturalisme contemporain," *La Nouvelle revue*, 6 (1884), tome 28, p. 84.
18. Gabriel Sarrazin, "La Littérature psychologique actuelle," *La Nouvelle revue*, 11 (1889), tome 57, p. 303.

zation."[19] Ferdinand Brunetière, defending the classical premise that art must be, or at least must begin in, an imitation of nature, denounced in 1888 the influence of Poe and Baudelaire as well as of E. T. A. Hoffmann on the new literature, the artificial literature of *décadence* and *symbolisme*.[20] Poe's influence on this literature appears in fact to have been largely supposititious; it was often confused in the 1880s with expressions of interest in his work or with mere ubiquity of reference.[21] For many, Poe evidently was less an author to be read—apart, perhaps, from a few standard pieces—than a motif. The motif, however, had been made singularly appropriate and timely through Baudelaire's portrayal of Poe as the victim of the counting-house mentality of a civilization that was, like ancient Rome, clearly on the road to extinction. Poe seems to have satisfied the need for a focal figure around which to organize the conviction that art—above all, the art of poetry—is the redeeming spiritual activity of man.[22] He appeared in this guise in the essays of Paul Bourget, the first important theorist of *décadence*, and in *A Rebours* as a kindred spirit to Des Esseintes.[23] In both

19. *XIXme siècle: Les Œuvres et les hommes: Les Poètes* (Paris, 1889), pp. 323–324. A summary of d'Aurevilly's comments on Poe is given in George D. Morris, *Fenimore Cooper et Edgar Poe* (Paris, 1912), pp. 89–95. See also Quinn, *The French Face of Edgar Poe*, pp. 47–49.

20. "Revue littéraire: Symbolistes et décadens," *Revue des deux mondes*, 58 (1888, 3ème période), tome 90, p. 222.

21. Joseph Chiari, *Symbolisme from Poe to Mallarmé: The Growth of a Myth* (London, 1956), pp. 69–71, 80, assembles statements by Léon Lemonnier, Mansell Jones, and others to refute Henri Mondor's positive view of Poe's significance to Mallarmé. Chiari, rating Poe as a minor Tennyson, rejects the possibility of Poe's influence on Mallarmé or on *symboliste* poetry in general (pp. 113–116). Quinn, *The French Face of Edgar Poe*, pp. 53–54, notes *symboliste* interest in Poe's poetry and critical ideas and the weight that Poe's name carried in *symboliste* discussions. He concludes that Poe was "the source of guidance and inspiration"—but not of influence—in the *symboliste* movement.

22. Angelo P. Bertocci, *From Symbolism to Baudelaire* (Carbondale, Ill., 1964), p. 44.

23. Bourget's essays were collected in *Essais de psychologie contemporaine* (Paris, 1885). C. P. Cambiaire, *The Influence of Poe in France* (New York, 1927), pt. 3, chap. 8, summarizes references to Poe in *A Rebours*.

Bourget and Huysmans an intense admiration of Baudelaire required that homage be rendered Poe as, variously, the priest of Beauty and the prophet of the autonomy of art, the exemplar of disciplined creativity (as opposed to "inspiration"), and the martyred victim of a corrupt civilization.

In Denmark the French reaction to Zolaesque naturalism seems at first to have gone largely unnoticed, but in 1890 Johannes Jørgensen, the author a few years later of an essay on Poe and one of Poe's Danish translators, wrote a long article on "Det nyeste Frankrig" [The newest France]. For two decades, Jørgensen wrote, "France was realism, positivism, naturalism—was Zola, Flaubert, Taine, and at its height, Goncourt. France was Pasteur, who performed miracles with the microscope; it was Charcot and Bernheim, who imitated scientifically the ecstasies and the stigmatizations of the Middle Ages. Only in the most recent years has this come into question." The article reviewed recent developments in French literature and concluded with a quotation from Edouard Rod on the modern need for something better than the relentlessly monotonous picture of ourselves given in naturalism.[24]

Jørgensen, active in the early 1890s as both poet and critic, is probably best known outside Denmark for his autobiography *Mit Livs Legende* (7 vols., 1916–1928; entitled *Jørgensen, An Autobiography*, in an abridged English translation) and for his lives of St. Francis, St. Catherine, and St. Bridget, all written after his conversion to Roman Catholicism in February 1896. In the second volume (1916) of the autobiography he looked back to the year 1890 and recalled from *Also Sprach Zarathustra* the lines "Die Welt ist tief, / und tiefer als der Tag gedacht" that had rung out from Georg Brandes's lectern in his celebrated lectures on Nietzsche. The poem,

24. Emil Frederiksen, *Johannes Jørgensens Ungdom* (Copenhagen, 1946), pp. 129–130.

he felt, provided a clear demarcation of the 1890s from the previous decades:

That the world is *deep*—it was this feeling that separated us who were twenty years old around 1890 from the two preceding generations. Neither [the realists] Schandorph nor Skram, neither Bang nor Pontoppidan, neither Esmann nor Nansen stood in any relation other than to the most patent realities. For them the world was more or less flat—often exceptionally flat; certainly it always had a bottom. Drachmann himself had only on occasion felt that existence is not easily understood—that life is a mystery.[25]

He added that in that same year his friend Sophus Claussen read to him a sonnet by a poet he had not heard of before, a poet for whom Brandes had found no place in *Main Currents*: Baudelaire.[26] Jørgensen published in the following year, 1891, an essay on Baudelaire, and by that time, he wrote, he was also reading Poe, Maeterlinck, Loti, Rollinat, Huysmans, d'Aurevilly, Villiers de l'Isle-Adam —all of them, Georg Brandes warned Jørgensen when he heard of this reading, "inimical to life." But even then, four years before his conversion, Jørgensen could see that on the contrary this was reading with such definite religious, specifically Christian, coloring that it moved him to write in his diary a New Year's Day prayer for 1892: "Seigneur, faites de moi un poète qui puisse chanter vos louanges dans ce monde bas et impur."[27]

25. Johannes Jørgensen, *Mit Livs Legende* 2 (Copenhagen, 1916): 19–20.
26. *Mit Livs Legende*, 2: 29–30. Frederiksen, *Johannes Jørgensens Ungdom*, pp. 97–98, notes, however, that Georg Brandes mentioned Baudelaire as early as 1877 in an essay on Emil Aarestrup, and that in the second number of *Ny Jord* in 1888 Emil Hannover strongly recommended the study of Baudelaire and the new poetry of France. The following number included translations of Baudelaire and of Bourget.
27. *Mit Livs Legende*, 2: 35–36. Jørgensen may actually have read Poe earlier than he recalls here. In 1:60 of the autobiography (which was written

A revolution in poetry was under way. Again from Jørgensen's autobiography: "Long enough had the commonplace and the everyday been preached to us—somber studies of somber reality, the uglier the better. Books like Amalia Skram's *Lucie* and *Constance Ring* were among those then most highly esteemed. It was against this bitter realism that we rose in protest. If life indeed were ugly, then lend it beautiful colors! If the day were cold and gray—then we chose to live in the night."[28]

As it appears from this passage, Jørgensen was not alone in protesting "bitter realism" in Danish literature. More than a few of his contemporaries had lost the zeal of the preceding generation— the Brandesian generation—for social and moral reform even though they did not discard such sentiments entirely. As a student at the University, Jørgensen soon found like-minded literary friends among the other students. Some of them were already beginning to publish their first efforts in verse or fiction and to write articles for the newspapers and for journals like the recently founded *Til-skueren* [The spectator] and the short-lived *Ny Jord* [New earth]. Jørgensen and his friend Viggo Stuckenberg were among those favored with invitations to Professor Høffding's "evenings" at his home in the Frederiksberg section of Copenhagen. Harald Høffding, who had recently been appointed professor of philosophy, was widely known for his studies in ethics and psychology, in which, under the continuing influence from his youth of Kant and Kierkegaard, he placed emphasis on the need to harmonize one's outer and inner life—to make philosophy significant in the development of personality. Although eventually as positivistic as Brandes, he op-

---

with the aid of diaries preserved from the early periods), he speaks of having looked forward as a new student at the grammar school in Copenhagen to reading the German romantics, to whom he had been introduced in *Main Currents,* and the French romantics, Poe, and Pascal.

28. *Mit Livs Legende,* 2: 38.

posed Brandes's radicalism and offered to his students instead the ideal of good citizenship and the exhilarating sense of their being part, without resort to religion, of a cosmic unity.

At Høffding's evenings, Jørgensen and Stuckenberg met Valdemar Vedel and Niels Møller, the latter of whom was to write in 1895 an essay on Poe. Both were ostensibly preparing for careers in the law, and both would become important poets and critics in the coming decade. Near the close of the 1890s, Vedel wrote two accounts that illustrate different aspects of the transition in Denmark from realism to symbolism. He recalled in one how the publication in 1884 of *The Wild Duck* had forced him and his fellow students to reappraise Ibsen's earlier plays and to conclude that the great doubter and agitator for reform was, rather, a creator, a true artist. The young men who founded *Ny Jord* in 1888 marked Ibsen's sixtieth birthday by designating him "den dristige skaber" (the daring creator).[29] In the second essay, Vedel recalled his student days prior to this reversal of attitude toward Ibsen, when everyone was excited by the prospect of seeing that scandalously "realistic" play *Ghosts* actually performed on the stage, and everyone was reading Herman Bang's *Haabløse Slægter* and Erik Skram's novel *Gertrude Colbjørnsen*, the Danish counterpart to *A Doll's House*. Vedel remembered, too, how he had been ready for a time to join the other students in democratizing Danish society. But he had discovered very soon that he had in fact little heart for reform, and rather than joining the young radicals and the emancipated women students in their pince-nez and straight skirts who flocked to hear Georg Brandes lecture, he cherished the opportunity at Professor Høffding's evenings to discuss art and literature and theories of

29. Valdemar Vedel, "Ibsen og Danmark," in *Firsernes førere: Karakteristiker og kritiker* (Copenhagen, 1923), pp. 17–51. Vedel had made many of these same points in 1888 in an article in *Ny Jord*, "Om Henrik Ibsens digteriske Manddomsgerning" (1:244–251).

association and of the unconscious with future jurists, civil servants, and writers.[30] From this group there emerged the idea for the fortnightly *Ny Jord*, which carried as its leading article in the first issue of January 1888 an essay by Høffding, "Om vor Tid og dens Ungdom" [Our era and its youth]. Our era is one of contradictions, Høffding wrote; there is on the one hand the continued assertion of religious authority, and on the other the demand for utter freedom of thought and for the unconditional right to put all values to the test and determine one's own beliefs. Unlike students of the previous generation, those of this era are bewildered by the array of conflicting ideas and programs thrust at them. Yet pessimism and resignation are surely not the answer. Work and learn! Høffding admonished his young readers—youth will find a way.[31]

But on the following pages there were signs enough to disabuse Høffding of his hopes for the acceptance of this gospel of work. Viggo Stuckenberg's poem "Landskab" [Landscape] described a sunset over mile-wide meadows as the lonely death of the day over a barren wasteland ("og over dette arme Øde dør saa Dagen / en ensom Død"), and in a long essay Valdemar Vedel criticized the English novelist Laurence Sterne for a failure in true feeling and a failure in creativity. An essay further on by Gustav Hetsch deplored the naturalists' confusion of art with science, for science, he declared, has nothing to do with feeling. Art cultivates what is unique in the individual; it is not meant to discover universal laws or to storm citadels but "to look at life, pervaded by a feeling, filled with a sentiment, all in accordance with what the eye has rested upon."[32]

Not unexpectedly, therefore, the new poetry that appeared in the next few years eschewed audacity and bitter protest and occupied itself instead with sentiment and mood, preferably those ex-

30. Valdemar Vedel, "Studenterminder fra 1880erne," in *Firsernes førere*, pp. 1–11.

31. *Ny Jord* 1 (1888): 1–5.

32. "Lidt om kunst," *Ny Jord* 1 (1888): 64.

perienced in seclusion in a natural setting and at night. It adopted free forms and irregular meters, following the example of Jacobsen's arabesque poems perhaps, but more likely that of Baudelaire's *Petits poèmes en prose*, for the translation of which Jørgensen had been in part responsible. Jørgensen's own volume of mood poems, *Stemninger* (1892), though bearing many traces of his reading of English romantic poetry, was one of the principal achievements of the new movement.[33] Another was the journal *Taarnet* [The tower], founded in 1893 and edited by Jørgensen. *Taarnet* announced in the second number its welcome of symbolism as the poetic means of renewing a reverence for life and for restoring profundity to the arts.[34]

Jørgensen relates in his autobiography how he came to edit *Taarnet*. A stranger named Karl Buhl had approached him in 1892 on behalf of a group of young Danish enthusiasts of *symbolisme* and asked him to help them publish a journal. He and Buhl had walked for hours through a misty November night discussing the project. They had found common ground very soon in lines from "Ulalume": "That night became the cornerstone for *Taarnet*—laid 'by the dank tarn of Auber, In the ghoul-haunted woodland of Weir,' laid in the name of Baudelaire, in the name of Poe, in the name of Verlaine. . . ."[35] Through Buhl, Jørgensen had met the others, "a youthful circle decidedly *symboliste-décadent*-minded,

33. Emil Frederiksen, "Til Johannes Jørgensens 'Stemninger' 1892," in *Festskrift til Valdemar Vedel*, ed. Knud Frederik Plesner (Copenhagen, 1935), 115–131. Shelley and Byron are frequently mentioned in connection with Danish poetry of this period.

34. The name of the journal carried several connotations. In Huysmans's *Là-bas*, the characters converse in a steeple on the only subjects worth talking about—art and religion. Des Esseintes, as Jørgensen pointed out in an essay on Huysmans, finds peace in the steeple of a church under the bells that call to him in the voice of the Middle Ages. (Frederiksen, *Johannes Jørgensens Ungdom*, p. 224). *Mit Livs Legende*, 2: 40–41, relates a mystical experience that occurred in the tower over Jørgensen's rooms.

35. *Mit Livs Legende*, 2: 58–59.

who had formed a cult of Oscar Wilde and the English Pre-Raphaelites. They drank tea, read Swinburne aloud, dressed in flowing garments, and adored white flowers."[36] Convinced, Jørgensen wrote, that the age required not only symbolism but metaphysics after the dry years of realism, he was to give a Catholic turn to *Taarnet* and thus doubly provoke the wrath of Georg Brandes.[37]

It is against this background that the Danish essays on Poe from the 1890s should be read, for in isolation they may seem slight and certainly they lose much of their significance. The first of them is the introduction that Jørgensen supplied for his translation of "The Narrative of Arthur Gordon Pym of Nantucket."

One of the several short-term newspaper posts that Jørgensen held in the beginning years of his literary career was with a financial newspaper, *Kjøbenhavns Børs-Tidende*. Ernst Brandes, the third of the brothers, was the editor and permitted Jørgensen to insert essays on literary subjects as well as translations of authors whom he had found of interest. The stockbrokers on the Copenhagen bourse were thus able toward the end of 1890 to read that Niels Møller's new book *Hændelser* [Events] reminded Jørgensen of Poe's and Pierre Loti's fiction, and in October and November of 1891, in an article on "New Denmark," to read that the longing for the remote and the unknown by writers like Stuckenberg, Møller, Vedel, and others had already begun to take form in published poems and fiction. The new Denmark was giving evidence of *décadence,* and the stockbrokers could deduce from this that "civilization" had become a bankrupt concept.[38] In that same November, *Børs-Tidende* began serializing Jørgensen's translation of "Arthur Gordon Pym"; it ran until February 1892 and then was published in book form with an

36. *Mit Livs Legende,* 2: 59–60.
37. *Mit Livs Legende,* 2: 67–68.
38. Frederiksen, *Johannes Jørgensens Ungdom,* pp. 131–132.

introduction by the translator. (In 1910 the volume was reissued with a new title page.)[39] Jørgensen had translated from English before—selected sketches by Mark Twain in 1888–1890—but this had been hackwork,[40] whereas the Poe translation, like his translations of Anatole France and Paul Bourget for *Børs-Tidende,* was a free choice willingly undertaken.

Jørgensen's introduction commented on the form and content of "Arthur Gordon Pym." In form, he wrote, it is a hoax, a "mystification," like several other of Poe's stories. As such it is remarkable for scientific verisimilitude, which has been obtained through the use of minutely exact details. In content, the story is related to Poe's first-person narratives. The Pym-mask is gradually discarded and the author's "strange and melancholy" face may be glimpsed in the references, for example, to Pym's excitable temperament and to the glowing powers of his imagination. Jørgensen had evidently read Poe's fiction as though Poe were speaking of himself directly in the first-person narratives and indirectly, through thinly disguised characters, in the others; for Jørgensen, the content of the fiction, quite simply, was the experience of Poe himself. He wrote that the subjects touched on in the Pym story are typically Poe's own concerns: "the exceptional moments in the life of the unconscious [Sjælelivets Undtagelsestilfælde], the nightmare of horrible dreams, the dread of death, and the terrors endured by those buried alive, the bewilderment of thought, the delirium of the will." Pym, like all Poe's heroes and heroines, is wholly chaste:

39. "Arthur Gordon Pyms Hændelser," *Kjøbenhavns Børs-Tidende,* 14 November 1891–9 February 1892. Reprinted, with introduction (of five unnumbered pages), as *Arthur Gordon Pyms Hændelser* (Copenhagen, 1892); reprinted with a different title, *Bryggen "Grampus" Sydhavstogt eller Arthur Gordon Pyms Hændelser* (Copenhagen, 1910). Jørgensen also translated "Silence—A Fable" ["Tavshed"] for *Illustreret Tidende,* 31 December 1893; in the same magazine two anonymous Poe translations appeared: "The Sphinx," 25 June 1893, and "The Cask of Amontillado," 22 July 1894.

40. *Udvalgte Skitser* (Copenhagen, 1888–1890). See letter 9 August 1888 to Viggo Stuckenberg, *Breve,* ed. Jørgen Andersen (Copenhagen, 1946), p. 36.

Love in the ordinary sense does not exist for these creatures, all of whose longing is directed to a remote and fantastic ideal. . . . The point is that this hero, like all of Poe's heroes, is a monomaniac. Nothing exists for him in this world worth desiring but that remote unknown; he is therefore carried off, just as the great oceanic currents on Mercator's old maps of the world are carried off toward the mysterious opening at each pole, through which they disappear into the bowels of the earth. The whole figure of Pym is really only the embodiment of man's attraction to the marvelous and the abominable. It was Poe's deepest urge and the reason why his life, as though sucked into a maelstrom, was drawn into destruction.[41]

The identification of character with author is complete; both symbolize the exceptional, the unpredictable and irrational, the unknowable "Outside" that in Poe's stories can be apprehended only in terror and with the danger of extinction to the self.

The awareness, whether awesome or blessed, of man's spiritual state was the theme of a series of essays that Jørgensen published in *Tilskueren* the following year. The series was called "En ny Digtning" [A new poetry] and consisted of essays on Edgar Poe, Paul Verlaine, Stéphane Mallarmé, and J. K. Huysmans.[42] Their work was said to stand in affirmation of a cardinal truth which the realists had lost sight of, that "life is a miracle, a riddle, a sanctity."[43] In the Poe essay, which led the series, Jørgensen announced that the new

41. "Indledning," in Edgar Allan Poe, *Arthur Gordon Pyms Hændelser* (Copenhagen, 1892).

42. "En ny Digtning: I. Edgar Poe, II. Paul Verlaine, III. Stéphane Mallarmé, IV. J. K. Huysmans," *Tilskueren* 10 (1893): 375–386, 469–480, 603–607, 770–782. The introduction (pp. 375–377), slightly reworked, was incorporated in the reprinting of the Poe essay in *Essays* (Copenhagen, 1906), pp. 45–56, as part of a long section entitled "Fra [from] Baudelaire til Strindberg." My citations from the Poe essay are from the reprinting of this version in *Udvalgte Værker* 6 (Copenhagen, 1915): 59–72.

43. "En ny Digtning: IV. J. K. Huysmans," *Tilskueren* 10 (1893): 771.

poetry is "the protest of the human spirit against the age and the world." It seeks "salvation and peace in the eternal realms of beauty and on the shores of an endless dream." There had been intimations of such a protest in Flaubert, Zola, and the Goncourts, "but its first and mightiest appearance was in the land where the rule of money and the aversion to beauty were both early and great—the model state of this century's mammonism, the birthplace of dollar-worship, advertizing, and humbug: North America."[44]

In the brief sketch that followed of Poe's life and work, Jørgensen emphasized the universality of Poe's escape from everyday reality into the dream world of his imagination. "The Philosophy of Composition" is an example of "mystification" but perhaps also a self-protective device designed to be so dazzling as to ward off unwanted intrusions into Poe's private life. That life was dramatically unhappy; Poe was persecuted and abused; he was a stranger and an enemy in the philistine society of the United States. But Poe had not submitted to their gods; he had sought the beauty that transcends earthly care and is a token of the eternal life. He sought the strangeness that Bacon had declared was a necessary element of beauty. Repeating in part his introduction to the translation of "Arthur Gordon Pym," Jørgensen continued:

> He worshiped the unusual, the extraordinary, the mystery, the wonder, and the beauty that passes all understanding. His preference was for depicting the exceptional moments of the mind, the nightmare of horrible dreams, the fear of eternal extinction, the dread of death and the agony suffered by the living dead. He adored all singular and unusual states of mind, the terror of loneliness, the excitement induced by the use of opium, the perverse impulses of the Will. He demanded to taste of all the rare and strange fruits on the tree of life.[45]

44. *Udvalgte Værker,* 6: 60, 61.
45. *Udvalgte Værker,* 6: 64.

Hence Poe dreams of remote times and remote places. Jørgensen saw in this a universal attribute visible alike in the terrifying visions of "Arthur Gordon Pym" and in the common experience that comes like the scent of violets on a spring day of longing for distant lands across boundless seas. The fragrance of violets and visions of shipwreck, hunger, imprisonment, and death among barbarians make an unlikely juxtaposition, but Jørgensen seems to have been intent on giving the broadest possible range of significance to the implications he had found in Poe's fiction.

Poe appears finally in Jørgensen's essay as the protosymbolist of modern times. He moves imperceptibly from dreams of the remote to the enchantment of the "pure" dream.

> It is as though the poet more and more understands that reality is the same in all its habitations and that only in the inner world may be found the perfect harmony that his soul seeks. Thus it is that he dreams his ideal landscapes that are formed by an artist's hand and are ordered in terms of what is decorative. The further he removes himself from original nature the more nearly he approaches the theatrical.[46]

In Poe's visions Jørgensen found the elements of symbolism: the inward search for perfect harmony, the essential unity of a world only apparently chaotic, and the theatricality of the artist's powers of mind in giving expression to these mysteries. Their philosophical justification lay, he thought, in Schopenhauer's concept of the world as a mirror of the Will. The concept had been anticipated by Poe in lines quoted by Jørgensen from "Eureka":

> In this view [that God's existence is diffused in the material world], and in this view alone, we comprehend the riddles of Divine Injustice—of Inexorable Fate. In this view alone the existence of Evil becomes intelligible; but in this view it

46. *Udvalgte Værker,* 6: 67.

becomes more—it becomes endurable. Our souls no longer rebel at a *Sorrow* which we ourselves have imposed upon ourselves, in furtherance of our own purposes.[47]

Some twenty years later Jørgensen again compared Poe and Schopenhauer. Required in the course of writing his autobiography to search for the "I" behind the narrative persona, he had had confirmed, he wrote in his preface, a favorite idea of his that "whither one wishes in his inmost soul to go, there will he in fact arrive."[48] The idea is supported, he continued, in Schopenhauer's dictum that all things issue from the Will, and he cited the same passage from *Die Welt als Wille und Vorstellung* that he had used in the Poe essay. Now, however, the Poe reference was not to "Eureka" but to Arthur Gordon Pym's visions of disaster:

Life consists of an unbroken series of dilemmas, great and small—and man chooses according to his inmost nature. Now, this continual series of small choices, always in the same direction, determines the direction of his life. There are men who wish to be happy—fewer, perhaps, than one believes. There are natures which need unhappiness—more than one believes. It is not only Arthur Gordon Pym (in Edgar Allan Poe's book) who can say of himself: "My visions were of shipwreck and famine; of death or captivity among barbarian hordes; of a life-time dragged out in sorrow and tears upon some grey and desolate rock, in an ocean unapproachable and unknown." There are many whose ideal state is unhappiness.[49]

Poe's imagination, theatrical in expression, is seen here nevertheless

47. Edgar Allan Poe, *The Complete Works,* ed. James A. Harrison 16 (New York, 1902): 313.
48. *Mit Livs Legende* 1 (Copenhagen, 1916): 9.
49. *Mit Livs Legende,* 1: 9–10, but I quote from the English translation, *Jørgensen* (London, 1928), pp. 6–7, which at this point is unabridged.

to be essentially neither capricious nor meretricious. Its insights are of a moral condition.

The fervor of Jørgensen's literary interests was redirected and in some respects diminished as he approached the crisis of his conversion in 1896. Despairing of his readiness for the event, he remembered Poe's imp of the perverse as he was obliged to confess that despite his flight from Denmark and the scenes of the past there remained in his heart a perverse attraction to perdition and the devil. In Italy he and a Catholic artist friend, Mogens Ballin, were allowed to live at a monastery near Assisi while Ballin restored the treasures of the church. As Ballin did his work, Jørgensen sat nearby and prepared a translation of Poe—"serenely, but with no great interest."[50] With the money earned for the work, he visited Florence.[51] The translation is not identified; it may have been a volume of tales that was never published, or perhaps it was "Landors Hjem" ["Landor's Cottage"], which did not appear in print, however, until February 1909.[52] In any case, translating Poe had obviously become as early as 1895 hardly more than the hackwork that translating Mark Twain's sketches had once been. For the rest of Jørgensen's long life (1866–1956), the priests, prophets, and saints of the church supplanted the poets in all matters of the spirit and became, moreover, his principal subject.

Of the other writers of "the new poetry" of the 1890s in Denmark, only Niels Møller was also to write on Poe. An essay on Poe might have been expected from Sophus Claussen, the most fully committed of his generation to *symbolisme* and a friend of Verlaine

50. *Mit Livs Legende* 3 (Copenhagen, 1917): 105–106.
51. *Mit Livs Legende,* 3: 156, 165.
52. "Landors Hjem," *Gads Danske Magasin,* 1908–1909, pp. 323–327. Emil Frederiksen faintly recalls, I am told, that Jørgensen told him that he was working on translations of tales for a volume to be called *Sælsomme Fortællinger.* Cammermeyers published such a title in 1897, but it was translated by an unknown C.S.

and his disciple F. A. Cazals, but Claussen owed his allegiance wholly to Danish and French poetry. He wrote in a memoir dated 1918 of conversations held in the late 1880s with Jørgensen: "From Heine's 'Junge Leiden' to Edgar Poe's 'Ulalume,' from Byron to Beyle and Baudelaire, we had many confidences to exchange, confidences that to our amazement we have since seen were those that occupied a whole generation the world over."[53] But Claussen had been no unreserved admirer of Poe's idea of the "pleasurable sadness" in poetry,[54] and although he thought that he knew the worth of Shelley and Poe (who "has written the sweetest and saddest songs"), without France, he was convinced, poetry is unthinkable.[55] Niels Møller had won Jørgensen's praise in Taarnet for fictional sketches in the "new" manner that he had published in 1890 and 1895. Møller, Jørgensen had written, depicts the hidden, psychic life of man, "the strange and vague moods, visions from the border-land between dream and waking, violent seizures of meaningless wilfulness. He reveals a taste for the strange and the marvelous which places him with Poe and with Maeterlinck."[56] But when Møller published his essay on Poe in Tilskueren in 1895, two years after Jørgensen's in the same journal, he did not make of it a protest against naturalism but a sober academic appraisal of Poe's life and work.

Møller, who was to become one of the most learned critics of European literature of his generation in Denmark, had read not only Jørgensen's essay but also Ola Hansson's, which will be discussed in chapter 4, as well as the memoirs of Poe by Baudelaire and John H. Ingram. He was obliged to take exception to statements of biographical fact in all of them, for he had also consulted

53. Sophus Claussen, "Jord og Sjæl," in Jord og Sjæl, ed. Stig Krabbe Barfoed (Copenhagen, 1961), p. 175.
54. Emil Frandsen, Sophus Claussen (Copenhagen, 1950), 1: 197.
55. Frandsen, Sophus Claussen, 2: 133.
56. Quoted in Hakon Stangerup and F. J. Billeskov Jansen, Dansk Litteraturhistorie 3 (Copenhagen, 1966): 439.

George E. Woodberry's biography of Poe published in 1885 and Woodberry's reprinting of Poe letters in *The Century Magazine* in 1894. "In recent years," Møller began, "the symbolists and other opponents of naturalism have exalted Poe to the skies. They have taken him in heritage from Baudelaire . . . and worshiped him with deep devotion. . . . For them, Poe is one of the prophets stoned by mankind; he has done his work as a god does his work. . . However, these recent accounts [by Hansson, Jørgensen, and Ingram] are not to be relied upon."[57] Møller then reviewed Poe's life, reducing the martyr and prophet described by Baudelaire and Hansson to a hard-pressed, hard-working American writer stripped of Norman ancestry, Byronism, moral saintliness, vast classical learning, and all the other mythical qualities that the authors of "recent accounts" had ascribed to Poe. Woodberry's factuality had obviously had its effect. Møller's concluding remarks reflected in still other ways his reliance on Woodberry's biography: "Poe is no deep or original esthetician," Møller wrote. "He can lend vitality to events, but his characters do not live. They are shadows he makes dance on the wall. They have neither flesh nor blood, but at most, nerves." And again, "Poe had a keen eye for morbid and perverse behavior, but scarcely any particularly deep or reliable psychological insight. His taste was far from certain, even though he represented himself as the apostle of taste. There is much false gentility and romanticism in his work, and at times his subjects or details can be downright repugnant, as in 'Berenice.' He offends also by his willingness to make himself greater than he is."[58] Even Georg Brandes's distaste for everything *décadent* would scarcely have permitted such harshness. By relying for his judgments on Woodberry, Møller in effect removed Poe completely from the European scene of his triumph

57. Niels Møller, "Edgar Poe," in *Nattevagter, Udvalgte Afhandlinger* (Copenhagen, 1923), pp. 229–231. This is a reprinting, except for the omission of two short paragraphs, of the essay in *Tilskueren* 12 (1895): 589–615.
58. *Nattevagter*, pp. 247, 251, 252.

as a seminal figure in "the new poetry." He had reduced Poe to the stature then being permitted him in American scholarship.

By the time Møller's essay appeared, however, symbolism had already emerged victorious from the disputes and debates surrounding its introduction into Denmark, and its advocates and adversaries had gone their separate ways. Møller's essay, useful though it surely was in setting straight a good part of the garbled record of Poe's life, was unfortunately timed. Even Johannes Jørgensen had lost interest.

CHAPTER 3

NORWAY AND SWEDEN

The "new literature" being published in Copenhagen in slim volumes of verse and poetic prose or as contributions to *Ny Jord* and other magazines in the form of essays, stories, and poems, found readers in Norway and Sweden who were as eager as the Danes for change. In both countries a reaction to the dominance of naturalism similar to that in Denmark was gathering force, and the lead taken in Copenhagen seemed to most young Norwegian and Swedish writers at least as provocative as the somewhat muted strains of *décadence* and *symbolisme* reaching their ears from a more distant Paris. As early as 1888 Norwegians and Swedes began making important contributions to *Ny Jord*, the first issues of which had been almost exclusively of Danish composition. In place of agitation for reform and the preoccupation of the past with the realistic surfaces of life, they too longed to realize an ideal of beauty in their art and looked to a new literature displaying a heightened sensitivity to "moods"—to obscure and *strangely* beautiful psychological states. The major lyric poets and writers of psychological fiction and drama who emerged in Norway and Sweden in the 1890s were very much aware of the new movement in Danish literature, and some of them, in consequence, were soon making their personal discoveries of Edgar Allan Poe.

Norwegian interest in Poe was as limited, however, as the relatively tepid reception given in Norway on the whole to *décadence* and *symbolisme*. Norway's habitual liberalism had by no means exhausted itself in the realistic fiction and drama of "the big four" —Ibsen, Bjørnson, Alexander Kielland, and Jonas Lie—and it continued into the 1890s to be productive of major work and to temper enthusiasm for the "new literature" coming from Denmark and France. The towering figures who now emerged in Norwegian art and literature were Edvard Munch and Knut Hamsun. Both were dedicated to an art closely resembling at many points that of the "new literature," especially in its dedication to an ideal of beauty and its determination to penetrate to the mysterious and revelatory nuances of "the unconscious life of the soul," to use a phrase of Hamsun's. But both were strongly motivated in their art by ethical considerations, which owed, when they were not indigenously Norwegian, much more to Russian than to French and Danish influences. Hamsun and Munch knew of Poe, however, and spoke favorably of him, Munch indeed with particular emphasis, for it is reported that he once declared that Poe and Dostoevski had made "the greatest impact" on his life.[1] The remark was not elaborated, unfortunately, and one is left to speculate how much "impact" the two writers may have had on the powerful symbolic expressionism coming to the fore in Munch's paintings at the end of the 1880s, so different from the anecdotal, decorative expressionism of his contemporaries in Germany.

1. Ingrid Langaard, *Edvard Munch, Modningsår* (Oslo, 1960), p. 266. The literary character of Munch's painting has long been noticed. August Brunius related Munch's art to the symbolism of Maeterlinck and Stefan George: "Hence we see the literary character in Gauguin many times more strongly emphasized in Munch; for both their association with authors had been a fateful one." *Färg och form* (Stockholm, 1913), pp. 94–95. A Poe influence on Munch at several removes is suggested in Gösta Svenæus's conjecture that the idea represented in Munch's pencil sketch "In uns sind Welten" (dated 1894) had been formulated for him in Odilon Redon's lithograph "Le Souffle qui conduit les êtres dans les spheres" (*A Edgar Poe*, V [Paris, 1882]), which had in turn been inspired by Poe's "To Helen." The idea assumed major importance for Munch, who was threatened with the loss of sight in one eye. Gösta Svenæus, *Edvard Munch, Das Universum der Melancholie* (Lund, 1968), pp. 212–219.

Knut Hamsun published in 1890 an essay in *Samtiden*, the Norwegian counterpart to *Ny Jord* although not so exclusively literary, in which he stated, in effect, his literary credo. The essay envisions a future literature very much like that which Ola Hansson was then describing in his long essay on Poe (see chapter 4). Hamsun wrote that literature must examine psychological subtleties hitherto neglected: "quite inexplicable sensory states: a mute rapture without cause; a twinge of psychic pain; . . . a sudden, unexpected view of once secret realms now revealed; the intuition of impending danger even in the midst of a carefree hour"—all those mysteries of "the unconscious life of the soul" that "crude and simple huckster mentalities cannot comprehend."[2] For all its resemblance to Hansson's views of literature, however, this program did not lead to an enthusiasm like Hansson's for Edgar Allan Poe. Hamsun would surely have heard talk of Poe during his frequent bouts of talking and drinking with Johannes Jørgensen and his

2. "Fra det ubevidste Sjæleliv," *Samtiden* (Bergen) 1 (1890): 332. *Samtiden* paid direct attention to "the new literature" in an unsigned article, "Strømninger i fransk aandsliv," 1 (1890): 153–162, which cited Edouard Rod's *Les Trois cœurs* as the principal representative of the movement. Unlike the naturalists, the new writers "show greater interest in the development of the idea produced by an object than in the object itself" (p. 159). However, at the conclusion of a survey that then followed of Paul Bourget's work, the writer of the article showed his displeasure with Bourget's characterization of democracy as "odious," and with other examples of Bourget's feigned aristocratism. Bourget's pessimism appeared to the writer to be the result of an unresolved conflict between masculine and feminine elements in his personality. His work is "interesting" and represents "a necessary phase in French literature"—but nothing more. The article was by no means programmatic for *Samtiden*, which covered a very wide range of topics and literature, including the "new" literature, in subsequent issues. Late in 1890, in keeping with latest trends, the magazine published Ola Hansson's essay "Litterære produktionsmaade" (see chap. 4, n. 45). Georg Brandes lectured in Kristiania on 12 May 1890 on the growing French opposition to Zola, principally by Edouard Rod, Bourget, and Huysmans, and by summer the controversy was well under way when Norwegian versions of *Les Trois cœurs* and *La Bête humaine* appeared in the same number of the radical *Kristiania Intelligentssedler*. Harald Noreng, *Nils Kjær* (Oslo, 1949), p. 59.

friends in Copenhagen,[3] but he apparently made his acquaintance with Poe not in Jørgensen's circle in Denmark but in America, where he had made two unsuccessful attempts to launch his career as an author. In his derisive lectures on modern American culture given on his final return from America in 1888 and published in expanded form the following year under the title *Fra det moderne Amerikas Aandsliv* [The cultural life of modern America], Hamsun declared that he had found little in America to merit the name of literature. From this stricture he excluded "Mark Twain, that pale pessimist, . . . [and] I exclude a little of Poe, a little of Hawthorne, a little of Harte."[4] He seems to have had nothing more to say about Poe. Characteristically, he chose as his representative American writers Whitman and Emerson, to each of whom he devoted a lengthy essay, as indeed on another occasion he had also to Mark Twain.

Hamsun had also published in *Ny Jord* in 1888 a portion of *Sult* [Hunger], the novel which on its publication in complete form in Copenhagen in 1890 brought to him at last the recognition that he had failed to get from his early literary efforts in Norway and in the Scandinavian settlements of the American midwest. *Sult*, to be sure, is a novel of "moods," and its depiction of a writer's insistence on asserting the sovereignty of his will over even the ravaging effects of hunger on his body and mind may surely be construed as a reply to the emphasis which the naturalists had placed on hunger as an immitigable biological force. But by the same token the protagonist in *Sult* is no world-weary *décadent*. Almost at once Hamsun was widely regarded in Norway as the principal figure in the "new" yet distinctively Norwegian literature of the 1890s, not necessarily to supplant Ibsen, but to take his place beside the great dramatist who

3. Johannes Jørgensen, *Mit Livs Legende* 1 (Copenhagen, 1916): pp. 176–177; 2 (Copenhagen, 1916): 37–38, 61–62.

4. *The Cultural Life of Modern America*, trans. B. G. Morgridge (Cambridge, Mass., 1969), p. 33.

had already shown in *The Wild Duck* and *Rosmersholm* the originality and independence of Norwegian symbolism.

The clearest expression in Norway of *décadent* ideals is to be found in the lyric poetry of the period. *Samtiden* published in its first issue "Fandango," a poem by Vilhelm Krag that displayed diction and sentiments sufficiently exotic and *décadent* to have created a small sensation when it was read aloud before the Student Union of the University in Kristiania. But neither Krag's other poems of the early 1890s nor those of contemporaries like Nils Collett Vogt and Sigbjørn Obstfelder give evidence of indebtedness to Poe. Obstfelder, like Hamsun, had tried unsuccessfully to settle in America; he might be expected to have shown particular interest in the American poet then being widely discussed, but it was Whitman rather than Poe who seems to have captured his attention.

Obstfelder, Krag, and other university students in Kristiania foregathered at the home of fru Dons, whose son was one of the group, and there discussed the new trends in literature and read aloud their own latest efforts. Included among them was a young aspirant in prose, Tryggve Andersen, who long afterward was reported to have declared "frankly that Poe was his great model."[5] Andersen, who is described in the same source as "the most fastidious stylist in modern Norwegian prose," seems not, however, to have taken any direct influence from Poe, nor is Poe included in his list of authors in whom he took particular interest: Cooper and Scott in his youth, and later, the German romantic writers, especially E. T. A. Hoffmann.[6] Some of Andersen's stories contain supernatural elements—wraiths, premonitory apparitions, or restless ghosts—but these stories are narrated at a relatively low pitch and with a restraint not suggestive of Poe, and they attribute the apparent return to life of the dead to traditional causes: "intense

5. Halvdan Koht, *The American Spirit in Europe* (Philadelphia, 1949), p. 119.
6. Christian Gierløff, *Tryggve Andersen* (Oslo, 1942), pp. 78–79.

46

passions, ominous warnings, fateful events,"[7] rather than to the distorted perceptions of an excited or unbalanced mind. So it is with such stories as "Veteranen" [The veteran], "De siste nættene" [The final nights], and "Nattevakten" [The night watch]. An exception is a frame story entitled "Den døde mand" [The dead man], told principally in the first person, as in many of Poe's stories but rarely in Andersen's. Intentionally or not, the story burlesques the melodramatic excesses of decadent heroes, in this case a pale, red-haired, bearded lawyer who tells drunkenly of the terrors of what Poe called "the incorporeal silence" to a reluctant guest in a remote hotel. He insists also on reciting an unfinished poem on his mental state in rough meter and with admittedly banal rhymes, and he begs the guest to think of the anomalous situation of the living dead: not yet ill-smelling but brought by the fresh fragrance of flowers to realize with disgust his own impurity, not yet decayed and desiring still the love of women but able to give only lust in return, tossed about in the wild dance of life but branded by death, and so on, until at last the guest meekly inquires whether it isn't time they both retired for the night. Offended, the lawyer retreats. He is, it turns out, one of Andersen's apparitions, not from the grave in this story but, as the guest later learns, merely a well-known local eccentric who makes an odd appearance from time to time. He and his story thus exemplify a kind of regionalism which Andersen adopted and on which his best work is founded.

Arne Garborg, another leading prose writer of the period who was persuaded of the need to base his fiction on regionalism not only, however, in subject but also in language, had been before the 1890s one of the most painstaking of Scandinavian naturalists. In a sharp departure from past practice, he published in 1891 a novel entitled *Trætte Mænd* [Weary men] which is often cited as a novel of *décadence*. The spiritual and physical decline of its hero Gabriel Gram was so vividly depicted and was so convincing to Garborg's

7. Tryggve Andersen, *Samlede fortællinger* (Kristiania, 1916), 3: 6.

contemporaries that the novel became the chief evidence of decadent literature in a debate organized by the Student Union of the
University in 1892. The debaters felt constrained to denounce the
folly of *décadence* and several times proclaimed the efficacy of work
as its proper corrective. But Garborg would not have disagreed; he
had ironized in the novel over the decadent dissipations and the
weary resignation of his hero as constituting an ethically mistaken
mode of life. He was no ripe *décadent* eager to embrace the new doc-
trines and its saints. And when Ola Hansson visited him at his home
at Kolbotn in 1889 and Hansson's mind, presumably, was still full
of his reading of Poe and of the essay on Poe that he had just finished writing, the talk seems rather to have been taken up principally
by his newest enthusiasm, Nietzsche. Garborg responded to this enthusiasm the following year by translating several of Hansson's
essays, including one on Nietzsche, as well as Hansson's forty-page
booklet on the philosopher. Poe, then, seems to have left no mark
on Garborg's work.

It was left to Nils Kjær, in later years feared as the witty, dis-
respectful literature and drama critic of a leading newspaper in
Kristiania, to write the only Norwegian essay on Poe from the 1890s.
Kjær had been a member of the group that met at fru Dons's home,
and even before passing his examinations at the university in 1892
he had begun contributing articles on *décadence* to the newspaper
Dagbladet. Later, he wrote also for the radical paper *Tidssignaler*
and in 1893 contributed articles and translations to Hans Tambs-
Lyche's *Kringsjaa*, of which Kjær later served for a brief time as
editor.[8] Tambs-Lyche had become a staunch Emersonian while
serving in the Unitarian ministry in America and in 1894 published
in *Kringsjaa* in four long installments his exposition of the master's
life and work. It is probably from this essay and from conversation
with Tambs-Lyche that Kjær learned about Emerson and decided
to include him for comparative purposes in his essay on Poe. The

8. Noreng, *Nils Kjær*, pp. 78–80.

essay was collected in 1895 with seven other newspaper pieces for Kjær's first book, *Essays, Fremmede forfattere* [Essays, foreign authors].

Like Niels Møller's Danish essay of 1895, Kjær's essay on Poe made use of Woodberry's scholarship, but it did not abandon a European point of view. It began,

> The New World, which in our prejudice stands as the example par excellence of money barbarism, a steaming, noisy world of hurtling speed and with a herd mentality, has to the surprise of old Europe already produced minds in this century which could more readily have been expected as the most recent and finest fruit of an old civilization than as the first growth of a crude pioneer society. One of these America regards as her finest writer, although he is as yet little known in Europe. The other has until very recent years been less appreciated in his homeland than in the old countries, where he has been and is the idolized poet of the young—he, who long after the authors of *Rolla* and *Manfred* have ceased to be read has his quiet admirers among young people dissatisfied with a plain and simple world and craving romance.
>
> These two Americans from the first half of the century differ markedly from each other. Ralph Waldo Emerson was much more hellenistic than any of the strenuous men of our iron age dare to be. He knew how to suck honey from the multifarious verdure of life, and to read him is like moving among roses. His profundity was wrinkle-free; he looks on the world with shining eyes, as only a child can or a grown man who is yet able to turn his gaze inward without misgivings. He is thus able to discover the harmony between inner and outer worlds—the great unity of all things—that most of us seek in vain. In his philosophy, the soul is the cosmic principle; the laws of the soul and the laws of nature

are two sides of the same thing; and on the basis of this correspondence he builds his noble, humane ethic.

America's other great metaphysical poet, Edgar Allan Poe, is of a completely opposite nature. His poverty and humble circumstances, which forced him constantly into that heart-rending, fragmenting activity called "magazine writing," would alone have made him different from Emerson. In contrast to the latter's harmonious, objective composure, his soul is impassioned, agitated, subjective, and above all, rich in fantasy—in a special sense productive, if Emerson can be characterized as reproductive. On the other hand, he is cursed with a sharper eye for reality and is therefore never, like the other, satisfied with reality but is always driven by its ugliness into those realms where he rules supreme: the world of dreams.[9]

Poe, Kjær continued, did not sentimentalize external circumstances as the cause of his unhappiness; he found the disharmony instead in his own being. In a world in which he felt homeless, he created dreams in his own image: "fantastic and secret, full of sorrow and guilt and wild fears, a tragic world, a monument to his suffering."[10] But he thereby created a new image of the world to serve as "a universal foundation for his suffering . . . a tragic view of life, or if you will, an esthetic view of life."[11] Poe must not be read as a realist; he is not trying to draw character or to describe passions.

But [his poetry] is itself an expression of a passion: the faltering search, the consuming unrest, the morbid attraction for the incomprehensible, the unreal, the eternal—this most irrational but for the same reason most inward and true

9. Nils Kjær, "Edgar Poe," in *Essays, Fremmede forfattere* (Kristiania, 1895), pp. 21–23.
10. *Essays*, p. 24.
11. *Essays*, p. 25.

passion of mankind. The purpose and meaning of this poetry is therefore to wrench the reader if only for a moment out of his secure and well-lighted reality and convey to him the intense feeling of endlessness out of which it arose.[12]

Kjær discerned three different intentions in Poe's tales: the presentation of incident, the development of an idea, and the evocation of a musical mood. These intentions were said, somewhat mystically, to combine "to communicate the intense feeling of endlessness which, esthetically speaking, signifies the soul's total deliverance in endless beauty."[13] But Kjær did not demonstrate what he meant by Poe's development of an idea. In discussing "The Fall of the House of Usher," "The Masque of the Red Death," "Ligeia," and "Eureka," he summarized incident and restated the hermetic, symbolic nature of Poe's work. Thus we learn that "Poe's premise . . . [is] that Beauty is the criterion of Truth. In the contemplation of beauty the soul is freed of every trammel; it feels itself to be absolute—'out of time, out of space,' and face to face with the eternal."[14]

Kjær then briefly examined the poetry, noting particularly its musical effects, and brought the essay to a conclusion consistent with his view of Poe as a symbolist. Evidence of Poe's puffing his wares does not, he suggested, bear on the value of his work (as Woodberry had implied it did). Nor are Poe's hardships pertinent to criticism (as they had been to every critic that Kjær had consulted): "it is undoubtedly incorrect of some critics to regard Poe as a martyr of American brutality, a lonely misunderstood aristocrat who was doomed to death in a society where life is engulfed in economic struggle. His loneliness, his fear of reality, his misanthropy would have been the same in every other country and in every other

12. *Essays*, p. 27.
13. *Essays*, p. 28.
14. *Essays*, p. 39.

age, for they had deeper roots in his nature than were determined by mere circumstance."[15] With this insight, Poe's separation from his American setting and his apotheosis as a symbolist were made complete.

Ola Hansson and August Strindberg were the first Swedish writers to be made welcome in the pages of Ny Jord. They were generally in sympathy with the aims revealed in such a declaration, for example, as Valdemar Vedel's that "the right art" is that which is able "with sensitive understanding of the functioning of the psyche . . . to have an effect on the reader's mind, to shape it according to one's mood, to play whatever melodies one wishes on its keyboard."[16] But the call for a new estheticism, for the cultivation of "tone" and "style" and "personal feeling," had only limited appeal to Ola Hansson and, considered as a literary policy, virtually none to Strindberg, who understood all too well what terrific forces might be concealed in "moods." He was scarcely ready to liken his work to the playing of melodies on a keyboard. For an early issue of Ny Jord Hansson wrote a brief survey of Swedish literary activity in 1887 in which he named Strindberg, then in bad odor in Sweden and unable to find either a theater or a publisher in Stockholm willing to take his work, the foremost living Swedish writer. He described Strindberg as a true "modern" who combines intuitive depths of insight and feeling with sharpness of psychological detail in a wide range of literature: drama, poetry, criticism, fiction, and autobiography. At the opposite pole Hansson placed fru Edgren (Anne Charlotte Leffler), a writer with only one subject, women's rights, and the founder of Swedish protest literature who headed a whole school of lesser goddesses.[17] Strindberg's own contributions

15. *Essays*, p. 45.
16. Valdemar Vedel, "Moderne Digtning," *Ny Jord* 2 (July–December 1888): 163.
17. Ola Hansson, "Den svenske Skønliteratur i Fugleperspektiv," *Ny Jord* 1 (January–June 1888): 291, 292.

to *Ny Jord* were no subjective notes struck on a finely tuned lyre; they included an article on the exasperating folly of the women's rights movement (an obsessive subject for Strindberg), another on the requirements of the modern theater, and two ferocious stories on the wiles employed in the struggle of one person for psychological mastery over another. "Analytical" literature of this sort, he believed, must surely supplant what Max Nordau had called the "synthetic," the merely "literary" performances of the past. When Strindberg arrived in Paris in the mid-1890s he was to find himself more in harmony with the *symbolistes* than he had ever been with their Scandinavian counterparts, for the French had formed, despite occasional digressions into verse technique as an end in itself and the idea of poetry as music, not merely a new estheticism but a radically romantic and mystical view of life. On the whole, it was not indeed until the latter half of the decade that typical French defenses against nineteenth-century social and intellectual upheaval —those adopted by such writers as Ferdinand Brunetière, Maurice Barrès, and Paul Bourget, and ranging from conversion to Catholicism to retreat into conservative nationalism—were to seem equally plausible in Scandinavia.[18] In short, Ola Hansson's and Strindberg's responses to the "new literature" at the beginning of the 1890s were different both in degree and in kind from those of other Swedish writers; they will be given separate consideration therefore in the following chapters.

Swedish writers interested in reading Poe would have had access by 1890 to a small body of Poe's fiction in translation and to one poem, "The Raven." A cheap and ephemeral "library of fiction" had included in its series in 1860 a translation of "The Murders in the Rue Morgue,"[19] but in 1881 and 1882 two small collections of translated stories had appeared, the latter with an introduction by

18. See Koenraad Swart, *The Sense of Decadence* (The Hague, 1964), pp. 142–143.
19. Gunnar Bjurman, *Edgar Allan Poe* (Lund, 1916), p. 411.

Henrik Schück, then a student at Uppsala University but very soon to be appointed to a professorship and to become one of Sweden's foremost literary historians. Schück used John H. Ingram's and Baudelaire's memoirs as his principal sources in outlining an inaccurate and romanticized life of Poe—"the old story," he wrote, "of the poet who is crushed under the juggernaut of a practical and prudent society." It is a story that shows us "the unfortunately so common drama of a richly endowed mind which on account of gaps in its intellectual and moral endowment is prevented from attaining that harmony in which all its powers would have had the opportunity to develop, and which comes to its demise without having left behind any permanent mark in the history of mankind." Poe drank intemperately and was also an opium eater; this may account in part, Schück wrote, for the grotesqueness of his fantasies, but they are basically the product of an overwrought temperament. Poe is a neoromantic, of interest nowadays in France where Sainte-Beuve and Mérimée and others have insisted on the poetic value of fantasy; like Love Almqvist in Sweden, he is a psychological experimenter. Only in his verse does he touch on the subject of love; the emphasis instead is on exceedingly fine gradations of feelings in the soul, not infrequently abnormal feelings.[20] This introduction

20. Henrik Schück, "Edgar Allan Poe," in Edgar Allan Poe, *Valda noveller* (Stockholm, 1882), pp. v, xii–xiv.

Poe's *Underliga historier* (Stockholm, 1881) appeared in two parts. The first part contained "The Gold Bug," "The Facts in the Case of M. Valdemar," "A Descent into the Maelström," "The Murders in the Rue Morgue," and "The Mystery of Marie Rogêt." The second part contained "The Purloined Letter," "The Premature Burial," "Some Words with a Mummy," "The Assignation," "The Black Cat," "Hans Phaall," "The Spectacles," "The Pit and the Pendulum," "The Fall of the House of Usher," and "Three Sundays in a Week." The two parts together constitute the fullest collection of Poe's fiction ever published at one time in Scandinavia.

Valda noveller, published the following year, contained "The Gold Bug," "The Facts in the Case of M. Valdemar," "The Murders in the Rue Morgue," "The Purloined Letter," "The Black Cat," "The Masque of the Red Death," "The Cask of Amontillado," and "William Wilson." It was this volume that Ola Hansson lent to August Strindberg (see p. 117, below).

to "probably the greatest American poet," when placed less than a decade later in Strindberg's hands, evoked a characteristic outburst of contempt for Schück's "stupidity."

In addition to the translations of fiction, Poe's "The Raven" had been translated, most notably by the poet and novelist Viktor Rydberg in 1877. Its publication in revised form in 1882 evidently aroused considerable interest and the poem was discussed among university students.[21]

Two major poets of the 1890s, Oscar Levertin and Verner von Heidenstam, collaborated in 1890 in the writing of a pamphlet satirizing what they called dreary "shoemaker realism." *Pepitas bröllop* [Pepita's wedding] was based in part on Levertin's familiarity with the current French reaction to naturalism, but neither he nor

---

Both the 1881 and the 1882 volumes were reviewed by C. G. E[stlander] in *Finsk Tidsskrift* 13 (1882): 448–449. Although Poe is not a new author, Estlander wrote, between readings of realistic prose one needs something to scare the sleep out of one's eyes, and this is Poe's specialty. "Naturally Poe was deeply unhappy, being a fullblooded romantic: he wearied a benefactor with his incorrigibility, dragged a wife through all kinds of misery, and died a ruined man after having wasted his exceptional talents" (p. 449).

21. It is not known when Rydberg first came to know of Poe. His translation, a tour de force of versification but lacking some of the concreteness of imagery of the original, is believed to have influenced his own verse, particularly such poems as the popular "Älvan till flickan" (Olle Holmberg, *Viktor Rydbergs lyrik* [Stockholm, 1935], pp. 215–220). Rydberg's later translation of "The Bells" became a popular recitation piece in Sweden.

Hjalmar Edgren, one time professor of Sanskrit at Yale University and later at the University of Nebraska, also translated "The Raven" for his anthology of American literature, *Ur Amerikas skönliteratur* (Göteborg, 1878), pp. 128–137.

Ingvar Holm, *Ola Hansson* (Lund, 1957), p. 100, has found evidence that translations of "The Raven" were being discussed by Hansson's acquaintances while he was a student at Lund University. Bjurman, *Edgar Allan Poe*, pp. 415–417, notes two additional translations of the poem: one by C. F. Peterson in *Budkaflen*, 8 April 1892, reprinted in *Hemlighetsfulla och fantastiska historier av Edgar Allan Poe* (Stockholm, 1908); the other by Hjalmar Sandberg in 1875 and published in *Fria tolkningar i bunden form* (Stockholm, 1882) with an introduction by Henrik Schück.

Heidenstam was to have more than a nodding acquaintance with Poe. A symbolist in poetry, Levertin would seem to have been well prepared for a sympathetic reading of Poe in the manner of the time. Almost alone of Swedish reviewers he had greeted Ola Hansson's early poetry with enthusiasm, and he had been allowed to read in manuscript Hansson's *Sensitiva amorosa*, the principal example of *décadence* to appear in Sweden. Levertin's novel *Livets fiender* [The enemies of life], published in 1891, presents a hero, Otto Imhoff, who is aristocratic and "nervous." The novel reflects Levertin's reading of contemporary French literature and psychology of the sort that helped Hansson prepare for his enthusiastic reading of Poe and that had contributed in France to the emergence of *décadence*.[22] But when Levertin might have heard about Poe from Hansson, they had had a falling out, as the reception of *Pepitas bröllop* reveals. Johannes Jørgensen in Denmark praised the little book, and Arne Garborg in Norway likened it to Valdemar Vedel's pronouncement in *Ny Jord* that art is not reportage but the creation of an effect. Ola Hansson, however, complained of the failure of Levertin and Heidenstam to take a stand against female authors, and he dismissed the work as a feeble, uninformed protest.[23] In the mid-1880s, before his opposition to naturalism had hardened, Levertin had had occasion to mention Poe in connection, strangely enough, with Zola, whose *Thérèse Raquin* Levertin compared in intensity with the work of Dickens and Dostoevski, but preeminently with that of Poe.[24] In 1893 he again mentioned Poe, this time in a newspaper review of Oscar Wilde's *The Picture of Dorian Gray*, but no more than to suggest, perhaps following Ola Hansson's preface to *Tolke og Seere* (see pages 100–101, below), that Wilde's theory of art as a re-creation of life is also the theory at the heart of both Poe's poetry and Arnold Böcklin's paintings. He later re-

22. Carl Fehrman, *Oscar Levertins lyrik* (Lund, 1945), p. 59.
23. Werner Söderhjelm, *Oscar Levertin* 1 (Stockholm, 1914): 283–285.
24. Söderhjelm, *Oscar Levertin*, 1: 163.

versed this opinion and criticized Wilde for being an esthete whose art is isolated from life.[25]

Heidenstam for his part had apparently nothing to say on the subject of Poe. He had already attacked naturalism in *Renässans* (1889) as unsuited to the Swedish temperament. He prophesied a renaissance in Swedish literature that would favor a distinctly Swedish sense of personal independence and joy. It would be subjective, but it would eschew the sickly subjectivity of *décadence*. If this were not enough in those days to discourage his reading of Poe, Heidenstam felt a lifelong hostility to America as a culture, in his mind the epitome of ruthless materialism in modern Western civilization. He allowed his dislike of America to be tempered only by a qualified appreciation of the humor of Mark Twain and Artemus Ward.[26]

Heidenstam's thematic contrast between Western barbarism and Eastern wisdom and beauty was recast by a third important Swedish poet to emerge in the 1890s, Erik Axel Karlfeldt. Karlfeldt's poem "Ungdom" pictured Sweden (and Europe) caught helplessly between "barbarism to the east," meaning Russia, and "billionairism to the west," meaning, of course, America. His uneasiness with the threatening world domination of American values and his ambivalence toward the poetry and fiction of *décadence* combined to preclude his taking any interest in Poe.[27]

A fourth major Swedish poet of the decade, Gustaf Fröding, had discovered his vocation on reading Heidenstam's first volume of verse, *Vallfart och vandringsår* (1888), an unprecedented achieve-

25. Söderhjelm, *Oscar Levertin* 2 (Stockholm, 1917): 392.

26. Harald Elovson, "Heidenstam och Amerika," *Edda* 33 (1933): 93–107. Underlying his famous essay on the Swedish temperament, "Om svenskarnas lynne" (1896), in which he called for a reconsideration of the Swedish national past as a defense against alien influences, particularly those from America, was Heidenstam's recurrent theme of the contrast between Western barbarism and the beauty and wisdom of the East.

27. For Karlfeldt's attitudes toward *décadence*, see Karl-Ivar Hildeman, *Sub luna och andra Karlfeldtessäer* (Stockholm, 1966), pp. 125–127.

ment, he believed, in poetic originality and musicality in Sweden. Then, when convalescing from alcoholism and depression in a sanatorium in Görlitz, he had come upon the Tauchnitz editions of English and American authors, including the tales and poems of Edgar Allan Poe. The experience came as a shock to an aspiring poet who had just a few months before written his sister and confidante:

> For that matter it is almost impossible to be a poet in these times, when either with or against your will you have to apply a scalpel to your feelings and not abandon yourself to them as in former times. My view is that poetry consists of warm and deep feelings expressed in a language that can evoke similar feelings in the reader. But analysis destroys the warmth and there are therefore no poets nowadays, only psychologists and observers. Poetry has lost its ties with music and instead has almost turned into a science.[28]

Now he was obliged to recognize that he was in the presence of a poet of great musical accomplishment who moreover seemed to know precisely what he was doing. Fröding wrote his sister, " 'Tales' exquisitely demoniacally horribly well done and 'Poems' in part marvelously musical—he is a true genius and a true bard, but poisoned by drugs."[29] The refrain of "The Raven" haunted his

28. *Samlade skrifter* 15 (Stockholm, 1922): 80.
29. *Frödingsminnen*, 2d ed. (Stockholm, 1925), p. 210. Fröding quoted the refrain in such a way in a letter to his sister—"the melancholy burden bore / Of never-never more" (*Posthuma skrifter* 3 [Stockholm, 1918]: 166)—as to make it clear the source was "The Raven" and not Shelley's "A Lament," which contains a similar line. In "Menageriet," *Karlstadstidning*, 28 October 1891, reprinted in *Efterlämnade skrifter* 2 (Stockholm, 1914): 35–43, Fröding described an unhappy hypochondriac in whose mind Poe's refrain constantly ran. In the same paper in 1892, Fröding contributed an exchange of letters, reprinted in *Posthuma skrifter* 1 (Stockholm, 1918): 216–226, between a sixteen-year-old girl with literary ambitions and a melancholy and like-minded

imagination, as it is said to have haunted the imagination of Gautier and Nerval and no doubt countless others; his friend Mauritz Hellberg on the staff of a newspaper in Karlstad with Fröding wrote in later years of Fröding's melancholia and his fondness for reciting the "melancholy burden" of "Nevermore." The two friends would repair to Fröding's rooms to read Poe and to ponder the sincerity of his account in "The Philosophy of Composition" of the calculated effects obtained in his poem.[30] But even before this, in a letter to Hellberg from Görlitz in March 1890, Fröding had announced that he would describe for his friend how he had written two poems ("Den höga visan" and "Skogsrån") "as Edgar Poe once described how it was that 'The Raven' was born."[31] It has since been suggested that Fröding's interest in Poe's prosodic techniques left traces in some of his own poems, including the highly popular "Säv, säv, susa," otherwise so close to folk song in manner and

young man with the name Nevermore. Citing these, Sverker Ek, "Frödings Balen," in *Festskrift tillägnad Werner Söderhjelm* (Helsingfors and Stockholm, 1919), p. 95, considered them evidence not only of an exaggerated youthful melancholy but also of a strain of real and pervasive melancholy in Fröding that had been deeply stirred by Poe's poem. Erik Vendelfelt, "Fröding upptäcker Poe," *Ord och Bild* 69 (1960): 306, suggests too that "the human thirst for self-torture" in Poe was admittedly pronounced in Fröding. In a marginal note in a Swedish commentary on Goethe, however, Fröding had written that despite his youthful sense of kinship with a character like Raskolnikov, in general he was never attracted to the morbid in literature or life: "Edgar Allan Poe has written some poems that have as greatly impressed me as they no doubt have other nervous and non-nervous persons, but for my part I do not think it was the morbid in Poe that appealed but the artistic virtuosity and the poetically beautiful." Quoted in Henry Olsson, "Goethelinjen i Frödings lyrik," in Carl Fehrman et al., *En Goethebok till Algot Werin* (Lund, 1958), p. 301.

30. As for Fröding's and Hellberg's debates on the sincerity of "The Philosophy of Composition," A. G. Lehmann, *The Symbolist Aesthetic in France, 1885–1895* (Oxford, 1950), p. 136, notes that the essay seemed to many in the nineteenth century so Machiavellian in coolness and dexterity that they hoped they could call it a hoax. It was no way for a poet to act.

31. *Posthuma skrifter* 3 (Stockholm, 1918): 95.

form.[32] Other poems with pronounced rhythmic effects and strong rhymes or giving evidence of prosodic experimentation might also be cited as having been possibly influenced by Poe,[33] but two long early poems, "Atlantis" and "Parken" [The park], have been singled out as unquestionably Poe-like—"Atlantis," on the subject of a lost civilization, influenced by Poe's "The City in the Sea," and "Parken" by no one poem unless perhaps "Ulalume," which Fröding had translated.[34] In a letter from Görlitz in March 1890 to a

32. Henry Olsson, *Fröding, ett diktarporträtt* (Stockholm, 1950), pp. 291, 370.

33. Many poems in Fröding's early volumes show a disposition for alternating masculine and feminine rhymes and for experimentation with closely rhymed short lines and with longer lines (occasionally hexameter) that bear traces, through assonance and alliteration, of internal rhyme, as for example, in "En visa till Karin":

> Mät mig ej med mått, men vät mig med tårar
> en dåre är jag vorden, en dåre ibland dårar
> [*Samlade skrifter* 4 (Stockholm, 1918): 100]

or in the pastoral "Corydon till Chloe":

> I dalens lugna famn en stilla bäck sig rörer
> i gröna mossan fram bland sköna blommors släkt
> och ifrån trädens valv man fågelsånger hörer
> och bladen böja sig för små zefyrers fläkt.
> [*Samlade skrifter*, 2: 141]

Although many times he comes close to writing doggerel, the poems in "Stämningar och bilder" show Fröding to be a master of the art of anaphora and reiteration. But all this may indicate no more than the delight such a poet would find in the poetry of Edgar Allan Poe.

34. John Landquist, *Gustaf Fröding, en levnadsteckning* (Stockholm, 1964), pp. 242–243, considers "Atlantis" superior to "The City in the Sea": "Poe takes us to a distant misty sea and presents the spectacle of the sinking and its results with great pathos. Fröding shows that Atlantis is close to us, that we share in its splendor and its downfall, and that the story of Atlantis is the story of mankind." In the use of anaphora, alliteration, alternating masculine and feminine rhymes, and a varied refrain, "Atlantis" does bear some resemblance to Poe's poem:

> Här är det ödsligt och stilla,
> här är det långt från det verkligas strand,
> drömmarnas svävande villa
> väves om vatten och land.

professor of literature at Uppsala University, Fröding had apologized for the quality of his attempts to translate poetry into Swedish and in particular mentioned "Ulalume." Sonority of language may itself convey meaning, he said in his defense. "Poe's 'Ulalume' is really absurd and peculiar, but in the original it has, through its strange harmony, a stronger effect than a more profound and grand but less sonorous depiction of sorrow."[35] The discovery and publication in 1931 of the manuscript of Fröding's translation of the poem served mainly to reaffirm the difficulties that Fröding had himself been aware of in translating poetry, especially the highly alliterative verses of "Ulalume."[36]

> Luta ditt huvud
> hit mot min skuldra,
> se över relingens rand!
>
> [*Samlade skrifter*, 3: 117]

But instead of intimating, as Poe does, what sinister forces rule the world, Fröding is closer in mood and theme to, say, Arnold's "Dover Beach" in the sad intimacy established by the speaker in the poem with his beloved, who is asked to see in the kingdom still shining beneath the sea a loss that stands for "our" loss.

Olsson, *Fröding*, p. 305, sees evidence of "Ulalume" and perhaps also of "The Raven" in Fröding's "Parken," the former in the anguished recognition of a place of former unhappiness, the latter in the theme of the death of a young woman. Stig Sjöholm, "Fröding och Byron," *Edda* 39 (1939): 180–181, suggests that Poe's influence, possibly Byron's also, is apparent in the development of themes in the last sections of "Parken." The poem is in twelve sections, each consisting of four quatrains rhyming *abab* in iambic pentameter, but without any alternating or other pattern of masculine and feminine rhymes, without internal rhymes, and with very little patterned use of alliteration or other reiterative devices. In the eighth section, each quatrain concludes with the words "ej mer" ("no more" or "nevermore"), but this melancholy phrase is not made the burden of the poem. Its subject, the dark labyrinth through which one wanders in life, is romantically gloomy and has no particular connection with Poe. The lushness of the vegetation in the park is evidently a realistic impression of a park in Malmö near the hospital in which Fröding was recovering from a bout of alcoholism.

35. *Posthuma skrifter*, 3: 93.

36. Gösta Attorps, "Edgar Allan Poes Ulalume tolkad av Gustaf Fröding: Ett märkligt fynd . . . ," *Svenska Dagbladet*, Julnummer 1931, pp. 2–3, 44.

Other translations of Poe's poems were appearing in the mean-time,[37] and in 1894 Johan Mortensen, a young graduate student and later professor of literature at Lund University, published an essay on Poe in which he located the origins of Poe's genius at the con-fluence of two currents of thought, German romanticism and Eng-lish positivism. Poe as a poet of "nerves" was shown to be typical of his time and a forerunner of the neoromanticism of the 1890s. Mortensen's sources included George E. Woodberry's biography of 1885; if it did not persuade him to abandon his Scandinavian perspective on Poe, neither did it serve to correct errors of fact de-rived from Baudelaire and Mrs. Whitman. The essay was rewritten and corrected for reprinting in 1908 in a volume of Mortensen's critical essays.[38] August Strindberg recalled the essay when he was

The translation is of the version in nine stanzas. Erland Lindbäck, *Gustaf Fröding* (Stockholm, 1957), p. 244, reprints with several verbal alterations the last three stanzas of the translation and suggests that much more than an exercise in translation, it expressed Fröding's own faith in the power of love and the melancholy, loneliness, and gloom he had himself felt.

37. Ivar Damm, "En öfversättning från E. A. Poe ["Sonnet—Silence," "Dream-Land"], *Svensk tidskrift* 2 (1892): 436–439. Bjurman, *Edgar Allan Poe*, p. 427, also names translations of "To Helen" and "The Coliseum" by Anders Österling; "Annabel Lee" by Birger Mörner; "Annabel Lee," "To Helen," "To One in Paradise," "Lenore," "A Dream Within a Dream," "El-dorado," and "Ulalume" by Sigrid Lidströmer (for *Stockholms Dagbladet* and *Svenska Dagbladet*). Bjurman also notes "obvious and strong" influence by Poe on two poems ("Elsa" and "Skräck") by the minor Scanian poet, Emil Kleen.

Johan Mortensen, *Från Röda rummet till sekelskiftet* (Stockholm, 1919), 2: 388–389, suggested the influence on Per Hallström's stories in *Vilsna fåglar* (1894) of modern English and American narrative technique, learned presum-ably while Hallström was in America. Helge Gullberg, *Berättarkonst och stil i Per Hallströms prosa* (Göteborg, 1939), pp. 20–21, narrowed the suggestion to the possibility of Poe's influence on one story ("En idé") in the volume; on the proof sheets of Gullberg's book, however, Hallström denied that Poe had ever interested him as a prose writer.

38. "Edgar Allan Poe," *Svensk tidskrift* 3 (1894): 160–180, reprinted in *Likt och olikt: Studier och kritik* (Stockholm, 1908), pp. 3–48.

introduced to Mortensen in the late nineties in Lund, and the two entered, as we shall see, into curious conversation about Poe and his significance to Strindberg.

But Strindberg first learned about Poe from Ola Hansson, and it is Hansson's reading of Poe that we turn to next.

CHAPTER 4

OLA HANSSON

Ola Hansson read Poe's prose and poetry in English in the winter of 1888–1889. The immediate result was the publication of three essays: a long study of Poe entitled simply "Edgar Allan Poe," and two short essays on other topics but adducing Poe and his work: "Andliga produktionssätt" [Methods of literary composition] and "Suggestion och diktning" [(Hypnotic) suggestion and poetry]. The two short essays will be discussed at the end of this chapter. The long Poe essay appeared first in an abridged German translation in Berlin in 1889; a complete Danish version the following year made it available to Scandinavian readers. Later, it was also translated into Norwegian and Polish and once more into German, again incomplete. The original Swedish was not published until 1921, for reasons that will become apparent. (The essay appears in the Appendix in English translation.)

The writer of the essay was at twenty-nine years of age probably the best informed Swedish critic in his time of contemporary French literature; he was also—or perhaps first of all—a poet whose work anticipated by several years significant trends in the "new literature" of the 1890s in Scandinavia. In consequence, he was, as was mentioned before, the first critic in Sweden to speak out against the dominance of tendentious naturalism. He expressed himself privately on this subject as early as 1885 when in a letter to his cousin Hans Larsson he wrote that he detected signs of the breakup of "Brandesianism" in Denmark and looked hopefully for them also in Sweden.[1] His achievements as poet and critic bear on the Poe essay, a work that Hansson laid out on a grand scale clearly intended to bring a measure of definitiveness to its subject. Hansson regarded it in later years as one of his principal writings, and Anders Österling, the distinguished Swedish poet and long-time member of the Swedish Academy, has called it Hansson's masterpiece of criticism.[2]

Although never made explicit in the essay, a major purpose in Hansson's undertaking to write it was to supply an alternative to Brandesianism in Sweden. This accounts in good part for the choice of Poe as the subject of the essay, as it does also for the emphasis given in it to Poe's art and psychology. But Hansson's anti-Brandesianism may also be detected in so slight a detail as his several references to the "night side" of the soul—the irrational, concealed side of human nature—and it will be useful to pause for a moment to examine these references, for they help introduce us to the nature of the essay as well as suggest its importance to Hansson in his opposition to the dominance of naturalism.

Whereas the night side of the soul, Hansson wrote, had been the distinctive subject of German romanticism, it was Poe's exclusive subject. Hansson borrowed the term and the titles which he cited in illustration of it from none other than Georg Brandes. Brandes's lectures of 1873 on the German romantics had noted what Brandes considered an inordinate interest in the night side

1. Cited in Hans Lindström, *Hjärnornas kamp* (Uppsala, 1952), pp. 25–26.
2. *Ola Hansson, Minnesteckning* (Stockholm, 1966), p. 41. Österling, who was, like Hansson, born in Skåne, felt a special sympathy for Hansson and his poetic evocations of the Scanian countryside. Hans Österling, the poet's father and a publisher in Hälsingborg in Skåne, accepted Hansson's *Sensitiva amorosa* as well as Strindberg's *Fadren* [The father] after Stockholm publishers, thrown into confusion by a popular outcry against immorality in literature, had refused both.

65

of the soul, which becomes visible to the sight of men, he declared, when a division of the self has permitted it to engage in self-observation: "One separates himself from himself, gazes upon himself as an observer, and soon has the appalling feeling which the inmates of a prison cell have when they look into the little glass peephole in the door and discover that the guard's eye is fixed upon them."[3] Brandes granted that the psychological insights provided by the "splitting" and "doubling" of the personality had at times been profound, but he deplored the onesided and morbid emphasis given them in German romanticism. "Struggle, will, determination," he protested, "make man whole"; the persistent probing by the Germans into man's "Naturside og Natside" was a serious fault.[4] For Hansson under these circumstances to specify the night side as Poe's exclusive subject was a clear gesture of contempt for Brandesian psychology. Brandes's belief in the efficacious will of man had brought him characteristically to a defense in 1883 of Ibsen's kind of pessimism as opposed to the gloomy pessimism then current in French literature. In the latter, he wrote, life itself is seen as evil and all is vanity and illusion, whereas Ibsen "finds the world evil but he does not call into question the goodness of life."[5] By way of illustrating this distinction, Brandes cited the contemporary French view of love as being mere illusion, whereas Ibsen is contemptuous of those who betray an ideal of love. To Ola Hansson this distinction merely provided additional evidence of both psychological and philosophical shallowness in Ibsen and his

3. "Den romantiske Skole i Tyskland," in *Samlede Skrifter* 4 (Copenhagen, 1900): 335. The term *night side* enjoyed considerable currency. Baudelaire used it in chapter 4 of *Salon de 1859*, having got it from the title of a work by Mrs. Catherine Crowe, *The Night-Side of Nature*. Mrs. Crowe cited her source for the term as "the Germans, who derive it from the astronomers" (quoted in G. T. Clafton, "Baudelaire and Catherine Crowe," *Modern Language Review* 25 [1930]: 287n).

4. *Samlede Skrifter*, 4: 351.

5. *Det moderne Gjennembruds Mænd* (Copenhagen, 1883), p. 86.

critic. Love could indeed be illusory, he was convinced; certainly it was not to be achieved through "struggle, will, determination." Ibsen, and Brandes after him, had failed to comprehend the very nature of life and the complexity and irrationality of human behavior; but it was precisely here, Hansson believed, that Edgar Allan Poe excelled. Brandes's view had led to the unfortunate acceptance in Sweden of the fiction of the "problem people," as Hansson called them—the reformers and progressive agitators who write the "tasteless, jargon-filled, wishy-washy, woodenly contrived problem-literature that is now in vogue."[6] The Poe essay was to do its share in deflating the reputation of such writing.

To corroborate on unimpeachable scientific grounds Poe's insights into the night side of the soul, Hansson brought into his essay the results of his contemporaneous study of recent treatises in psychology. He became in consequence Poe's first major psychological critic. He anticipated by more than a decade Emile Lauvrière in France and Karl Ferdinand van Vleuten in Germany, whose pretentiously "medical" diagnoses of Poe's abnormalities lack moreover the sensitivity and tact that Hansson brought as a man of letters to his psychological criticism. Admittedly, though of course not to Hansson's discredit, his reach exceeded his grasp, and he did not perfectly succeed in converting his psychological knowledge into cogent literary criticism. Yet he was not content, with van Vleuten and Lauvrière, to label Poe a dipsomaniac, "ein Kranker, der seine Delirien nicht vergaß,"[7] nor "le malheureux Poe," "le

6. *Samlade skrifter* 2 (Stockholm, 1920): 176, n. 1.

7. Karl Ferdinand van Vleuten, "Edgar Allan Poe," *Die Zukunft* (Berlin) 44 (1903): 184. The diagnosis was elaborated in Ferdinand Probst, *Edgar Allan Poe*, Grenzfragen der Literatur und Medizin, no. 8 (Munich, 1908). Although listing the German publication of Hansson's essay in 1889 (but not that of 1894 or 1895), Harro H. Kühnelt, "Die Aufnahme und Verbreitung von E. A. Poes Werken im Deutschen," in *Festschrift für Walther Fischer* (Heidelberg, 1959), pp. 198–199, describes van Vleuten's and Probst's essays as marking the turn in Germany away from emphasis on Poe's romantic life as

pauvre dégénéré," "le pauvre rêveur extatique,"[8] of their description.

Poe was for Hansson more than a case study in abnormality and certainly more than a pitiable, unhappy genius given to intermittent episodes of a special form of hereditary epilepsy. Poe epitomized for Hansson a "psychological-artistic" principle in literature. He was the ideal fusion of the perceptive and the conscious artist that Hansson himself aspired to be. Poe exhibited keen intuitive knowledge of the least accessible yet most determinative side of human nature, and he possessed unusual powers in giving it artistic form. In short, Poe's work pointed in the direction that the future course of literature would take. And in characteristic nineteenth-century fashion, Hansson thereby made of his subject a "great man" in an age of transition between the preoccupation of the past with the surface aspects of life and the coming scrutiny of vital truths that lie deep within man himself. Hansson could scarcely avoid coupling

---

"Dichter-Märtyrer" to emphasis on the psychological problems in the tales. Both van Vleuten and Probst, however, continued to identify the narrator in Poe's tales with Poe himself. More than twenty years before, in "Edgar Allan Poe," *Magazin für die Literatur des In- und Auslandes* (Leipzig) 51, no. 13 (25 March 1882): 169–172, the last of a three-part essay, Eduard Engel had spoken, with reference to "The Black Cat," "The Pit and the Pendulum," etc., of Poe's "Studien auf dem Gebiete der *pathologischen Psychologie*" (p. 169), but he had not elaborated.

8. Emile Lauvrière, *Un génie morbide: La Vie d'Edgar Poe*. Thèse . . . de l'Université de Paris (Paris, 1904), pp. 157, 231; vi, 283; 308; 429. Lauvrière's biography and his analysis in an accompanying volume of Poe's work are markedly "medical" in contrast to Hansson's literary study. Lauvrière used the last of the major works written in support of the degeneration theory, especially those of Magnan and Legrain. Strindberg knew Legrain's work, but if he owned it, he apparently did not lend it to Ola Hansson. Lauvrière's biography is essentially an elaboration of an article by Paul Moreau, "Edgard Poë, étude de psychologie morbide," *Annales médico-psychologiques* (Paris) 52 (1894): 5–26, in which the diagnosis is given of Poe's ailment as dipsomania by virtue of defective heredity. Poe was accordingly not to be thought mad in the ordinary sense: "Poe fut fou à la façon des dipsomanes, par intermittence" (p. 25). Lauvrière enlarged at length on this opinion (see especially pp. vi, 44): Poe's "folie" was of a special kind, *furor bibendi*, but was accompanied by several complications of a degenerative nature.

his acclaim of Poe, therefore, with his welcome of the new era of psychiatric truth, and as a result the essay is, paradoxically, a somewhat positivistic effort to declare war on the rule of reason in literature. Its faults are probably due more to this than to any other single cause.

Hansson's enthusiasm for Poe, although not unguarded, left him vulnerable in several ways. His frequent use, with only scanty explanation, of long quotations was a fault that his previous criticism had succeeded in avoiding; now, he relied too heavily on the sweep of his argument to carry lengthy quotations along with it. His election of Poe to be the prophetic voice of literature led to his ranging across wide areas of nineteenth-century thought, and the essay, although thereby freed of the narrowness that compromises, for example, Lauvrière's and van Vleuten's diagnoses of Poe's ailments, threatened to become mainly a mixed bag of ideas then coming to the fore in Europe. It is not that their presence in the essay is adventitious; they had been brought into it naturally enough, rooted as they were in deeply felt convictions that Hansson held about literature. But he became too much interested in them, and his attention was drawn away from Poe to theories that tended to obscure rather than to sharpen his perceptions.

Hansson's essay begins with a brief introduction outlining in broad strokes the picture of Poe that was to follow. Poe is termed, following Baudelaire, a prophet and martyr; as an intuitive genius, he is said to have anticipated the future development of the race; and in explanation of the psychological sources of his powers, Hansson describes him in his introduction as one of the world's "sick ones": he is "in *one* person the cloven trunk of madness and genius."

The body of the essay is divided into six parts. The first is a chapter in literary history and claims Poe's kinship with the German romantics in their revolt against French classicism and its shallow representation of individual character. The Germans' great discovery is said to have been the night side of human nature, which became in Poe an exclusive interest. Yet his esthetic is wholly rationalistic. His "perfected system of esthetics" is based on the triad of pure intellect, taste, and the moral sense, the cultivation of the second of which, the faculty of taste, justifies and explains the poet's doctrine of *l'art pour l'art* and his emphasis on technique.

Hansson's sketch of Poe's life in the second part of the essay tells a familiar nineteenth-century tale of Poe's misfortunes, which are described, however, as the misfortunes not of a scoundrel or of an alcoholic, but of a "morbidly nervous temperament." One of Hansson's biographical sources was Baudelaire's "Edgar Poe, sa vie et ses œuvres" (1856), the representation in which of Poe as a rarefied creature fascinated several generations of French writers; but Hansson was able to temper Baudelaire's indignant protest against the brutality of American materialism through the use of John H. Ingram's "Memoir of Poe," which prefaced the first of the four volumes of his edition of Poe's Works (Edinburgh, 1874).[9]

9. Baudelaire's memoir of 1856 prefaced the translations collected in *Histoires extraordinaires*. It was an extensive revision of "Edgar Allan Poe, sa vie et ses ouvrages," published in 1852 in *Revue de Paris* and incorporating in translation a survey of Poe's work and an obituary notice of Poe from the *Southern Literary Messenger* (see W. T. Bandy, "New Light on Baudelaire and Poe," *Yale French Studies* 10 [1952]: 65–69). Hansson would have had no occasion to seek out the 1852 memoir, which is, moreover, notable among Baudelaire's utterances on Poe for its concern with alcoholism, a subject of no interest to Hansson. It also included a long commentary, omitted in 1856, on "Berenice," to which Hansson's discussion of the story owes nothing. The tales that Hansson discusses or mentions follow no discernible pattern suggesting his use of *Histoires extraordinaires* (1856) or *Nouvelles histoires extraordinaires* (1857); he had in his possession the Swedish translations included in *Valda noveller* (1882) (see chap. 3, n. 20), which he lent to Strindberg, and John H. Ingram's edition of the Works (Edinburgh, 1874). That he followed the 1874 rather than the 1876 version of Ingram's "Memoir of Poe" is indicated by his identifying, as in the 1874 version, the source of an anecdote as Mrs. Helen Whitman rather than, as in the 1876 version, simply "one who knew him at the period," and similarly by his noting that Poe's grave was left unmarked, an error of fact corrected in a footnote in the 1876 version. Unfortunately, Hansson did not have access to Ingram's extensively revised memoir for the London

The brief third part of Hansson's essay nevertheless opens with echoes of Baudelaire's lament over Poe's sufferings in a hostile world and links Poe's creation of imaginary realms in his fiction to that of Des Esseintes in Huysmans's *A Rebours*. The picture of Poe's heritage is now complete in the manner of Taine: Poe's Norman (hence Gallic) origins, his Anglo-Saxon rearing, and his German literary heritage are said to have combined to bring French precision and Anglo-Saxon reason to his analysis of that distinctively German romantic subject, the night side of the psyche.

Poe's powers of reasoning, as displayed in selected sketches and tales of ratiocination, are shown in the fourth part of Hansson's essay to be the necessary complement of his acute visionary powers. "The Island of the Fay" and other tales are cited in illustration of Poe's ability to give definiteness to an abstract mood, a theory, or a vision.

The source and significance of Poe's abnormally heightened powers of the mind are discussed in the fifth and most original part of the essay. Here Hansson claims Poe's anticipation of modern psychiatric research (of the 1880s) in his studies of hypnotism, the loss of consciousness, and criminal psychology. Poe's characters are said to be examples of "degeneration," a technical term then much in vogue to signify an inherited aberrant condition potentially productive of either criminality or genius. "William Wilson" is called a study in the "doubling" of a personality in consequence of a malady (not specified) in the basic bodily organism. The narrator in "The Tell-Tale Heart" is said to have committed murder in consequence of a diseased will. "The Imp of the Perverse" is cited as Poe's authoritative statement of the underlying theory in these and other studies. The exposition of scientific authority for these observations occupies more of Hansson's attention in this part of the

edition in 1885 of the *Works*, in which, for example, the legend of Poe's exploits among the Greeks, which Hansson repeats, was reduced to a conjectural visit to Europe, and some less glaring errors were corrected.

essay than does Poe's fiction; unfortunately for the essay, it is science that, though slow to be forgotten, was soon outmoded as its contribution to the growth of present day psychiatric theory was supplanted by more and more clinical research. Hansson's extended effort to find scientific corroboration of his reading of Poe is, however, the first of its kind in Poe criticism and perhaps the first in the history of criticism. Hansson, to be sure, followed in this the lead suggested, as we shall see, by some of Poe's critics in France. He had benefited also from Baudelaire's remarks on Poe's abiding interest in "les *exceptions* de la vie humaine," on Poe's treatment of the usurpation by "hysterie" of "la place de la volonté," and on Poe's analysis of "ce qu'il y a de plus fugitif" in human life,[10] but Hansson's documentation, although grossly disproportionate to its application, is deliberate and extensive as never before.

In the sixth, last, and least satisfactory part of the essay, Hansson seems to have taken yet another cue from Baudelaire. Baudelaire characterized Poe's women as being "toutes lumineuses et malades";[11] Hansson describes them as shadowy, enigmatic figures: Eleanora is a "phantom," Ligeia a "will-o'-the-wisp," both betrayed by false, "degenerate" lovers. Berenice, on the other hand, is said to have been the victim of a brooding degenerate who loved not her but the ideal beauty that she symbolized. The morbid, tension-filled relationship of the sexes in Poe's work is declared to be indicative of his whole theory of life and of his doctrine of the "strangeness" that is a necessary component of Beauty.

At the time Hansson wrote the essay on Poe, he had suffered a stunning setback that made it seem to him impossible to continue his career in Sweden; beginning with this essay, he was henceforth to look first to Germany for publication of his work, and in two

10. Baudelaire, *Œuvres complètes*, ed. F.-F. Gautier and Y.-G. le Dantec 9 (Paris, 1928): 42, 43.
11. *Œuvres complètes*, 9: 44.

years' time he left Sweden for good. The Poe essay was the first strong indication that far from yielding he was ready to reassert even more firmly than before the literary principles on which he had built his career.

In an essay published in 1902 on his beginnings as a writer, Hansson wrote that he had two principal subjects: first, the countryside of his native Skåne, the southernmost province of Sweden where he had been born on a farm in 1860, and second, "the presence in human nature of the unconscious, so difficult of access, so difficult to apprehend."[12] Both subjects, he wrote, were metamorphosed into aspects of himself and had been reflected even in his first two volumes of verse, *Dikter* (1884) and *Notturno* (1885). But it was the volume of prose fiction entitled *Sensitiva amorosa* (1887) in which the theme of the unconscious had flowered in such "deep, dangerous, and beautiful" images, Hansson reported, that "Swedish criticism took it for granted that of course it could only have to do with sexual abnormalities, and that as far as *Sensitiva amorosa* was concerned, Gutenberg need not have troubled himself with his invention."[13]

The critics had indeed been harsh with a volume too strange in tone and content for them to know as yet how to "place" it. One had described it as "a kind of 'esthetic' for practitioners of certain unnatural vices," and another as "the most unwholesome and repulsive work ever proffered by a Swedish pen."[14] Their derision exacerbated a melancholy strain in Hansson and sent him into virtual isolation, from which he seems psychologically never to have completely recovered. He gained a measure of control over his despondency at first by assuming aloofness toward his critics in Sweden and in 1891 by turning his back on Sweden altogether. He

12. "Sensitiva amorosa," in *När vi började* (Stockholm, 1902), p. 159.
13. *När vi började*, p. 171.
14. Quoted in Gunnar Ahlström, *Det moderna genombrottet i Nordens litteratur* (Stockholm, 1947), p. 424, and in Ingvar Holm, *Ola Hansson, En studie i åttitalsromantik* (Lund, 1957), p. 142.

acquired a leading position as a critic in Berlin for a few years in the mid-nineties but then moved restlessly from country to country. When he died in Turkey in 1925 his sense of alienation from homeland and colleagues had become almost pathological.

Like Johannes in Kierkegaard's *The Diary of a Seducer*, the narrator in the first of the nine stories in *Sensitiva amorosa* declares his determination to avoid in the future the disgust that he has felt in his previous relations with women. He begins his story, "There remains for me only the one interest: to study and to enjoy the sex." He will, however, experience his enjoyment at a distance so that it will be uncorrupted by the vileness of the flesh and the *tristesse* that follows pleasure. He will take his pleasure rather in "the whole body and the whole soul." It will lead to a better understanding of women than through "actual relations" that often are "banal and painful," for he will be able to know many women and learn what subtle differences distinguish them from one another. This was a policy odd indeed at a time when the women's rights movement, particularly strident in Sweden, was swirling in controversy over the definition of male and female roles. Other stories, including one of a homosexual cast, tell of love that in dimly felt moods and strange disharmonies has inexplicably turned into hatred, disgust, or chilling indifference. In all, some failure in love or some incapacity for love has been revealed in a moment and a mood for which the stories—or sketches, rather—supply the context. What had caused these failures? One could scarcely say; the merest trifle, it would seem. In the recognition of that fact lay the sharpest contrast between these stories and the positivistic realism of "problem-raising" literature. The possible answers to the question of ill-fated love were to be sought across the whole spectrum of modern anxiety. Do the causes for this radical human failure, Hansson asked in one of the stories, lie in

> a purely psychological tendency, hidden morbid processes in the blood and nerves? . . . Is it mortality that has come closer

74

to man in our time, death that follows him like his own shadow and is ever to be heard treading behind him, its icy breath on his neck, the specter of death thrusting in his face its white toothless jaws and its empty black eyeholes? Or is it fate, insane and malicious fate, raising its Medusa-like head before the modern fatalist? Or the sight in our time of the struggle for existence, time's forward-rolling chariot and the millions of human vermin crushed by it to death? Is it perhaps the sickness at the heart of the universe that modern man with his quickened sensitivity glimpses within himself? [15]

The stories in *Sensitiva amorosa* were cast in fragile images, as Hansson later said. They seem indeed too delicate to bear the full weight of these questionings into the fate of modern, psychologically self-observant man—the "split" man of Brandes's description —in a world traveling "sickly" in its evolutionary course not toward progress and perfection but destruction. This sweeping, troubled vision, this "great pessimism," as he called it, permeates Hansson's study of Poe, whose tales, he tried to show, project the vision supremely and whose genius throws a ray of hope for man into the enveloping darkness ahead. Poe's tales perhaps can bear up no better under the heavy burden that Hansson placed on his own, yet in various formulations it is the kind of responsibility that all of Poe's modern critics—those who take him seriously, from D. H. Lawrence on—have asked them to assume.

15. *Samlade skrifter* 3 (Stockholm, 1919): 7, 8, 10, 43. The resemblance of Hansson's narrator to Johannes was noted by Sten Linder, *Ernst Ahlgren i hennes romaner* (Stockholm, 1930), p. 344. The Goncourts describe a recent acquaintance as dangerous on account of her immaterial, supernatural quality and her emaciation, "d'une finesse presque psychique, de cette distinction d'une femme de Poe parisienne," for whom a love like that in *Sensitiva amorosa* is conceived that is not to be physical but will bring possession of her heart, her head, and her imagination (*Journal*, ed. Robert Ricatte [Paris, 1956], 1: 1366– 1367).

Hansson came to the cosmic *décadence* of *Sensitiva amorosa* by various routes, some of them conspicuous still in the Poe essay. The recognition in the earlier work of the decisive role of intuition in human conduct had been apparent in the first volumes of verse, particularly in the yearning they had expressed for life organized naturally on some organic principle rather than bleakly and superficially on trust in reason.[16] The yearning took more precise form after Hansson's reading of contemporary French literature. In 1886, just before writing *Sensitiva amorosa*, he published a series of essays on French naturalists and *décadents*—Paul Bourget, J. K. Huysmans, Guy de Maupassant, Jean Richepin—which concluded in a fervent plea for the renewal of Swedish literature on the "psychological-artistic" principle illustrated in the work of these writers.[17] He noted approvingly Bourget's "scientific investigation of the present times . . . of the great malady of this century" that goes under many names: "the great neurosis, pessimism, nihilism," and consists, according to Bourget, of a weakening of the will, an attenuation of the moral energy, and the predominance of morbid rather than wholesome, restorative elements in life.[18] Hansson's review of Huysmans's art criticism and fiction concluded with an essay on *A Rebours*, "not a novel in the usual sense, but a scientific treatise based on a generally psychophysiological analysis," in which the author's purpose has been to depict by intuitive means "the subtleties of depravation in a modern personality as well as the concealed relation of the morbidly heightened senses to their enigmatic expression."[19] Hansson's attraction to this literature rested in good part on its readiness to seek validation in the new science that

16. Fredrik Böök, "Åttiotalslyrik," in *Från åttiotalet* (Stockholm, 1926), pp. 44–45; Erik Hedén, "Ola Hansson," in *Litteraturkritik* 1, vol. 4 of *Valda skrifter* (Stockholm, 1927).

17. *Litterära silhuetter, II: Det unga Frankrike*, in *Samlade skrifter* 2 (Stockholm, 1920): 282–284.

18. *Samlade skrifter*, 2: 159, 160.

19. *Samlade skrifter*, 2: 220, 221.

taught that one was to speak no longer of good and evil conduct but only of conditions, some of them beneficial, others destructive. The writer's task then would be to depict these "conditions" in detail, and in Hansson's view, to locate the source of the strange and often contradictory permutations of human behavior in the psychic processes of the bodily organism:

> Hence it is the enigmatic in human nature that attracts the scientist in Bourget. It is the ephemeral moments in the life of the soul that he painstakingly depicts, the least noticeable shifts of feeling and the most subtle operations of thought, everything lying within or beneath the threshold of the unconscious. It is the obscure in human nature, that which governs it and determines its whole life, yet is only felt in shifting moods or vague needs.[20]

This point of view, though distinctly naturalistic, was not in the least inconsistent with Hansson's opposition to the forms that Swedish naturalism had commonly taken, and it prepared the way for the use he was to make in the Poe essay of new psychophysiological evidence to argue for the validity and modernity of Poe's romanticism, that "blue flower," as he called it, using Novalis's phrase, from the Germanic past.

Not unexpectedly, this line of thought in Hansson's criticism of writers like Bourget and Huysmans and Poe represented yet another aspect of Hansson's discontent with Brandesianism. It derived, though perhaps only indirectly, from Taine, to whom Hansson also owed his panoramic view of the forces—the nations, philosophies, races—that come into play in the emergence of a literature. From Taine Hansson had obtained sanction for the detailed description of "une âme humaine" (but not, in Taine's continuation, of simi-

20. *Samlade skrifter*, 2: 183. Bourget's ideas in the *Essais* of the split in the soul of modern man and the sickness of the will were derived from Ribot. Hansson's *Sensitiva amorosa* draws on Ribot, of whom Hansson had learned through Bourget; later, he borrowed books by Ribot from Strindberg for the Poe essay.

larly describing "les traits communs à un groupe naturel d'âmes humaines").[21] Hansson had also had the benefit of Scandinavian precedents set in Herman Bang's *Haabløse Slægter* and J. P. Jacobsen's "arabesk" verse (pp. 17–23, above). However, it was no doubt through his reading of Huysmans and Bourget (and perhaps of other French writers too, for Poe's name was cropping up everywhere) that Hansson was moved in the first place to make his own study of Poe. It is possible that he had heard Poe discussed during his student days at Lund nearly a decade before,[22] but after the blows dealt him by Swedish critics of *Sensitiva amorosa,* he read Poe now with the assurance that his own work had been on the right track all along. His reading helped him recover his self-esteem and set him writing again. He saw that he was able to carry over into the Poe essay the "central principle" enunciated two years before in his essays on the new writers of France: the need for "psychological-artistic" literature.

A consequence of this continuity in his criticism, of vital importance to a man as disturbed by adverse criticism as Hansson had been, was that the rapidly mounting French interest in Poe as the proto-*symboliste* made little or no impression on him. He outlined in his essay Poe's "perfected system of esthetics," based on the separate functioning of pure intellect, taste, and the moral sense, but he appears to have been aware neither of Baudelaire's development in "Notes nouvelles sur Edgar Poe" (1857) of the same ideas into a theory of pure poetry nor of the new values being attached to these ideas in France in the mid-1880s in the extension

21. *De l'Intelligence,* 2d ed. (Paris, 1870), 1: 9. Bourget dedicated *André Cornélis* (1887), "un roman d'analyse," to the author of *De l'Intelligence.*

22. Holm, *Ola Hansson,* p. 100. Hansson's first mention of Poe occurs in essays from 1886 on the new literature of France (*Samlade skrifter,* 2: 226, 261). He describes Poe on Des Esseintes' list of favorite authors as "Edgar Poe with his investigation of the lethargy and stiffening of the human will in the enigmatic anguish of life and the fear of death." He calls "Edgar Poesk" Tombre's poem "Happy zigzags" in Richepin's *Brave gens.*

of *décadence* into *symbolisme*. Hansson's "central principle" of literature was dualistic, "psychological" as well as "artistic," and he would not allow the former to be subsumed in the latter. The doctrine of the self-sufficiency of art, the first axiom of the *symbolistes* although honored also by the *décadents,* was based on the wish to disengage poetry from the impurity of a fallen world,[23] but it was not at all in this direction that Hansson intended to go. On the contrary, he wished to implicate poetry deeply in life. The revelations of poetry were not for him, as they were for the *symbolistes,* spiritual correspondences lying beyond the criteria of science and history, but were—a major point in Hansson's essay on Poe—equally discoverable in science. It was distinctive of Poe's genius that he had anticipated the work of modern psychiatrists.

Nor did Hansson believe that the poet approaches divine status by virtue of his special function as creator. Poe was, rather, a man "differentiated" ahead of his time in the evolutionary process, hence superior in sensitivity and analytic powers to his fellows—a poetic superman. When Mallarmé wrote his friend Henri Cazalis as early as 1864 of the care he had taken with his poem "L'Azur" to achieve an effect "sans dissonance, sans une fioriture, même adorable, qui distrait," he had been guided, he said, by "ces sévères idées que m'a léguées mon grand maître Edgar Poe"[24]—ideas of the exacting discipline of art and (in a second axiom of the *symbolistes*) of music as the purest expression in art to which poetry might aspire. But Hansson, although one of the most conscious stylists of the period in Sweden, took only passing interest in Poe's theories about the music of poetry and none whatever in the corollary idea of art as ritual. Of the poems, he barely mentioned "The Raven," "The Bells," and one or two others.

23. See M. H. Abrams, "Coleridge, Baudelaire, and Modernist Poetics," in W. Iser, ed., *Immanente Ästhetik, Ästhetische Reflexion* (Munich, 1966), p. 132.

24. Quoted in Henri Mondor, *Vie de Mallarmé,* 6th ed. (n.p., 1941), p. 104.

On the other hand, Hansson could not say enough in wonder over the extraordinary combination in Poe's tales of ultra-romantic sensitivity and analytical reasoning. This was a psychological mystery that Baudelaire had also taken notice of in his 1856 essay on Poe but not, however, in the great "Notes nouvelles" of 1857. It was the latter which had lately become of peculiar significance to Baudelaire's French followers. In it, lessons which Baudelaire had learned from Poe about the transcendentalism of art were given a Swedenborgian turn and raised to a doctrine of the unity and spiritual correspondence of all things.[25] When Hansson, preparing to write his Poe essay, turned to Baudelaire, as he was directed everywhere in the literature to do, he consulted only the earlier essay, "Edgar Poe, sa vie et ses œuvres." Here he found many of the points he was to make in his own essay: the lament for the tragic life of a "caged" poet (but not, as in the 1857 essay, the prolonged cry of outrage against mediocrity in criticism, against democracy, and against the idea of progress, all of which Hansson surely would have embraced had he read it); the tale of Poe's winning the prize in the Baltimore competition; Willis's story (quoted) of Mrs. Clemm's looking for work for her dear Edgar; the characterization of Poe's women figures as "toutes lumineuses et malades"; and the observation that Poe's interest lies in *"l'exception dans l'ordre moral. . . . Il analyse ce qu'il y a de plus fugitif, il soupèse l'impondérable et décrit, avec cette manière minutieuse et scientifique dont les effets sont terribles, tout cet imaginaire qui flotte autour de l'homme nerveux et le conduit à mal."*[26] Indeed, the last sentence recapitulates nearly all the major elements in Hansson's essay.

To remark this direction taken by Hansson in his use of French sources on Poe is not to charge him with imperceptivity. For one

25. See André Ferran, *L'Esthétique de Baudelaire* (Paris, 1933), pp. 170–211, for a discussion of Poe's and Swedenborg's significance in the growth of Baudelaire's esthetics.

26. *Œuvres complètes* 9: 44, 42, 43. See note 9, above.

thing, the French themselves could still feel quite uncertain of the worth of the new poets who apotheosized Baudelaire and Poe.[27] The use that Hansson made of Baudelaire's 1856 essay on Poe ensued naturally enough from the interest he had taken, in his essays on Bourget and Huysmans, in the psychology of *décadence*, and the expression he had himself given it in *Sensitiva amorosa*. His mind moved most suitably in the natural world where poets were men, not gods, and poetry, far from drawing its images from the storehouse of a Swedenborgian universe, described and informed life. For Baudelaire, Poe had been a saint, a martyr and intercessor; for Hansson, he was a genius, not a "great man" in Brandes's definition of genius, but the culminating point of his age and place, yet mysteriously and miraculously in advance of both—a genius close to madness, a brilliant analyst of the night side of the soul who anticipated by intuitive means the work of a later generation of scientists.

The science that Hansson claimed for Poe was then called mental pathology. After he had finished with the more or less conventional discussion in the first three parts of his essay of Poe's relationship to German romanticism, his misfortunes in a materialistic society, and his multiracial heritage, Hansson clearly warmed, in parts 4 and 5, to his next subject, Poe's anticipation of modern mental pathology. Here he elaborated the characterization given in his introduction of Poe as "a prince of culture" who is "in *one* person the cloven trunk of madness and genius."

In an age typically preoccupied with the theme of the terror of man's separation from God, from his fellowmen, and even more drastically, from his "true" self, poets had become peculiarly sus-

27. See, for example, Maurice Peyrot, "Symbolistes et décadents," *La Nouvelle revue* 9 (1887), tome 49, pp. 123–146; and Gustave Kahn, "Les Poèmes de Poe traduits par Stéphane Mallarmé," *Revue indépendante*, September 1888, pp. 435–443.

ceptible to charges of madness as they were discovered to be at odds with the values of a rapidly growing, well-meaning, but philistine middle class. They for their part had become increasingly interested in the new science probing the fearsome powers of instinct and irrationality. Flaubert, Balzac, and Zola supported their own studies of character by recourse to physicians and medical and psychiatric publications; Sainte-Beuve took the position that certain writers—he named Rousseau, Baudelaire, Maupassant, and others —could not be fully understood without an acquaintance with the science of mental pathology; and Taine dutifully attended courses at the Salpêtrière on "l'alienation mentale."[28] It was the era of "nerves"; for Baudelaire, Poe had been par excellence the poet of "nerves." For two decades—well into the 1870s—adverse French criticism of Poe had been based on charges of his being insane or of having a sick, delirious mind, but thereafter the opposite strain had become dominant, and French critics began noting the peculiar advantages that Poe gained from being "un malade" or "un fou."[29]

28. Donald L. King, *L'Influence des sciences physiologiques sur la littérature française, de 1670 à 1870* (Paris, 1929), pp. 181–187, 193–197. Gunnar Brandell, *Strindbergs Infernokris* (Stockholm, 1950), pp. 174–175, notes the advantage to a poet in Paris near the end of the century, when Baudelaire, Poe, and Verlaine were being venerated, of being "détraqué," just mad enough to claim access to the higher forms of spiritual life. In 1890 Francis Vielé-Griffin, using arguments derived in part from Poe's "Fifty Suggestions" and in part from Lombroso and Taine, defended *symbolisme* against a socialist charge of its being too abstract and sickly: "hors, donc, la brute humaine il n'y a, rigoreusement, que des malades dans la humanité; l'artiste, *a fortiori*, est un monomane et un détraqué." "Les Forts," *Entretiens politiques et littéraires*, 1, no. 5: 163.

29. Léon Lemonnier, *Edgar Poe et la critique française de 1845 à 1875* (Paris, 1928), pp. 278–282, 289–290, cites numerous French commentaries from the 1850s and 1860s on Poe as *malade* and on his work as the product of a sick mind stimulated, it was sometimes said, by "les excès de l'intempérance et de la solitude," but more often by alcohol. But even as early as 1865 a critic (Arthur Arnould) declared that Poe "restera comme le malade le plus intéressant . . . de nos jours" (quoted in George D. Morris, *Fenimore Cooper et Edgar Poe* [Paris, 1912], p. 115). By 1886 Jules Lemaitre, in a criticism of Renan, was convening the shades of Plato, Shakespeare, and Poe in the Elysian

Hansson was following a well-established line in current opinion of Poe in France when he too designated Poe as a *malade*; it was one of the highest compliments he could pay the American.

But to support and clarify this designation, and to demonstrate thereby Poe's modernity, Hansson, unlike the French, enlisted scientific evidence. He consulted a variety of the best known authorities. The first he mentions is Joseph Moreau, author of *La Psychologie morbide* (Paris, 1859), from which Hansson quoted the doctrine that madness and genius are "congeneric" and have the same roots. It was ancient doctrine, repeated by Seneca, among others, and well-known to English readers in Dryden's couplet, "Great wits are sure to madness near alli'd, / And thin partitions do their bounds divide." Moreau himself claimed to be quoting his version from Johan Peter Frank, the author of a standard practitioners' manual in internal medicine widely used in the early part of the century.[30] The idea had acquired new vitality when Pinel,

---

fields and allowing the latter to say: "J'ai été un malade et un fou; j'ai éprouvé plus que personne avant moi la terreur de l'inconnu, du noir, du mystérieux, de l'inexpliqué," etc. ("Dialogue des morts," *Les Lettres et les arts* [Paris] 1 [January 1886]: 141). The assumption in all these comments, as in similar ones made nearly always pejoratively in America, was that the author and his work were essentially one, yet they reflect a growing acceptance of Poe as a writer making conscious use of the maladies ascribed to him. Hence it is not surprising to learn that Poe's interest in the marvelous was frequently taken in France in the 1850s as presaging modern research. *Le Figaro* wrote in 1856 that in many stories Poe "dramatise les points les plus obscurs de la science" (quoted in Lemonnier, p. 131). Ola Hansson was evidently the first to have tried to show what these points in fact were in the science of psychology.

30. Moreau does not use the term "dégénéré supérieur," but his purpose is to demonstrate "la corrélation héréditaire des deux conditions les plus extrêmes dans lesquelles l'esprit humain puisse se trouver: la folie et les aptitudes les plus élevées de l'intelligence" (*La Psychologie morbide dans ses rapports de l'influence des névropathies sur la dynamisme intellectuel*, p. 385). His citation of Frank (p. 143) as the source of the phrase also quoted by Hansson, "in radice conveniunt," is incorrect.

My survey of degeneration theories is indebted to Georges Genie-Perrin, *Histoire des origines et de l'évolution de l'idée de dégénérescence en médecine*

Fodéré, Lucas, and other alienists at the beginning of the century discovered a hereditary disposition for madness and removed it from the province of the moralists. Moreau's treatise purported to identify certain physical signs of such a disposition (some of them disquietingly slight: "l'irritabilité," "l'inégalité de caractère," and even "accidents en apparence").

Almost simultaneously with the publication of Moreau's book there had appeared the extremely influential *Traité des dégén-érescences* (1857) by Bénédict-Auguste Morel, the fountainhead in the nineteenth century of the degeneration theory of madness and genius. Although an experienced clinician, Morel took as his premise that God had created man for continuity and for immuta-ble perfection. It followed that all deviations from human perfec-tion are degenerations: "Les dégénérescences sont des déviations maladives du type normale de l'humanité, héréditairement trans-missibles, et évoluant progressivement vers la déchéance."[31] Morel was also willing to consider environmental and cultural influences on madness (he studied, for example, Swedish abuse of alcohol and Chinese abuse of opium), but his perhaps most famous follower, Cesare Lombroso, whose *L'Uomo delinquente* (1876) Hansson quotes in the German version *Der Verbrecher* (1887), did not merely indicate the signs of a "prédisposition morbide," but codified physiological irregularities that Lombroso was convinced were un-mistakable hereditary concomitants of madness. Morel's work had prepared the ground for a psychiatric nosology later in the century; Lombroso's work, though useful in spreading the idea of *le criminel-né* and thereby of criminality as an illness rather than sin or willful wickedness, took the degeneration theory up a blind alley in the

---

mentale (Paris, 1913); also to George Rosen, *Madness in Society* (London, 1968), pp. 254–255, and Henri Foucault, *Folie et déraison: Histoire de la folie à l'âge classique* (Paris, 1961), pp. 453–455.

31. Quoted in Genie-Perrin, *Histoire*, p. 54.

history of psychiatry. His *Atlas* of cranial measurements of criminals and his studies of handwriting, of which something will be said later, were for many years of much interest to amateurs of psychiatry and to sociologists, although now only curiosities.[32]

Lombroso vulgarized Moreau's idea of genius as a kind of "névrose," but another of Moreau's followers, Honoré Saury, also cited by Hansson, developed, particularly in his *Etude clinique* (1886), the idea of "le dégénéré supérieur." This is the exceptional man who is yet not a criminal although his genius too has a physiological basis. Like the criminal, he is a degenerate (in the technical sense), a biologically differentiated being. The genius and the criminal, indeed, may share certain irregularities of feature, personality, and behavior—the line between the two is often indistinct; hence the popular abuse of genius through the ages by the unthinking mob. The argument fitted perfectly into Hansson's conclusion that the closeness of the two types explained the uncanny insights of the genius Poe into the psychology of the criminal mind. It also explained in yet another way the hostility of his contemporaries toward him.

Hansson learned another kind of lesson in modern psychiatry from his reading of treatises by Théodule Ribot and Angelo Mosso. Neither was a theorist of degeneration, but both, like the degenerationists, sought a physiological basis for mental illness. Hansson quoted from Mosso's popular work on the physiology of fright and pain, *La Peur* (1886), on the aptness of Poe's descriptions of fear and saw in his study of the concomitants of fear a resemblance to the expressive theory of emotions held by the Danish psychologist

32. An augmented English version of Lombroso's *Der Verbrecher* appeared as *Crime, Its Causes and Remedies* (Boston, 1918). Equally influential, but not cited by Hansson, was Lombroso's *Genio e follia* (1863). The preface by Dr. Ch. Richet to the French version (*L'Homme de génie*, 1889) lists Poe and Baudelaire among the great men who have been known to be insane (E. A. Carter, *The Idea of Decadence* [Toronto, 1958], pp. 67–68).

Carl Georg Lange.[33] Hansson had already learned from his earlier reading of Bourget's *Essais* and fiction a great deal about Ribot's theories of the emotions. Bourget had drawn on case studies reported by Ribot in *Les Maladies de la personnalité* (Paris, 1885) and *Les Maladies de la volonté* (Paris, 1883)—as well as other works, but these were not now consulted by Hansson—and had profited from Ribot's descriptions of the subtle changes that can

33. Usually called the James-Lange theory, Lange's and William James's publications on the subject (see *Principles of Psychology* [New York, 1890], 2: 449–467) having appeared almost simultaneously. The entire passage on Poe in Mosso, *La Peur, étude psycho-physiologique* (Paris, 1886), p. 156, reads in the English translation of E. Lough and F. Kiesow (*Fear* [London, New York, and Bombay, 1896], pp. 247–248):

> One of the greatest physiologists of fear was Edgar Allan Poe, the unhappy poet who lived in morbid hallucinations, and died at the age of thirty-seven in a hospital, a victim to intemperance, amidst the horrors and convulsions of *delirium tremens*.
>
> No one has ever described fear more minutely, none have so ruthlessly analysed, or made us feel with more intensity, the pain of overwhelming emotions—the throbbing which seems to burst the heart and crush the soul, the suffocating oppression, the awful agony of him who awaits death. No one ever plunged the mind of man into more horrible abysses, or led it into darker, gloomier wildernesses. None have ever inspired such horror with storm, tempest, the phosphorescence of decay, the lightning-flashes in the dead of night, the sighs and moans losing themselves in the darkness, the grip of fleshless hands amid the mystery of graves and ruins.
>
> Who can forget those midnight terrors, those streaks of lurid light, those faint footfalls in the dark which make us shudder, those murders which paralyse the limbs, the groans, the strangled cries from the depths of a soul in agony? And those pulsations of the heart, deep, rapid, restrained, sending forth, like a muffled bell, a dull sound which spreads in the silence of the night, beating, throbbing even after death? How useless becomes even the courage of despair before these motionless spectres which fill us with terror! And the tortures and horrors for which words fail us, which still the heart, close the staring eye and numb the trembling limbs, stretch us senseless on this rack of fright and kill us with agony!

It is a passage to which Hansson was much indebted in his Poe essay, not least in style and imagery. In a review article on Mosso's book in *Journal des Savants*

inexplicably occur in personality. Hansson had been particularly struck with Ribot's idea, which Bourget had adopted, of "la multiplicité du moi." Ribot argued that the self is wholly organic, hence constantly in flux, a fact usually obscured from the individual himself in the complexities of modern civilization. The doctrine was summed up in the slogan that Hansson quotes in the Poe essay from Ribot: "tel organisme, telle personnalité." The evolutionary process that had taken man to ever higher levels of achievement was also serving to attenuate his consciousness of the deeply primitive, organic self: he has lost his sense of wholeness and fails to recognize the collective nature of his every act. As Hansson reports Ribot's argument, "It is feelings that govern men," not some "indissoluble entity" called the self. It is only conceit in man that allows him to speak of acting on his convictions or of exercising free will.

There were exciting possibilities in these ideas for a critique of Poe's fiction, but by the time Hansson turned in his essay to a discussion of "William Wilson" and "The Tell-Tale Heart," Saury and Lombroso and their notions about degeneration had intervened, and Ribot had been all but routed. All that remained of his doctrine was the term *ratio sufficiens,* which Hansson found useful in defining the irrational element in behavior that Poe had called

---

(1886), E. Caro took special note of the literature of fear in the fiction of Anne Radcliffe, E. T. A. Hoffmann, and Poe. "Edgard Poë a poussé l'illusion [of one's experiencing fear when reading his tales] si loin qu'il a mérité d'être loué par le savant le plus compétent dans cet ordre de phénomènes," and goes on to quote Mosso on "ce poète malheureux" (p. 438).

Other references to Poe in psychological literature were very brief. Lombroso, *The Man of Genius* [*L'Uomo di genio*] (London, 1891), pp. 316, 318, 320, 325–326, misread Baudelaire's passage on the "sardonic" American's view of Poe and thus cited Poe as an example of vagabondage and alcoholism in men of genius. Henry Maudsley, "Edgar Allan Poe," *American Journal of Insanity* 17 (October, 1860): 152–198, was perhaps originally responsible for the medical diagnosis recurrent in the century of Poe as a victim of defective heredity. For other references, see Philip Young, "The Early Psychologists and Poe," *American Literature* 22 (1951): 442–454.

"perverseness." The narrator in "The Tell-Tale Heart" was thus described as "a degenerate who commits murder with no *ratio sufficiens* whatever." He murders compulsively, and still the degenerate, he also reveals his crime compulsively. It is his personal nemesis.

This is typically as far as Hansson took any of his criticism in part 5 of the essay. For a moment he seems, when he speaks of Poe's specialty as *livsångest* (dread of life) and *dödsskräck* (fear of death), to have perceived that Mosso's theories had in Poe's fiction been perhaps somewhat more existential (and *décadent*) than psychophysiological. And for several pages his exposition of Ribot's theories gives promise that a fruitful and original examination will follow of whatever signs of "la multiplicité du moi" may be in evidence in Poe's fiction. The commentary, when it comes, however, falls off instead into meager commonplaces decked out in current psychiatric jargon. Certainly, Hansson's criticism had the merit of insisting that Poe's tales be read, so to speak, from the inside, as dramatizations of crises in the life of the soul, and not as meretricious contrivances for inducing feelings of horror nor, as Hansson said, merely as allegories "of the conflict of good and evil within the individual." Even so, he was held back from any deep and sustained penetration of the tales (such as even Lauvrière was to venture upon) by his eclecticism and fondness of theorizing, and perhaps most of all by his commitment to the rationalism of the studies of irrational behavior that he had consulted. He lived still under "la lune pâle des nuits du Nord," but its spell was broken here; his attention had been wholly diverted from the *décadent* idea of death that Bourget had been fascinated by in Baudelaire, "l'horreur de l'être / Dans l'amour profond de la mort."[34] Hansson's attention had been directed instead to the categorizing speculations of the infant science of mental pathology. It is a failure regrettable in one so

34. Bourget, *Poésies* 1876–1882, quoted in Kenneth Cornell, *The Symbolist Movement* (New Haven, 1961), pp. 24–25.

well prepared by temperament and interest to distinguish between the experience of literature and the theories of scientists. Yet if failure it is, it was characteristic of the age to confuse the two, and it had been from the beginning Hansson's habit to take enlightenment wherever he found it, even in the notoriously tangled confusion of nineteenth-century psychiatric thought.

There were contradictions even among the few theories that Hansson happened to use in the Poe essay.[35] They vanished, however, as we shall see, under the shelter given them in the essay by the theories of Carl Du Prel, a German spiritist and author of *Die Philosophie der Mystik* (Leipzig, 1885),[36] which enjoyed considerable prestige for a decade. But even without this, the several psychiatric theories cited by Hansson did have the psychophysiological principle in common. They all recognized the existence of a secret and psychically primitive self with roots in the human organism. They suggested, it is true, different paths whereby to penetrate to the inner man: studying and charting his biological heritage (family

35. In a letter to Strindberg Hansson noted a contradiction between the degenerationists' view of mental illness as a kind of atavistic relapse and the reverse view, held by Saury, of such illness as the result of evolutionary development (see p. 130, below). Another sort of contradiction was that between Ribot's dynamic pre-Freudian theory of the multiple, shifting self and, on the one hand, the degenerationists' view of mental illness as a deviation from perfection, and on the other hand, Du Prel's notion of a more or less stable though submerged "Subject." Ribot rejected flatly "l'idée d'un *moi* conçu comme une entité distincte des états de conscience" (quoted in Lindström, *Hjärnornas kamp*, p. 120). Du Prel's idea of a transcendental subject appears not to have been an early conception of what is now commonly called the "unconscious," but an occult version at several removes (Schopenhauer, Hartmann) of Kant's "original and necessary consciousness of the self" (quoted in *Encyclopedia of Philosophy* [New York, 1967], 4: 312). Loren Eiseley, *Darwin's Century* (Garden City, N.Y., 1958), pp. 299–300, has called the degenerationists' position "the last stand of the special creationists against human evolution."

36. Hansson wrote an essay on Du Prel in 1885 but it was not published until 1930: "Carl du Prel och somnambulism i romanen," in *Efterlämnade skrifter i urval* (Hälsingborg, 1930), vol. 3. Du Prel's book was translated into English as *The Philosophy of Mysticism* (London, 1889).

disorders and signs of degeneration), defining his instinctive life, discounting the cultural accretions of personality in favor of the fundamental tone of the psychic mechanism, and so forth. The causal hypotheses and the methods varied, but the object in each was always the discovery of man's elusive soul in the presence of his flesh, blood, and nerves.

Already, however, there were researchers who were becoming increasingly convinced that the psyche reveals its secrets most tellingly in dreams or in the artificially induced equivalent of dreams, the hypnotic state. While medical studies of hypnotism were being conducted by Charcot at the Salpêtrière and by Bernheim at Nancy, at the popular level hypnotists, mesmerists, and old-fashioned animal magnetizers were enjoying a tremendous vogue in the 1870s and 1880s. Carl Du Prel seized on the revelatory potentiality of all "somnambulistic" states (his blanket term for hypnosis, dreams, revery, etc.) and thereby provided Hansson in the Poe essay with a broad, quasi-philosophical sanction for any and every sort of undertaking aimed at exploring the true, inner self of man.

Du Prel, insisting that the great merit of his theory of personality was its monistic basis rather than the usual body-mind dichotomy, owed more to philosophical Idealism and nineteenth-century spiritism than to clinical psychiatry. His theory posited the existence of a "transcendental" nucleus of personality (called the "Subject") not unlike the metaphysical (as opposed to psychological) entity that Eduard von Hartmann had called "the Unconscious." The "Subject" was presumed capable of perceiving regions of experience lying beyond the range of ordinary sensory organs. Du Prel was convinced that by imperceptible mutations in the long slow process of biological differentiation the sensory organs were increasing their power, with the result that new inroads were continuously being made by man on the invisible, inaudible, nonsensate world. The process was to continue, according to Du Prel, until even higher stages of biological refinement would be reached, the nature of which is already intimated in the disclosures given in dreams and abnormal states, like delirium and mental illness. In such "somnambulistic" conditions the threshold of sensation is lowered to the point where the "Subject" can at last be apprehended. This shift from the clinical to the mystical level of the search for the nuclear self permitted Hansson to correlate his various psychiatric theories and take biographical and other evidence of hypersensitivity in Poe as proof of his being the man of the future, "one of the mystic seers of the world who arrive at the new truths not through thought but through vision." Possessed of organic refinements that would become common only in future generations, Poe was a kind of psychological as well as poetic superman, an artist preternaturally aware of his "transcendental," "nuclear" self, doomed to suffer the harshness of the sensate world and to be confounded by the hostile incomprehension of ordinary men.

Though lamenting with Baudelaire Poe's wretchedness in America, Hansson saw the conflict between artist and society as unavoidable and even as necessary in the evolutionary growth of human sensibility. Later, the conflict would assume for him some of the fierceness of the Nietzschean superman's struggle with his environment, but now he regarded it simply as the inevitable fate of genius that is uncomfortably close to madness—as the romantic destiny of the "lonely ones" in an age of pessimism. This was the stage to which Hansson's Du Prellian combination of Darwinism, décadence, and psychiatry had brought the idea so innocently pondered in one of Poe's marginalia:

I have sometimes amused myself by endeavoring to fancy what would be the fate of any individual gifted, or rather accursed, with an intellect *very* far superior to that of his race. Of course, he would be conscious of his superiority; nor could he (if otherwise constituted as man is) help manifesting his consciousness. Thus he would make himself enemies at all points. And since his opinions and speculations would widely differ from those of *all* mankind—that he would be considered a madman, is evident. How horribly painful such a condition! Hell could invent no greater torture than that of being charged with abnormal weakness on account of being abnormally strong.[37]

Even as he was preparing the Poe essay, Hansson had begun reading Nietzsche with renewed interest under Strindberg's encouragement. There are signs of this in the essay: the use of the slogan *Umwerthung aller Werthe*, the reference to the nonsensical egalitarian principles of the Enlightenment, and the references to Nietzsche by name. Nietzsche's great impact, however, came afterwards and caused Poe to be entirely eclipsed as an influence on Hansson's mind. Before the year was out Hansson's bride, Laura Mohr, had translated his pioneering booklet *Friedrich Nietzsche, seine Persönlichkeit und sein System*. Yet when in a few years' time Hansson looked back to this period, he recalled in a letter to Viktor Rydberg the release of creative energy he had experienced from his reading of Poe:

At that time I became acquainted with two spirits: Poe and Nietzsche. With the former I lived out [lefvde jag ut] a long period of my life—was liberated from something that surely had been part of the best in me and could therefore have made me in the best sense productive, but that had also been a hypnotic power and terror. I was made free and felt something of a new strength within me, a strength that did not know what to do with itself, a strength that evidently had not yet really awakened to self-consciousness. Then came Nietzsche.[38]

37. Edgar Allan Poe, *Works*, ed. James A. Harrison (New York, 1902), 16: 165.
38. Quoted in Holm, *Ola Hansson*, p. 117.

The new allegiance was not a betrayal of the old, but an addition to it that provoked, of course, an electrifying rearrangement of its emphases. Strains of thought to which Hansson had been responsive had found their way into Nietzsche's writings as well; one thinks particularly of the insistence they both shared that man renounces at his peril the influence of the irrational, unconscious forces of the mind; or more narrowly, of the Lombrosian doctrine in *Götzen-Dämmerung*, which had appeared in Berlin bookstores a few months before Hansson's Poe essay, of the criminal as a strong man, a potential genius frustrated by the mediocrity of society.[39] As Ingvar Holm points out, Hansson's construction of a philosophy of personal development as it was exemplified in the Poe essay in the connection drawn between genius and madness allowed him in a letter to note with satisfaction the circumstances of Nietzsche's madness, and later, to name "nerve-sickness" in his family as the source of his own hypersensitivity.[40]

In a posthumously published essay on Nietzsche, Hansson aligned the philosopher on his and Poe's side as "an opponent of naturalism, a subjective lyricist, a seer into the future, a prophet in the style of the Old Testament in the midst of a century of commerce and utilitarianism."[41] By these standards, at any rate, Hansson's essay on Poe may be described as Nietzschean.

Despite the liberation that Hansson reported he had experienced on reading Poe, the direct effect on his fiction was very slight. In 1920, when commenting on his correspondence with Strindberg, Hansson spoke of having written the eight stories in the collection *Parias* [Pariahs] at the time he was working on the Poe essay. The

39. *The Portable Nietzsche*, ed. Walter Kaufmann (New York, 1954), p. 549. *Götzen-Dämmerung* appeared in the bookstores in February 1889 (*Gesammelte Werke* [Munich, 1926], 17: 381). Nietzsche had sent Strindberg a copy before the end of 1888.

40. Holm, *Ola Hansson*, p. 108.

41. "Friedrich Nietzsche och naturalismen," in *Efterlämnade skrifter i urval* 4 (Hälsingborg, 1931): 102.

collection was first published in Danish and German translations in 1890. Except for the sixth and eighth, the stories in it tell of crimes committed, as Hansson would say, without *ratio sufficiens*. The sixth tells of the ironic self-destructiveness of a visit to a prostitute, and the eighth is an essay rather than a narrative on the multiplicity of possible hidden motives in a case of suicide. It closes with a statement of thesis applicable to the entire book: "We have built our lives, our society, our laws on an illusory world [of rationality] that we have ourselves created and that is, however, only a caricature of the real world, which we never attain."[42] This marks no advance in Hansson's work; like everything else in the book, it is a reiteration of a major theme of more than two years' standing, although Hansson's reading of Poe and his study of scientific literature in connection with the writing of the Poe essay may have helped clarify these old ideas. They seem certainly to have suggested further applications.

The first story in the volume *Parias* is nevertheless of special interest. It lent its title "En Paria" [A pariah] to the entire collection, but it had been first printed as a separate story in *Ny Jord*. Its appearance there in November 1888 caught Strindberg's eye and led to the exchange with Hansson that is discussed in the following chapter. It is a frame story in which the primary narrator takes no active part. He tells of his week-long acquaintance with a Swedish-American entomologist who has returned to Sweden to collect specimens for a museum in Minnesota. The two men see little of each other, but at the end of the week the entomologist confides that he is a marked man, a pariah, having needlessly and unintentionally forged a document by compulsively, unthinkingly copying the signature from a letter. Later, he just as compulsively revealed his crime, he says, and was sentenced to a prison term. At his visi-

42. *Samlade skrifter* 3 (Stockholm, 1919): 137. Hansson's remark on the writing of *Parias* appeared in "En brevväxling med August Strindberg," *Göteborgs Handels- och Sjöfartstidning*, 22 May 1920.

tor's departure, the primary narrator concludes the tale by lamely noting that his visitor may have lied, "but it is not at all impossible that he had told the truth."

Perhaps the visitor's vocation was suggested by Legrand's ento-mological interests in "The Gold Bug," but it is of no consequence in Hansson's story. The compulsive criminality, however, and the equally compulsive need to confess (which is described in the story in words close to those Hansson used in the Poe essay) may have had their source, though certainly not their sole warranty, in "The Imp of the Perverse" and "The Tell-Tale Heart." The lame con-clusion and the flat style in which both the frame and the inner stories are narrated are quite unlike anything in Poe, yet they stand perhaps as Hansson's attempt at the analytic method he so much admired in Poe. The net effect is nevertheless much closer to that of the dispassionately reported case studies in Hansson's psychiatric sources. Parallels to Poe have been sometimes noted in Hansson's later fiction, but all, as might be expected from so eclectic a reader as Hansson, have been shown to have had at least one other possible source.[43]

43. Bjurman, *Edgar Allan Poe*, p. 424, and Erik Ekelund, *Ola Hanssons ungdomsdiktning* (Stockholm, 1930), pp. 161–162, detect the doppelganger motif from "William Wilson" in Hansson's "Husvill" (*Samlade skrifter* [Stockholm, 1920], 4: 103–140), but Holm, *Ola Hansson*, p. 234, points out other possible sources in *Peter Schlemihl* and in a case reported by Ribot. In another of Hansson's stories, "En modermördare," a degenerate's matricide is prompted by his fascination with the movement of the mother's Adam's apple —a variation, possibly, of "The Tell-Tale Heart," but also of a case reported by both Ribot and Saury (Ekelund, *Ola Hanssons ungdomsdiktning*, p. 157).

In the sixteenth of the prose poems in Hansson's *Ung Ofegs visor* (Stock-holm, 1892; translated as *Young Ofeg's Ditties* by "George Egerton" [London and Boston, 1895]), some details from "The Raven" perhaps are visible in the midnight setting of an encounter between the narrator and a stranger who has burst into his room to proclaim a motif from Hansson's essay on Poe: "Living, I am called mad; dead, I am called genius" (Holm, *Ola Hansson*, pp. 112–113, which includes the unconvincing suggestion that Hansson's use of anaphora derives from Poe's use of refrain).

Despite the meagerness of Poe's direct influence, Hansson continued to hold Poe in special regard even after Nietzsche had become the predominant influence. In a letter to Viktor Rydberg in 1892 Hansson declared that "to him [Poe] I will surely be faithful to the end of my days; beyond him I am able to glimpse nothing." He had wanted from Rydberg, he wrote in another letter at this time, his opinion of the Poe essay: "Along with the prose pieces enclosed in manuscript [*Ung Ofegs visor*] and *Sensitiva amorosa*, it is the poem [dikt] that is most precious to me."[44]

At the beginning of this chapter two short essays were cited as having been, with the long Poe essay, among the immediate results of Hansson's study of Poe. The first of these, "Andliga produktionssätt" [Methods of literary composition], was published in German translation in Frankfurt in the autumn of 1889 and in Norwegian translation the following year in *Samtiden*, where it contributed to the discussion in Norway of the "new literature." It appeared in Swedish for the first time in 1921 as part of Hansson's collected works. The essay describes two "methods" of composition: the inspirational, the method of Strindberg (as Hansson could testify from firsthand experience) and of the romantics, and the systematic, the method of the naturalists. The two methods, he wrote, reflect basic differences of mind, hence may be as characteristic of the scholar as of the poet. Nietzsche works by the first method, Hansson felt certain, and Darwin by the second. Occasionally an exception to this rule appears, as it does in Edgar Poe, who works with Darwinian thoroughness and objectivity on materials that are wholly conceived in his imagination. Poe presents us with the dilemma of choosing between what seems the certain evidence in

44. Both letters are quoted in Holm, *Ola Hansson*, p. 115. Rydberg was highly complimentary of Hansson's essay on Poe: "Your translation of Edgar Poe's work [dikt] testifies to the mastery in one person of the art of language and of poetry. Indeed in places your essays are also the work of a poet" (*Viktor Rydbergs brev*, ed. Emil Haverman [Stockholm, 1926], 3, no. 270).

"The Raven" that he works by inspiration and the asseverations in "The Philosophy of Composition" that the poem was constructed artificially through a series of "combinations." "It is as though we met someone, felt the warmth of his body, peered into his eyes, saw him move and heard him speak—and then the most competent of all witnesses appeared and assured us that we were dealing with a finely wrought statue. For a mechanically assembled construct is essentially different from an organic living being, even among the products of the human mind."[45] Poe had nevertheless succeeded in using two polar methods of composition, and he had accordingly established a rigorous standard for all future literary composition.

The second essay, "Suggestion och diktning" [Suggestion and poetry], in which the example of Poe is cited in illustration of the force of suggestion in the creative process, was published in 1892 as part of a chapter in a German treatise on the psychology of hypnosis. The essay did not appear in the original Swedish until 1897.[46] It begins by distinguishing between "classic" authors like Goethe and Schiller, whose work is normative and appeals to reason and morality, and "the others," like Kleist and Love Almqvist, but most notably that *enfant perdu* Edgar Allan Poe, whose poems are constructed not of ideas but of moods. Poe and these other "impressionist suggestionists" capture impressions as they emerge from the unconscious. These poets create through the moods and rhythms of their inner being a realm in which suggestion rules although beneath the threshold of consciousness. Here and elsewhere in the essay Hansson seems to have been approaching a *symboliste* concept of poetry as the embodiment of a mystical reality intractable

45. *Samlade skrifter,* 9: 189–190. The essay appeared under the title "Litterarische Produktionsarten" in *Frankfurter Zeitung,* 24 September 1889, and "Litterære produktionsmaader" in *Samtiden* (Bergen) 1 (1890): 314–321.

46. *Samlade skrifter,* 9: 262–263. The essay first appeared in German translation and with the addition of prefatory and concluding remarks as "Beitrag Ola Hansson's" in Hans Schmidkunz, *Psychologie der Suggestion* (Stuttgart, 1892), pp. 260–275.

to ordinary discourse. The truth discovered by the visionary poets, he wrote, is not of the same order as the truth of science; it serves rather "to free what is fettered, to awaken what is slumbering, to give consciousness to what is unconscious."[47] It is poetry of intensity of feeling rather than of breadth of learning; at its best it yields entirely to the power of suggestion.

> One of those most susceptible to suggestion, the most sensitive of all, an inexhaustible source for examining the relationship between suggestion and poetry, a trove of psychic secrets, and one for whom the least thing can turn into perversity and the perverse into the obvious, is Edgar Poe. All his work is suggestion; he moves out of one state of hallucination and clairvoyance into another; he is everywhere more at home and knows how to bring greater clarity to us than the sober light of day in which we all wander. His habitation is the realm of compulsive ideas, of perverse impulses, of irrational conduct, of minimal impressions, which expand into a whole structure of experience; with Darwinian meticulousness he worked with material that had no other existence than in his imagination. A reflection on dark water became in his mind the figure of a woman in white, then an oar that she paddled with, then a boat in which she stood; and his imagination begets still more by the power of suggestion: the figure becomes a fay and the fay an incarnation of grief over mortality. A shadow, a melancholy half-light, filters into his soul and becomes a pensive mood; the mood takes leave of him and becomes a point of darkness in the room; the dark point takes form and becomes a raven; and the raven, with its nihilistic "Nevermore," demolishes all hope of life, the means by which the poet tries to cling to existence.[48]

47. *Samlade skrifter*, 9: 257.
48. *Samlade skrifter*, 9: 273–274.

Hansson continued with an outline of "The Philosophy of Com-position," which he regarded, however, not as an esthetic for sym-bolism nor even as a hoax—two common interpretations of the 1890s, but as a defensive maneuver by the poet grieving over the death of his beautiful young wife. It is

> a rather obviously transparent device by which someone on whom the power of suggestion has operated [den suggere-rade] tries to turn attention away from his Achilles' heel by exerting his own powers of suggestion [suggerera] on his read-ers. People who live deeply the unconscious part of their lives are more or less deliberate dissemblers.[49]

Evident here is the view taken in the long Poe essay of Poe as the exceptional man, the Poe to whom Hansson had said he would remain faithful to the end of his days:

> If we consider how infinitely full the world is of potential suggestion and how infinitely few and crude the suggestions have hitherto been that are discernible to the undifferenti-ated nerves of the average man, we may obtain an approxi-mate notion of the condition of the chosen ones, like Poe, whose organs are so sensitive and finely constructed that they detect a physical and spiritual reality and feel it playing about them even while we others see nothing of the sort.[50]

Hansson would have been much surprised to learn that these ideas won the strong approval of his cousin Hans Larsson, a profes-sionally trained logician and one of his closest friends from his home province of Skåne and university days at Lund. Larsson be-came a professor of philosophy at Lund and a prominent estheti-cian. In an essay on "The Intuitive Life" published posthumously in 1944, he took care to acknowledge that Ola Hansson and he had

49. *Samlade skrifter*, 9: 276.
50. *Samlade skrifter*, 9: 276.

differed from the start in their views of art and literature. In the present instance they also seemed to disagree, Hansson looking on the problem of poetic composition as a play of the emotions, Larsson as a problem in logic. But with this one reservation Larsson found himself in perfect agreement with Hansson. "The Philosophy of Composition" seemed to him too an unacceptable account of the creative process; and he agreed—unaware, of course, of the biographical facts—that Poe's real motivation in writing "The Raven" was his grief over the death of his young and beautiful wife. "It was in this circumstance that the power of suggestion lay." Larsson insisted, however, that the "precipitation" of Poe's grief included a wider range of experience than Ola Hansson had allowed: "all the thoughts associated with what his wife meant to him, and how empty life would now be, countless memories, fantasies, all converging in the ineluctable finality of 'Nevermore.' "[51] Yet it was true, as Hansson had said, that although a poem may be analyzed after the fact by rational analysis, it cannot be so brought into being, and Larsson accepted Hansson's description of the role of suggestion in poetic composition as a legitimate though partial statement of a central point that he had made in his own esthetics.

In the early years of the 1890s Hansson again had occasion to indicate the value he placed on Poe's work and methods despite the strong appeal that Hansson had since felt in Nietzsche and in the cultural teutonism of Julius Langbehn, author of the anonymously published *Rembrandt als Erzieher* (1890). Hansson placed his long Poe essay first in a collection of six essays published in Kristiania in 1893 in Norwegian translation under the title *Tolke og seere* [Interpreters and seers]. This volume served as the basis for two editions in German, *Seher und Deuter* (1894, 1895), for a Polish

51. "Det intuitiva livet," in *Postscriptum*, ed. Johanna Hans-Larsson and Ivar Harrie (Stockholm, 1944), p. 196. Reidar Ekner, *Hans Larsson om poesi* (Stockholm, 1962), pp. 33–34, 219, relates Larsson's commentary at this point to his basic ideas on the intuitive nature of art.

edition in 1905, and for a greatly augmented Swedish edition in 1921 as part of the collected works. The six essays in the Norwegian edition took as their subjects, besides Poe, Vsevolod Garshin, Friedrich Nietzsche, V. K. S. Topsøe, Max Stirner, Paul Bourget, the author of *Rembrandt als Erzieher*, and Arnold Böcklin, all of them "genuinely modern minds," Hansson wrote in a preface to the volume, who represent ideas and ideals widely held by the present generation of young writers and artists.

How many present day minds have not proceeded from the breach between the altruism which beat so strongly and morbidly in Garshin's all too generous heart, and the individualistic egotism which received its most bizarre and at the same time most powerful expression in Stirner's metaphysics and Nietzsche's moral doctrine and poetry—how many have not proceeded from this point as did the irresolute, spineless, maudlin reactionary whose prototype may be found in Bourget, in his personality as an author as well as in the heroes of his books. And I believe that many will—in reaction to the spirit which, beginning with the Gallic cultural revolt of 1789 and by means of the Gallic-influenced Jewish-South German movement of 1848, penetrated the Nordic countries after 1870 through Georg Brandes's personality and his disciples—recapture their true selves in the Pan-Germanic culture founded on instinct which is described in *Rembrandt als Erzieher* as a landscape lying in the first feeble rays of daybreak. And we who wander through life and our pursuits in the shadow projected by the colossal figure of mysticism looming ahead of us on the horizon, will perhaps, one by one, feel the painful anguish of Poe's mysticism find its resolution in the profoundly peaceful harmony of Böcklin's mysticism.[52]

52. *Samlade skrifter*, 10: 6–7.

Far from being a local Scandinavian phenomenon, Brandesianism has acquired here a long history and is seen as the culmination in Scandinavia of historical forces of revolt and political distress that must be met by the more powerful forces that emanate from the secret depths of the individual soul and are shaped by the action of race and milieu. This is incipient aryanism that is obliged to reject now the "irresolute, spineless, maudlin" *décadence* of a Bourget, even though Poe, for whose acquaintance Hansson, as we have seen, owed much to Bourget, remains somehow invulnerable to the same charges and is indeed given pride of place in the essay collection. It is confirmation of the heavy investment Hansson had made in this "prince of culture," as he had called Poe in the long essay, and of his continued faith in the "psychological-artistic principle" which Poe had so brilliantly displayed for him.

CHAPTER 5

AUGUST STRINDBERG

August Strindberg's acquaintance with Poe's work dates from the beginning of his friendship with Ola Hansson. He wrote to Hansson 16 November 1888, the same day that Hansson's story "En Paria" [A pariah] had appeared in *Ny Jord*. Hansson was then languishing at his brother's farm in southern Skåne, badly shaken by the adverse criticism of *Sensitiva amorosa*. He contemplated earning a doctorate in literature, but in his loneliness and isolation he soon dismissed the thought.[1] But then from across the Öresund he received Strindberg's letter urging him to make a one-acter of his story. Strindberg was trying to start up a "little theater" in Copenhagen on the model of Antoine's Théâtre libre in Paris. He had already written for it two remarkable plays, later to be among his most admired, *Fröken Julie* [Miss Julie] and *Fordringsägare* [Creditors], and was now looking for more material. Hansson, with little interest and no experience in the theater, demurred, and eventually Strindberg undertook the dramatization himself. But correspondence had begun and soon meetings would take place between the dramatist living in self-imposed exile from Sweden and the poet and critic soon to choose a similar destiny for himself. Strindberg heard, among other things, of Hansson's project to write on Edgar Allan Poe, lent him books for the purpose, and borrowed from him a

1. "En brevväxling med August Strindberg," *Göteborgs Handels- och Sjöfartstidning*, 15 May 1920.

volume of Swedish translations of Poe's tales. Shortly thereafter he wrote in a letter to Hansson of his enthusiasm: "The next epoch will be E. P.!"[2]

The rest of the letter was equally enthusiastic and even more tantalizing. It has provoked discussion by nearly every Strindberg scholar on the nature and extent of Poe's possible influence on Strindberg. A demonstration of such influence on one of the seminal figures in modern drama would open up the possibility of tracing yet another line of descent from Poe to the twentieth century, not as Edmund Wilson and T. S. Eliot traced it through Baudelaire and the *symbolistes* to twentieth-century English and American poetry, but through Ola Hansson and Strindberg to O'Neill, Pirandello, Albee, and the theater of the absurd. Strindberg's letter, unfortunately for such speculation, says both too much and too little. The references in it to a dozen works of literature that Strindberg related to his reading of Poe evidently came instantaneously to mind, but he neglected to supply the links that even Hansson might have been grateful to have had in following Strindberg's train of associations. The letter and a handful of passing references to Poe in later letters make up the sum of Strindberg's utterances on the subject. In isolation, they seem startlingly significant, though perhaps for the wrong reasons. When placed in the changeful context of Strindberg's growth as an artist, his remarks on Poe tend to lose some of their individuality and take on the complexion of the broad range of ideas in which Strindberg was then immersed. Although their significance, in consequence, will probably always be more or less conjectural, an assessment is worth attempting, given the stature of the two writers and the variety and amount of specu-

2. *August Strindbergs och Ola Hanssons brevväxling*, 1888–1892 (Stockholm, 1938), p. 15. This correspondence is hereafter cited as *Brevväxling*. A similar prophecy is recorded in the Goncourt journal 16 July 1856: "Après avoir lu Poe. Quelque chose que la critique n'a pas vu, un monde littéraire nouveau, les signes de la littérature du XXe siècle." *Journal*, ed. Robert Ricatte (Paris, 1956), 2: 216.

lation that the question of Poe's influence has engendered and left scattered in numerous books and articles on Strindberg. For this purpose, a short preliminary explanation is required of Strindberg's complex interests at the time he read Poe. Much of it will probably be familiar to every student of Strindberg's work, but it is repeated here in a manner suited to the present purpose of supplying a context in which to understand Strindberg's enthusiastic exclamations over his reading of Poe. Present in this context are the strains and stresses that marked Strindberg's friendship with Ola Hansson; they constitute a factor in his professed enthusiasm for Poe that has not been sufficiently recognized.[3]

Strindberg wrote to Hansson in one of the most trying periods, personally and professionally, of his life. Having put Sweden behind him after his trial there in 1884 for blasphemy, he traveled south on the continent and then in November 1887 came up from Germany to Denmark to attend the premiere of his play *Fadren* [The father] at the Casino Theater in Copenhagen. Since then he had been living in various suburbs of the city trying to ward off with his pen the economic ruin that was threatened chiefly by the boycott of his books in Sweden on grounds of indecency. His marriage to Siri von Essen was after a decade fast deteriorating; in a few years' time they

3. Poe's significance to Strindberg has been frequently noted. Ola Hansson and Johan Mortensen (see n. 46, below) were followed by Gunnar Bjurman, whose dissertation on Poe declared that Strindberg's letter of 3 January 1889 to Hansson "quite clearly" showed that Poe had undoubtedly stimulated Strindberg's interest in "the rather obscure and mystical aspects of existence, above all in the psychological realm, particularly with respect to psychic phenomena that tend toward horror, compulsive thinking, and madness." *Edgar Allan Poe* (Lund, 1916), pp. 442–443. In 1926 Strindberg's biographer was both more general and emphatic: "Mystic and scientist, hypersensitively compassionate and nervously cruel (in his work), Poe was indeed like Strindberg." Erik Hedén, *Strindberg* (Stockholm, 1926), p. 212. In more recent books on Strindberg, attempts have been made to supply particulars. For example, Lindström, *Hjärnornas kamp*, pp. 278–279, suggests that the burial chamber scene in "Samum" was perhaps inspired by "The Black Cat" and "The Cask of Amon-

would be divorced. Nothing had come of the acclaim given *Fadren* at the time of its premiere, and in the summer and fall of 1888 Strindberg had been at work on plays suitable for the experimental theater that he hoped would retrieve his professional situation by bringing new dramaturgical standards to Scandinavia. He had spent a taxing, disturbing summer at "Skovlyst," a decayed mansion near Holte, just north of Copenhagen; later in the year, while living in a hotel or a nearby house in Holte, he wrote *Tschandala*, a novel based on the strange events of the summer at "Skovlyst."[4]

The interpretation given in *Tschandala* to those events of the past summer and to the ideas that were finding their way into all of Strindberg's work at this time and that would color his response to Poe had been in the process of rapid formation for two or three years.[5] After long vacillation, he had renounced socialism and all similar attempts to reorder life for the lower classes as sentimental Christianity. This new position had received strong support from

---

tillado." Karl-Åke Kärnell, *Strindbergs bildspråk* (Uppsala, 1962), p. 86, speculates on Poe's "A Predicament" as the source of a photographic-anatomical eye image in one of the tales in Strindberg's *Utopier* (1885). Other suggestions may be found in David Norrman, *Strindbergs skilsmässa från Siri von Essen* (Stockholm, 1953), pp. 30–31, 81 (Poe stimulated Strindberg's interest in psychic mysteries, scientific narration, and scientific experimentation); Stellan Ahlström, *Strindbergs erövring av Paris* (Stockholm, 1956), p. 116 (support from Poe in Strindberg's Nietzschean reaction to Zolaesque naturalism); and most interesting of all, Gunnar Brandell, *Strindbergs Infernokris* (Stockholm, 1950), pp. 205–206, on Poe's possible influence on the compression and the use of bizarre effects in the one-act plays (see pp. 134–136, below).

4. Harry Jacobsen's *Strindberg i Firsernes København* (Copenhagen, 1948) gives details of Strindberg's stay at this time in Denmark; the same author's *Digteren og Fantasten* (Copenhagen, 1945) examines the circumstances of his residence at "Skovlyst." Information related to this period is available in English in Evert Sprinchorn's introduction to *A Madman's Defense* (Anchor Books, Garden City, N.Y., 1967), an excellent translation of Strindberg's *Le Plaidoyer d'un fou*, the emotional account of his marriage written in the winter of 1887–1888.

5. This and the two succeeding paragraphs follow Torsten Eklund, *Tjänstekvinnans son* (Stockholm, 1948), pp. 350–351, 376–399.

his reading of Henry Maudsley's *The Pathology of Mind,* which dismisses Christianity as ancient superstition that has failed to confront the facts of modern life. It is futile, Maudsley argued, to regret the failures of the weak, for had the weak succeeded, mankind would not have been in a position to offer the opportunities now accorded the strong to make proper use of their strength. Strindberg had also discovered new sympathies with Herbert Spencer's corollaries to evolutionary doctrine. Here too it was argued that it is useless to waste sympathy on the weak and the poor, for that is their fate, and it is unrealistic to suppose any lasting good can come from tampering with the social organism—by attempting, for example, to raise women to equality with men. Max Nordau's *Paradoxes* (1885) added fuel to the fire. Strindberg had delighted in its heavy-handed ironies and mockery of "degenerate" authors and the folly of those others who generalize about so-called natural laws. From Nordau's chapter on the psychophysiology of genius Strindberg had learned that, by ranking human intelligence on an "organic" basis, it necessarily follows that no women and few men are capable of "cogitation," the highest functioning of the intellect, as distinguished from its lowest functioning in automatic responses. Poetry and art are chiefly characterized by the latter, and true, discriminating genius by the former.

Vast new energy had already begun to pour into these attitudes from the pioneering lectures on Nietzsche given by Georg Brandes in Copenhagen in April and May of 1888. Strindberg was finding in Nietzsche a man much if not altogether after his own heart on such issues as women's rights, democracy and socialism, the poor and the weak, and Christianity. The Strindbergian superman who eventually and most notably emerged from these developments was Axel Borg, the inspector of fisheries in the novel *I havsbandet* [By the open sea], completed in 1890. The erudite Borg, however, is to be distinguished from the Nietzschean superman in being, as in Ola Hansson's concept of Edgar Allan Poe, a "differentiated" man whose highly sensitive sensory organs render him capable of niceties of perception unknown to ordinary people.

The turn away from social issues and reform had also led Strindberg to an intensive study, beginning in 1886, not only of Maudsley's *The Pathology of Mind*, but also of psychiatric literature of the kind that he later passed on in quantity—"a whole little library," he wrote the writer Geijerstam[6]—to Ola Hansson for use in writing his essay on Poe. Ribot's theories of the relativity of personality had made an especially deep impression on Strindberg and are apparent in the famous foreword to *Fröken Julie* on the "characterless" character and all through the autobiographical novel *Tjänstekvinnans son* [The son of a servant]. At one place in the novel, for example, the hero Johan reports having sensed in himself a split personality, described thus: "The victim is obsessed: he wills one thing but does another; he suffers from a longing to do himself harm and almost takes pleasure in the self-torture."[7] Coincidentally with Strindberg's study of psychiatric literature, a chapter in Nordau's *Paradoxes* on the power of suggestion on the weak-willed had renewed his interest in hypnotism. He attended séances and read the literature, especially that originating in Bernheim's researches at Nancy, where it was held that everyone, not merely cases of hysteria as Charcot maintained, was more or less susceptible to suggestion according to his strength of will, even in "the waking state." The most striking outcome of this study had been the development of a concept that almost obsessed Strindberg's imagination for a decade or more and was never entirely relinquished. This concept was of personal rela-

6. *Brev* 7 (Stockholm, 1961): 350.

7. *Samlade skrifter* 18 (Stockholm, 1913): 53; cited by Eklund, *Tjänstekvinnans son*, p. 350, who observes that Strindberg names as precedents Ribot's *Les Maladies de la personnalité* and Goethe's *Faust*, but not Poe, in whose sketch "The Imp of the Perverse" Strindberg could have found an almost identical description of the phenomenon, nor Kierkegaard, whose concept of dread contains the ambivalence of attraction and repulsion: "*en sympathetisk Antipathie og en antipathetisk Sympathie.*" *Samlede Værker* 6 (Copenhagen, 1963): 136.

tionships as a kind of psychic power play, or as Strindberg formulated it in 1888 in the short story that is its *locus classicus*,
"Hjärnornas kamp" [The battle of brains].

The concept was both fruitful and commodious. It brought together and gave shape to many different strains of thought: Ribot's
"multiplicité du moi," with its implication that the self, being
relative and in flux, is susceptible to influences that can alter it;
Bernheim's concept of suggestion as a power capable of operating
subtly on the human will; Eduard von Hartmann's idea of the unconscious, described by Strindberg in *Tjänstekvinnans son* (part 3,
chapter 3) as the life-force on which the conscious will operates;
Carl Du Prel's idea of a transcendental "Subject" that is apprehended only in "somnambulistic" states; Maudsley's distinctions
between the "insane temperament" and genius as resting on the
definition of their impulsiveness; Lombroso's and Nordau's ideas
about the inferiority of women and of most men, and their somewhat different concepts of degeneration; and finally, evolutionary
differentiation, especially as taught by Spencer, of the strong from
the weak, or of "the great" (*de stora*) from "the small" (*de små*),
terms that as a university student at Uppsala Strindberg had learned
from reading Georg Brandes's lecture on Shakespeare. The concept
of the battle of brains gave shelter to all these ideas in varying
emphases.

The story "Hjärnornas kamp" was, as we shall see, the first title
of his own work that came to Strindberg's mind after he had read
Poe's tales. Though simple in structure, it is resonant with the many
chords of thought that are simultaneously struck in it. The narrator,
an author, tells of being sought out by a young man named Schilf,
ostensibly for an interview. But Schilf persists instead in arguing the
advantages of socialism, and the narrator "shrewdly" perceives that
he is in fact under attack in a battle of brains. At first he reports
weakening under Schilf's onslaught, but after a good night's sleep
he begins the counterattack. He employs Schilf to be his photog-

rapher on a botanical tour to the Mediterranean, all the while finding new ways daily to rebut his arguments. Schilf weakens and sick-
ens under this treatment; the narrator grows stronger, his mind
more powerful, until at last Schilf begs to be excused from his
duties. When the narrator discovers evidence that Schilf has damaged the photographic plates—in revenge, he suspects—he dismisses
him triumphantly. "What did this man want of me?" he asks himself, and finally, "Who was this man?" uncertain of everything but
some sort of victory over him. "I do not know, for I saw him alter
character according to altered circumstances as people do until
they enter the age of inflexibility and unchanging situations. He
was young and had not yet been able to settle upon his role in life;
he was therefore fairly pliable and easy to study and perhaps I was
therefore able to bend him until he realized—or perhaps this was
the reason—that my mind was the stronger!"[8] In other stories and
in some of the plays the stronger mind, we learn, can radiate influence from a distance, like the clairvoyant "somnambulist" of spiritist literature. Usually, however, the contest, as for example in
Fröken Julie and *Fordringsägare* as well as "Hjärnornas kamp," is
principally enacted face to face, where the power of suggestion can
have the force of hypnotic influence.

The concept of the battle of brains was not merely intellectual.
It was highly charged with emotions generated in Strindberg's personal relationships and was then imposed onto these relationships,
lending them both clarity and a fatal monotony. Probably the most
disastrous example of the process is Strindberg's deteriorating rela-

8. *Samlade skrifter* 22 (Stockholm, 1914): 157. Schilf was apparently
modeled on Gustaf Steffen, whom Strindberg had engaged to accompany him
on a photographic tour of France. Steffen's mother was a medium and his
father, Strindberg believed, was the Librarian of the Royal Library and a zealous
student of hypnotism in Stockholm in the 1880s. Strindberg had held a post
under him from 1874 to 1882 and attended séances he had arranged (see
Lindström, *Hjärnornas kamp*, p. 220).

tionship with his wife. Whatever their immediate, personal difficulties had in fact been, she necessarily stood to lose, as a woman and as one of "the small," in the uneven contest with her husband. Gunnar Brandell has noted Strindberg's growing paranoia in this decade preceding a series of marked psychotic crises between 1894 and 1896, the so-called Inferno period, when Strindberg imagined threats and danger on all sides. In his fiction and as early as November 1887 in his letters he testified to a growing inability to distinguish between dream and reality and between what he had written and what he had personally experienced.[9]

A close examination in this context of Strindberg's first letters to Hansson, in which Poe was discussed, suggests that Strindberg was willfully waging a battle of brains with his new friend. If this is so, his exclamations of enthusiasm for Poe, although no doubt perfectly spontaneous, are to be regarded as having originated in highly mixed feelings and not solely in delight with the discovery of a congenial author.

Strindberg had opened the correspondence, it will be recalled, with an appeal to Hansson to dramatize the story "En Paria." ("En Paria" should be kept distinct from "Paria," Strindberg's dramatization of it, and from *Parias*, Hansson's later collection of tales in which "En Paria" appeared without title as the opening story.) This letter, which launched a friendship that was to end four years later in bitterness in Berlin, got off to an uncertain start, for Strindberg spelled his correspondent's name "Hansen," the Danish form of the name. Ola Hansson was no more than nettled at first by this strangely careless error, but later, in one of his three commentaries on the correspondence, he claimed that it had been deliberate, the first move in a Strindbergian psychic battle. He had arrived at that conclusion, he said, after witnessing the drastic changes that Strindberg had made in the dramatization of his short story:

9. Brandell, *Strindbergs Infernokris*, pp. 60–62.

I saw "Paria" in Malmö and was seized by a disagreeable realization. What was this all about? Why had Strindberg turned this simple theme topsy-turvy and completely spoiled it? This was based on no "idea" of Ola Hansson [as Strindberg had announced it]. Strindberg had also urged me to *act* in the play with him on the stage, and I did not know that it was going to be a duel between two criminals. He had also had in mind to call the play "Aria och Paria"—Strindberg, the strong Aria, would then have crushed, *coram populo*, Hansen, the weak Pariah. A year later, in a letter of 24 April 1890 to Berlin and in connection with his book *Tschandala*, he again called me "Hansen" and amused himself by writing over the name the word "Tschandala" in pencil. I found out later that the gypsy, whom he had blasted for the Tschandala that he was, bore the name Hansen.[10]

First, as to the references to *Tschandala*, which with "En Paria" has particular associations with Poe in the Hansson-Strindberg correspondence. The title, the novel tells us, is the name given in the Laws of Manu to the casteless of India (Kəndàla in the English translation of the Laws). The name is applied in the novel to Peder Jensen, caretaker of an estate, because he is discovered in the course of the narrative to be really a gypsy, a classless rover. Strindberg modeled Jensen on Ludwig Hansen, the caretaker at "Skovlyst,"

10. "August Strindbergs Breve til Mig fra Holte," *Tilskueren* 29 (July 1912): 40. The letter of 24 April 1890 to which Hansson refers did contain the same misspelling with "Tschandala!" written above (*Brev* 8 [Stockholm, 1964]: 39), but there is no evidence in the letters of Strindberg's having habitually confused "Hansson, Hansen, Jansson, etc.," as Hansson claimed in his article (p. 32). Hansson's retrospective view of the friendship has to be used cautiously, colored as it was by the bitterness of its conclusion. In his commentaries on the correspondence in *Tilskueren* and *Die neue Rundschau* (see note 12, below) in 1912, the year of Strindberg's death, and in *Göteborgs Handels- och Sjöfartstidning*, 15 May 1920, he emphatically disclaimed having had any common ground with Strindberg or any liking for or particular interest in his work. This is in part belied by his article in *Ny Jord* in 1888 praising

where Strindberg had spent the previous summer. The altercations between Ludwig Hansen and Strindberg, which had led to the former's arrest, Strindberg's flight to Berlin to avoid a court hearing, and sensational reports of sexual irregularities at "Skovlyst" in the Copenhagen press that summer, were transformed in *Tschandala* into a battle of brains between members of two social classes, Professor Törner of Lund and Jensen, who is suspected of thievery and worse. The battle is fought in an atmosphere dense with suspicion and distrust, deception and subterfuge. The professor's foe is shown, rather melodramatically, to be capable of vile deceits, but they are ultimately no match for Törner's higher intelligence and vast erudition. At the last, in a scene that Ola Hansson was to describe as "Poe of course," Törner lays plans to trap the gypsy by taking advantage of his lower class superstitiousness and presumptuousness. He sets his plans in motion one night by first overwhelming Jensen in a five-hour-long display of learning; then having softened his victim, he takes up the subject of ghosts. When he has thoroughly alarmed the gypsy, Törner projects lantern images of persons and

---

Strindberg and by the correspondence itself. Strindberg's misspelling of his name is, however, indisputable, as are the pencil notation of "Tschandala" and the proposal to call the play "Aria och Pariah" (*Brev*, 7: 196).

Hansson described his first meeting with Strindberg several times in increasingly critical sketches of his behavior. In an incomplete continuation of Hansson's autobiographical novel *Resan hem* [The journey home], Strindberg appears under the name Viggman as the overwrought and bored host of young Truls Andersson ("Tio år i exil," in *Ur minnet och dagboken*, ed. Emy Ek [Stockholm, 1926], pp. 119–139). In another sketch in the same posthumous volume Hansson described a visit twenty years later to Strindberg's apartment in Stockholm and again emphasized Strindberg's eccentric manner. He recalled Strindberg's cryptic references in their early correspondence to the madhouse at Gheel and believed that he could now see that beginning at this point some sinister purpose was at work in Strindberg's attentions to him. For this, he wrote, Strindberg had made preparation by sending to him "some of Edgar Poe's spookiest, most morbid, and most sharply doubled-edged stories" (p. 152). It was, on the contrary, Hansson who had lent Poe's stories to Strindberg. The entire passage reveals the tension present from the start in this relationship.

animals into the darkness; in the smoke of the gypsy's bonfire they seem animated, and the gypsy is completely deceived. When next the image of a dog is shown, he is so reduced that he gets down on all fours and barks at it. But at this the eight real dogs on the estate rush at the gypsy, on whom Törner has now cleverly projected the dog image, and bite him to death. Tschandala, having failed to observe caste distinctions, has met a deservedly ignominious death. Strindberg's epithet *pariah*, though perhaps suggested by Hansson's derived use of the word in a quite different context, was doubly correct: "Pariah was dead, and the Aryan had won" [Paria var död, och ariern hade segrat].[11] From this conclusion to the novel stemmed Strindberg's proposal that his dramatization of Hansson's story be called "Aria och Paria," a rhyming variant of *arier* [Aryan] and *paria*.

From this it seems clear that Strindberg had cast his new friend Ola Hansson in the role of Tschandala-Jensen, but whether compulsively or not is impossible to say. If there were moments when the fantasy held sway and the confusion of identities was all but complete, at other times no doubt he knew it was fantasy and was either bemused or amused by it, testing it to see what it might reveal. In most of the correspondence, and especially after the beginning dozen or so letters, Ola Hansson's reality seems to have come through unhindered and undistorted.

If at first Hansson did not perceive what was going on, he understood a great deal, if not all, later on. He certainly perceived and was offended by Strindberg's wanting to have the two of them appear in "Paria" and act out Strindberg's private fantasy in public. Hansson could not then have realized, and may never have fully understood,[12] that Strindberg's dramatization was a battle of brains

---

11. *Samlade skrifter* (Stockholm, 1913), 12: 375.

12. Hansson seems to have understood enough in 1912 to disallow excuses for Strindberg's misspelling on grounds of his posing as *un détraqué*: "Dies war keine Monomanie, die Strindberg wie so vieles andre nur simulierte. Dies war ein Berechnung, wie überhaupt durch die ganze Reihe seiner Briefe ein

—that it illustrated a concept all too useful in structuralizing Strindberg's personal relationships, and that it exemplified a literary theme then being rigorously explored. The accidental similarity of Hansson's name to Ludwig Hansen's had triggered reactions in Strindberg that cast Ola Hansson all unsuspectingly in the role of one of "the small," the part played by Schilf in "Hjärnornas kamp," by Tschandala, and now by Herr Y in "Paria."[13]

In the transformation of "En Paria" to "Paria" that had shocked and bewildered Hansson, Strindberg had been obliged for the purposes of this new battle of brains to raise Hansson's nonfunctional first-person narrator to whom the Swedish-American entomologist tells his story of involuntary criminality and imprisonment to an active and superior position in the drama, to make him a worthy opponent to the entomologist. He becomes Herr X, an archaeologist, who in response to Herr Y's tale of forgery (one of the few remnants in the play of Hansson's short story) confesses to having killed a man. For the rest of the play, X and Y jockey for position as Y tries to extort money from X on the threat of exposure of his crime, and X discredits Y's tale as having been stolen from a book on his own shelves (Bernheim on suggestion). Toward the end of the play, Y likens the contest to a game of chess: Who will make the move to put the other in checkmate? It is X who wins at the last, not that Y, he admits, is more or less guilty than he is or stronger or weaker, but because Y has been shown up as stupid—stupid for having stooped to forgery when he could have begged,

---

bestimmter Zweck geht." "Erinnerungen an August Strindberg," *Die neue Rundschau* 23 (1912): 1551.

13. For this reason the argument against the identification (suggested by Holm, *Ola Hansson*, pp. 48–49) of Hansson as the model for Herr Y, advanced by C. R. Smedmark in "Ola Hansson och Herr Y i Strandbergs Paria," *Meddelanden från Strindbergs-sällskapet*, no. 39 (May 1967), pp. 6–10, seems to be on the wrong grounds. The identification does not hinge on the amount of knowledge about Nietzsche that Herr Y is permitted to have in the play and that Hansson actually may or may not have had at the time the play was written, but was associative and, as I suggest, perhaps not altogether conscious.

stupid for having supposed that X would not know that his tale of involuntary wrongdoing was plagiarized, stupid for having supposed that he could even his score with society by making X into a thief also, and stupid for having supposed that X had not had the foresight to protect his position in advance. The harangue crushes Y, who meekly retreats as the curtain falls. This pariah has not been eaten by dogs, but he has been soundly vanquished. The Aryan had won again.

Strindberg's drastic reworking of the story amounted to fairly sharp criticism of Hansson. As Ingvar Holm points out, Hansson's use of the word *paria* had conveyed no moral judgment by the author of the outcasts pictured in this or any of the other tales in *Parias,* unless indeed it was to show sympathetically how undeservedly their fate as outcasts followed upon their well-intentioned or involuntary actions. Hansson's "En Paria" is a psychological tale in which the forger is held not responsible for a crime committed deterministically, hence without criminal intent. In Strindberg's dramatization, on the other hand, Herr X insists that although the individual himself may not be responsible for his actions, society nevertheless requires retribution and cannot let the act go unpunished. The play illustrates a principle not of criminal psychology but of justice.[14] But X is not content to demonstrate the inadequacy of Y's explanation of his criminality; he accuses him of plagiarizing it, just as in 1894, at a time of severe mental stress, Strindberg would write a friend that Ola Hansson had stolen the tale. The source named then was not Bernheim but Poe, probably in consequence of Strindberg's lingering association of Hansson's Poe essay with the psychiatric literature he had lent Hansson for it.[15] But the charge itself, both in 1889 and in 1894, was a regression to Strindberg's conviction that Ludwig Hansen was an unprincipled thief, a "gypsy."

14. Holm, *Ola Hansson,* pp. 46–49.
15. *Brev* 10 (Stockholm, 1968): 202.

The portion of the Hansson-Strindberg correspondence that bears on Edgar Allan Poe confirms this view of their relationship. Even though confidences were freely exchanged and Strindberg was cordial and helpful and at times as charming as many testimonials have made him out to be, the friendship was an uneasy one from the start, a little too cordial for Hansson's taste, it would appear, and perhaps all too urgent with confidences. Hansson repeatedly averred in later years that he never understood what made Strindberg approach him in the first place or why he then persisted in his attentions despite their widely different interests. Nevertheless, despite Strindberg's "error" in misspelling Hansson's name, his letter brought Hansson to Denmark for a visit. Hansson returned to Skåne with an armful of books, including Mosso's *La Peur* and Ribot's *Les Maladies de la personnalité*, both of special interest, he next wrote Strindberg, in putting him on solid ground for an essay he now planned to write on Poe, "who takes up by preference the same things—William Wilson, for instance, the double man."[16] After what then appears to have been silence on Hansson's part in reply to two communications from Strindberg, Strindberg wrote 23 December 1888 asking for a copy of Poe in Swedish. He was genuinely curious, but it appears that he wrote also in the hope that by showing interest in Hansson's projected essay, he would reengage him in correspondence.

Hansson sent him in reply a copy of *Valda noveller*, the Swedish translations published in 1882 with an introduction by Henrik Schüch (see pp. 53–55, above). Of the eight tales in the volume, Strindberg was to name only "The Gold Bug" by title. Ten days later, 3 January 1889, Strindberg wrote Hansson in exuberant praise of the tales. This letter, which will be quoted in full since it constitutes Strindberg's only extended statement of Poe's significance to him, linked Poe to "Hjärnornas kamp" and other works, both by Strindberg and by others. It was as though Strindberg were pre-

16. *Brevväxling*, p. 10.

pared to find Poe everywhere he looked—but not, be it noted, in Hansson's "En Paria." Strindberg reported in the letter that he had felt very restive for many days after his first meeting with Hansson, at which time Hansson had mentioned Poe and Strindberg had assumed some connection in "En Paria" with Poe. His restiveness had been decisive in asking for the loan of the tales, but he had needed to read no further than "The Gold Bug," the first story in the volume, to be released, he reported, from his restiveness, for he could see no connection between "The Gold Bug" and "En Paria" except in the detail of a butterfly net and the vague general appeal that both Hansson's story and Poe had for him.

Now, although there is an entomologist in both "The Gold Bug" and "En Paria," in each of which stories he tells an inner tale to a first-person narrator, there is no mention of a butterfly net in either one. (It was to appear only later as a stage prop in Strindberg's dramatization of "En Paria.") Strindberg seems to have singled out this incorrect and quite trivial detail to insinuate a distinction between Hansson's "En Paria" on the one hand, and on the other, Poe's tale and the work of the other authors named in his letter. Hansson was apparently not to suppose that Strindberg had failed to see how Hansson had attempted unjustifiably to claim Poe for his own. In short, Strindberg's letter conveyed not merely spontaneous praise of Poe; it was *aggressively* enthusiastic. Its extravagant claims of relationship to Poe were in effect a declaration in a battle of brains of a superior and ultimately even of a *prior* right to assert kinship with the writer of "the next epoch."

3 January 1888 [error for 1889]

Dear Ola H,

The night between the Second and Third Day of Christmas [26 and 27 December] I read Edgar Poe for the first time! And made a note of it in my notebook! I am astounded! Is it possible that he, dead in '49, the same year I was born, has been able to work his way down [pyra sig ner] through layers of mediums all the way to me!

What are "Hjärnornas kamp," "Schleichwege" [Circuitous ways], even *Gillets hemlighet* [The secret of the guild] (for which I read the Danish proofs today) other than E. P.!

And "The Gold Bug"?—Do you know I immediately connected it with my fascination with your "[En] Paria"! Do you recall you mentioned the name Edgar Poe! the last time we met! That I was enchanted by your "[En] Paria." Was restive in my whole body for many days until with no further motivation I requisitioned the book from you! Then when I got through "The Gold Bug" I was liberated [förlöst]![17] Your "[En] Paria" is not there, but the butterfly net—everything that attracted and appealed. It would be remarkable if you do not now believe in "spirits." It is thus that souls (brain vibrations) continue in other souls, and therefore there is a *certain* immortality in the fleeting soul!

I have so much that is new, psychological to talk about. And I think I would be able to enlarge at length upon Edgar P. I fancy I could find treasures without ciphers and such—come here some day and I'll tell you about it!

And much more new—psychological! Extremely remarkable things!

Now I am working on your "[En] Paria"!

Don't you think we should be able to read [E. T. A.] Hoffmann's tales with profit now? E. P. is regarded by that stupid Schück merely as a neoromantic alcoholic, and yet it is he who has fertilized Bourget, Maupassant—in *Pierre et Jean*—*Rosmersholm*, *Fadren*, not to mention all mind readers and hypnotizers! The next epoch will be E. P.!

If you knew what I have gone through since I read E. P. —gone through—because it captured my attention!

17. *Brevväxling*, p. 15, reads "förläst," an error corrected in *Brev*.

And how far ahead of its time is *Fordringsägare*! When he *produces* epilepsy! I did not know how right I was—but now I know!

I have so much to talk about, but I cannot get away! Should you feel disposed—come on over in a couple of weeks when your "[En] Paria" will be finished! We'll read it—and have a good chat!

Now, Happy New Year!

> Your friend,
> Aug. Sg.[18]

The references to metempsychosis (here in an assertion of a special tie with Poe), mind reading, hypnotism, and the kinds of parallels that Strindberg draws to "E. P." indicate the nature of his fascination clearly enough. He had made many of the same points a few days before in a letter to Karl Otto Bonnier, the publisher. The "genre" of Edgar Poe would be that of the next decade, he had then written; it "began with Bourget, continued in Maupas-

---

18. *Brev*, 7: 217–218. When the letter was first printed in 1912, Hansson commented: "Diese Begeisterung für Edgar Poe entsprang aus einem einzigen kleinen Bändchen der von Professor Schück ins Schwedische übersetzten Erzählungen Poes [*Valda noveller*, 1882]. Die vier dicken Bände der englischen Ausgabe hatte ich unterdessen zu Hause für meine Arbeit." "Erinnerungen an August Strindberg," *Die neue Rundschau* 23 (1912): 1541. When the letter was printed a second time in a Göteborg newspaper in 1920 in the original Swedish, Hansson commented on the concentrated style of the letter and continued (*Göteborgs Handels- och Sjöfartstidning*, 15 May 1920):

At the same time we can see his reaching out into the unknown, his yearning outward beyond matter, his searching for something which he cannot find words for but which surely exists for his spirit. This attracts him to Poe; this made him into the occultist, into the mystic, and in his less happy moments into the humbug such as we find him in "Guldmakaren" [The maker of gold]— . . . What he found in Poe and what is to be found there in rich measure—natural forces that so to speak acted on their own, emancipated from matter but not yet placed

sant's *Pierre et Jean,* was imported to us in *Rosmersholm* and *Fadren* . . . and now splendidly by Ola Hansson!"[19] In the letter to Hansson there has, however, occurred a slight but significant shift. An imagined and trivial detail (the butterfly net) is made to seem the extent of Hansson's profit from reading Poe; "En Paria" is dismissed as not being "E. P."; and Strindberg has a suddenly renewed interest in dramatizing the story himself. Given the rich texture of "The Gold Bug" and especially the subtle interplay between its two leading characters (the narrator and the entomologist), which though certainly not a battle of brains has elements of intellectual sparring and swagger, it is not surprising that Strindberg would have thought Hansson's story undramatic and its sympathies misplaced. Now he saw it solely in terms of a full-fledged battle of brains. This view of Hansson's story was either inspired or confirmed by his reading of "The Gold Bug," which seems to have reawakened his urge to play Professor Törner to Hansson's Jensen as he extravagantly claimed Poe to be the seminal figure in modern literature. From that literature he excluded Hansson's "En Paria" though not his own plays *Fadren* and *Fordringsägare* and most certainly not his drastic revamping of "En Paria" into the one-acter "Paria."

Strindberg names only "The Gold Bug" in his letter, a tale a good deal less likely to exacerbate the battle-of-brains syndrome than two or three others in the volume he had borrowed from Hansson. Schück's introduction to the volume contained no mention of Poe's endless disputes with editors and writers or of his crypto-

---

under the rule of the spirit,—that peculiar intermediate condition that we find in the literature of Asia—this was not exactly what I found in Poe.

That there was a division of opinion between Hansson and Strindberg on the subject of Poe is readily apparent, as I show, from their correspondence, but Hansson's explanation in 1920 of Poe's appeal to Strindberg moves the latter's occultist period back by about seven or eight years.

19. *Brev,* 7: 212.

graphic challenges of his readers. But in "The Murders in the Rue Morgue," "The Purloined Letter," and "The Cask of Amontillado" there are battles of brains of a sort that presumably would have caught Strindberg's attention if he had read beyond the first tale, "The Gold Bug," in the volume. He said nothing about them, nor about "The Facts in the Case of M. Valdemar," the story that makes a daring and grisly application of mesmerism, a subject of intense interest to Strindberg. It is not, as has been suggested, that Herr X's exposure of Herr Y has "the impeccable logic and systematic thoroughness"[20] of Poe's Dupin, but that Herr X is, as Dupin says of himself and of Minister D—— in "The Purloined Letter," both mathematician *and* poet. Herr X outguesses Herr Y much as Dupin can outguess his opponent by his uncanny ability to follow the train of associations in the other's thought processes. It permits Dupin to exceed the merely mathematical rationality of the police. He cites in "The Purloined Letter" the example of the schoolboy who won at "even and odd" by identifying so thoroughly with his opponent's intellect in each contest as to mimic his facial expressions and so induce in his own mind the level of intelligence in the other. And in "The Murders in the Rue Morgue" Dupin demonstrates his awesome and subtle powers of associative thinking while out walking with the narrator of the tale. Poe prefaces this tale with a commentary once more on the strategy for winning at games. The successful player will go beyond mere skill in the mechanism of play and closely observe the countenance of his partner and that of his opponents, the slight details of their handling the cards, the words they utter as the game proceeds trick by trick, and the hesitation or eagerness they show, for "all afford, to his apparently intuitive perception, indications of the true state of affairs." In short, "the analytical power should not be confounded with simple ingenuity."

20. Børge Gedsø Madsen, *Strindberg's Naturalistic Theater* (Copenhagen, 1962), p. 118. See also Gunnar Ollén, *Strindbergs dramatik* (Stockholm, 1961), p. 84.

Analytic power rather than mere ingenuity similarly operates in Strindberg's stories of the battle of brains. There is nevertheless a vast difference between these stories and Poe's tales of ratiocination. It is true that Dupin's efforts in retrieving the purloined letter from a man who had once done him an evil turn are not disinterested, and the motive of revenge is central to the action in "The Cask of Amontillado," but in neither is it the principal object to claim a moral triumph in unmasking a charlatan or destroying his power in the assertion of one's own. Strindberg's Herr X emerges victorious over a dissembler of whom he has been darkly suspicious from the first, when he told Herr Y that he looked like a doppelganger, in the sense of his being someone other than he pretends to be, hence someone whose duplicity, literally and figuratively, must be ruthlessly revealed. Strindberg's battle of brains is typically a battle for mastery waged in aggrieved self-defense against darkly suspected threats of danger; it concludes in the assertion of personal power as a kind of moral triumph over evil. The Poe stories, on the other hand, explore the workings of a sophisticated mind endowed with the imagination to take another point of view or kind of intelligence into account as it reasons its way to victory. They are stories of the triumph of mind and sensibility; Strindberg's tell of the triumph of mind and will. Perhaps it was also some realization of this difference that caused Strindberg to stop short in his letter to Hansson with specific mention only of "The Gold Bug," a story with a cipher, as he noted. A cipher, as a later letter to be discussed reveals, is in Strindberg's vocabulary a device containing a secret whereby to test the psychic strength of one's opponent.

In addition to "Hjärnornas kamp," Strindberg, we recall, referred in his letter to Hansson in praise of Poe to other fiction and to drama by himself and others, some of it falling obviously into the category of a battle of brains, some of it only by a stretch of the imagination as great as Strindberg himself displays. "Schleichwege" had appeared in *Neue Freie Presse* in the fall of 1887 (it was translated into Swedish after Strindberg's death for inclusion in the collected works).[21] It tells of the contest between Tekla, a medium, and the victorious hero of the tale, a famous author named Karl Billgren, who is clearly Strindberg in thin disguise. Billgren skeptically rejects spiritualistic evidence produced by Tekla at a séance and detects in the claims of women mediums to spiritualistic power an ulterior motive, that of circumventing the natural inferiority of women to men. (Soon after Strindberg read Poe, Tekla reappeared as an accused witch in "En häxa" [A witch], one of three tales in a volume set in the Swedish past, *Svenska öden och äventyr* [vol. 3, 1890]. It gives no evidence, as has been claimed, of influence from Poe; it purports essentially to be the inside story of a case of witchcraft. Given what we are permitted in the tale to know of Tekla's humble origins, her innate vanity and laziness, and her aspirations to rise in the world, the question posed at the end is whether she was not more sick than criminal in her wild imaginings and accusations. Although Strindberg blurs the issue by allowing Tekla certain witch-like powers, the answer was supplied by Strindberg's reading not of the horrors of punishment described by Poe but of the literature of criminal psychology that lies behind the writing of the story.) [22]

Gillets hemlighet, for which Strindberg happened at the time to be reading proof for the Danish translation, is a history play that had been produced in Stockholm nearly a decade before, in 1880. It

21. *Samlade skrifter* 54 (Stockholm, 1920): 7–114. Tekla was modeled on the mother of Gustaf Steffens, the model for Schilf in "Hjärnornas kamp." See note 8, above, and Lindström, *Hjärnornas kamp*, pp. 235–236.

22. By concentrating her desires, Tekla causes the young baron to appear before her and is about to seduce him, according to the custom of witches, when her rival interferes (*Samlade skrifter*, 12: 194). Lindström, *Hjärnornas kamp*, pp. 278–279, suggests that the torture chamber scene in "Samum" as well as the burial chamber scene in "En häxa" was inspired by Strindberg's reading of "The Pit and the Pendulum" and "The Black Cat" in translation in the two volumes of selected tales published in 1881 as *Underliga historier*, but there is no evidence that Strindberg knew these volumes.

is based on the rivalry between members of the builders' guild in Uppsala as to who will have the honor of continuing work on the cathedral. Perhaps Strindberg now looked back on the rivalry as an incipient battle of brains and thus grouped the play with "Hjärnornas kamp" and "Schleichwege" as being "E. P." Perhaps, too, he had in mind the parchment containing the secret writing in "The Gold Bug," for in his play there is a parchment containing the secret of the guild that is indecipherable to the rival who possesses it because he is illiterate. The writing is not invisible, however, and at the last it is revealed to be a cross in red designating the ground plan of the cathedral that had been lost sight of, followed by an admonition to build always on the cross of God, the church, rather than on one's own strength.

The other associations with Poe proposed in Strindberg's letter went well beyond the immediate context of the battle of brains. Bourget is named but without reference to any one work and probably as a writer that Hansson and Strindberg had discussed as a psychological novelist of interest to them both. The reference to Maupassant's *Pierre et Jean* is even less clear. "Le Roman," the much discussed preface to the novel, had been published separately in the literary supplement to *Le Figaro* (7 January 1888) and translated at once for publication early in 1888 in *Ny Jord* (1: 221–233). Maupassant had dissociated himself in the preface from "les partisans d'analyse" (like Bourget) who write novels as though they were psychological tracts, but in the novel itself, which had appeared in book form in the spring, Strindberg might have found "E. P." in Pierre's reflections on his uneasiness after having learned of his brother's inheritance. Pierre wonders whether his "physiological problem" has not been caused by a train of envious feelings set in motion in his instinctive being although such feelings are inimical to his better, rational self.[23] It is an instance of compulsive

23. Guy de Maupassant, *Œuvres complètes* (Paris, 1929), 19: 40–41.

feelings and of restiveness, both certainly present in Poe's fiction, but what is more to the present point, both are described by Strindberg in his letter to Hansson as his own reactions on learning of Hansson's claim of a Poe "inheritance" in "En Paria."

Ibsen's *Rosmersholm*, to which Strindberg's letter also refers, had been published in November 1886 and all through 1887 had been going a round of performances with little success in the principal Scandinavian cities. Strindberg had evidently seen the Copenhagen production in November 1887, and though detesting Ibsen as a women's rights man and a "bluestocking," he approved at least of August Lindberg's direction of the play[24] and, it would appear, even of the play itself. It will be recalled that in *Rosmersholm* the presence of Beata, though she is deceased, is felt among the living; her influence has continued even after death. No doubt Strindberg saw at least hints of a battle of brains both in Rebecca West's confession that it was she who by intimation and suggestion lured Beata to her death, and in her desire to redeem Rosmer by counteracting the enervating influences of his heritage. Like *Pierre et Jean* and *Rosmersholm*, Strindberg's own play *Fadren*, which had had its premiere in Copenhagen a little more than a week before *Rosmersholm*, portrays the breakup of a marriage under the pressure of "influences." The most striking use made in the play of the power of suggestion occurs in the final scene, where the Captain is eased by his old nurse into a strait jacket, but suggestion has operated throughout the play.

Finally, Strindberg associated Poe in his letter with his play *Fordringsägare*, written at "Skovlyst" late the previous summer. It again ruthlessly analyzes the deterioration of a marriage. The wife's former husband returns to avenge an insult and sets out to destroy her character to her present husband. Again the most striking use

24. *Brev* 6 (Stockholm, 1958): 337. But Strindberg did not think that the production had succeeded (*ibid.*, p. 318).

of the power of suggestion occurs near the end of the play when, as Strindberg notes in his letter to Hansson, the former husband in a battle of brains with his successor induces epilepsy in him by having him mimic the symptoms.[25] Mimicry used to induce a state of mind is present, as we have noted, in "The Purloined Letter," but the induction of an illness by means of mimicry has no precedent in Poe—"Ligeia" and "The Oval Portrait" are of another order and meaning altogether—yet Strindberg apparently wished Hansson to understand how the rightness of such a scene had been confirmed in his reading of Poe.

Even after the extravagance of Strindberg's letter praising Poe is tempered by the realization that the letter itself figured in a minor battle of brains, the special nature of his enthusiasm is apparent. The dramatization of "En Paria" and the allusions in the letter to Bourget, Maupassant, Ibsen, and particularly to stories and plays of his own that conclude, actually or in effect, with the destruction of one character by another through the force of suggestion make it fairly clear that Poe was wholly subsumed in Strindberg's concept of the battle of brains. In its most characteristic and dramatic form, it was, as for example, in "Paria," "Hjärnornas kamp," and *Tschandala*, a duel between two persons; in this fact alone it has obvious parallels to the tension-filled contests between two persons in such tales as "The Purloined Letter," "The Cask of Amontillado," and even, as has been suggested, "The Gold Bug." But Strindberg's battles end in gloating triumph over stupidity, duplicity, and deceit, not in the satisfaction of revenge, or simply of intellectual mastery, obtained through the brilliant exercise of "the analytical power." Poe had become grist for a powerful mill. If "E. P." were indeed

25. Martin Lamm, *August Strindberg*, 3d ed. (Stockholm, 1968), p. 192, designates the source as a ghost story by Erckmann-Chatrian in which an old woman in a French village induces her victims to hang themselves by getting them to mimic her actions.

"the next epoch," it was only because Strindberg seems to have been convinced that he and Poe were armed with psychological truths that Ola Hansson had somewhat presumptuously laid claim to.

Strindberg's subsequent correspondence with Hansson touched on the subject of Poe only in passing, yet it continued to apply his ideas about Poe to current and past work and to his relationship with Hansson. On 19 January 1889, Strindberg, having just reread *King Lear* and *The Tempest*, reported that "There is Edgar Poe in *Lear*! Read where Gloucester *believes* he has fallen off the cliff, and Edmund fears this belief could have had the same effect as a fall." [26] He kept Hansson posted on the progress of a planned production of "Paria," and on 28 January labeled a section of his letter "Edgar Poesque!" as he enclosed a letter he had received from Ludvig Josephson, the Swedish co-owner of Nya teatern. "Do not read this letter from Josephson," he enjoined Hansson, "but examine it and you will see Arabic letters. The man is an Arab and his handwriting adduces ancestral memories!" [27] This exposure of the Swede's identity as an Arab (that is, a non-Jew, as Strindberg later explained), Strindberg permitted himself apparently on the strength of Lombroso's practice of tracing evidence of criminal tendencies in handwriting samples. This sort of decipherment was now called "Edgar Poesque." The letter was followed by one offering a lengthy analysis of the Swedish poet Carl Snoilsky as a "gypsy" and a pariah. The decipherment of character persisted to such lengths that Strindberg posed a mind reading experiment for Hansson in a letter dated 1 February:

> Let us try some simple mind reading!
> Solve this!
> Fjabkvebcjmsffhp.
> It is Edgar Poe!

26. *Brev*, 7: 229.
27. *Brev*, 7: 236.

And let me know how much time you needed!
Then send me one like it!
If you are afraid, say only *that* you understood![28]

Hansson did not accept the invitation to play this game. In 1912, when the letter was first published, Hansson commented, "There then followed an exercise in mind reading that I neither understood nor was interested in and whose significance he heightened in the words, 'If you are afraid, say only that you understood!' "[29] Hansson was apparently not to be afraid that he might not solve the cipher but that, in attempting it, he would somehow expose his true identity, undergo an unmasking and defeat of the kind that always concludes a battle of brains. That this was Strindberg's intention is supported in the passage that without interruption followed the mind reading proposal, as though in explanation of it. Here he recalled a friend from his service at the Royal Library "who only needed to look at me and I understood at once what he wanted: a reply, tobacco, the time of day, my opinion of the latest book, play, official appointment." Ola Hansson could gather from this how superior were Strindberg's psychic powers and therefore how vulnerable he himself was. Strindberg's association of Poe with mind reading experiments was made through the use of decipherment, in this instance of a real cipher, as in "The Gold Bug"; but it carried broader implications, for in previous instances, Strindberg had associated Poe with character unmasking (Josephson and Snoilsky) and the analysis of handwriting and ancestry, as in Lombroso.

Hansson's long reply on 4 February betrayed, however, no sense of injury. It discusses a case of matricide reported in the psychiatric literature that Strindberg had lent him. It goes on to exclaim,

28. *Brev*, 7: 241. Strindberg's cipher has proved to be too brief for decipherment by professional Swedish cryptographers to whom, through the kind offices of General Nils Sköld, it was submitted.

29. "August Strindbergs Breve til Mig fra Holte," *Tilskueren* 29 (July–December 1912): 39.

What a phenomenal genius Poe really was! I am now studying him quite thoroughly in English in order to write an exhaustive essay about him. And I am thunderstruck to see how that man anticipated our time by purely intuitive means. He must have had the same soul structure as we men of today have—in even greater degree than [Marie-Henri] Beyle. He not only foreshadows the great mystic; he also is the culmination ahead of its time of the modern psychological novel. He has a little story about a heretic in a torture chamber of the Inquisition in which he writes pages about a state of mind that endures only a fraction of a second. He is the master in this of both Bourget and Dostoevski.

And in another little sketch, "The Imp of the Perverse," he presents exactly the same phenomena that I have just come upon in the books I have borrowed from you, just as thoroughly and correctly presented. He is the only writer I know who has penetrated all the way to the bottom of this theory of the absence of real *ratio sufficiens* in those actions that originate in a certain kind of psychic condition, namely that found in *les dégénérés*. Indeed he goes so far—perhaps unconsciously, granted—yet he goes so far as to touch upon the difference existing, for instance, between Lombroso and Saury as they set about explaining this kind of person, who constitutes the link between the criminal and the sick. It does not heighten the contrast itself, but one can do this himself, in that the one [Lombroso] sees in all these manifestations of criminality and sickness *atavistische Rückgänge*, whereas the other [sees] a type developed little by little through generations until it has come to perfection in the present concluding moment.[30]

The letter bears on climactic points that Hansson was to make, as we have seen, in his essay on Poe. A second letter a few days later,

30. *Brevväxling*, pp. 25–26.

of which only a portion is extant, rehearsed additional passages that would appear in part 5 of the essay as Hansson concluded that Poe's conception of perverseness is nothing other than Saury's idea of degeneration, and that what is most deeply hidden in the nature of man finds expression most strikingly "in the great artist and in the great criminal."[31]

As usual, Strindberg made no attempt to reply item by item, but drily noted in his next letter, "Degeneration is as vague a concept as germs."[32] He had often thought he was degenerate, he added, but has since decided instead that he is a giant who from overexertion has had periods of weakness when, for example, longing for cessation of strife, he had been attracted to the false gospel of socialism. At Hansson's instigation, he had been reading Huysmans, a writer like Poe, or for that matter, he now conceded, like Hansson himself, in transition between "synthetic literature" (as Max Nordau termed

31. *Brevväxling*, p. 27.

32. *Brev*, 7: 247. Strindberg's idea of degeneration, though basically Lombrosian, had pejorative connotations and differed from Hansson's use of the term. In a letter to Nietzsche, for example, he took exception to the view taken in *Götzen-Dämmerung* of the criminal as a strong man frustrated by society; Lombroso's photographs of criminals made it clear, he wrote, "que le fourbe est un animal inférieur, un dégénéré, un faible dépossédé des facultés nécessaires pour éluder les paragraphes de la loi" (*Brev*, 7: 190). Max Nordau's usage was markedly pejorative also; see, for example, his excoriation of modern artists and writers as "degenerates" devoid of genius and even of good sense in *Degeneration*, 7th ed. (New York, 1895). Strindberg's curious comparison of degeneration with germs [bacterier] perhaps derived from an analogy drawn in *Utopier*, a collection of tales published in 1885, in the preface to which Strindberg had rejected evolutionary perfectionism and declared his purpose in the volume to show the need for social reform. He argued on a bacterial analogy: "Society is an organic product, it is said, and everything that is, is nature. The cholera bacillus is also an organic product, but not therefore something we should cultivate . . . There is wholesome and unwholesome nature." *Samlade skrifter* 15 (Stockholm 1913): 7. Upperclass culture, based on exploitation of the working classes in order to obtain leisure to produce useless works of art, is a form of unwholesome nature or degeneration. After his trial for blasphemy in 1884, Strindberg abandoned these ideas though not, it would seem, the conjunction of degeneration and bacteria.

fiction, drama, and poetry) and psychological treatises. At the last, he noted that he was now reading the Danish proof for *Tschandala*: "It is Poe before Poe! Complete!" He had said as much though less ringingly more than a month before to K. O. Bonnier when he classified *Tschandala* in the Poe "genre."[33] In his next letter, however, he had misgivings about *Tschandala*: "It is not as good as it could have been, in part because I could not make use of reality and present time for the setting, in part because I had not then read Edgar Poe."[34]

He had sent off the Swedish manuscript of *Tschandala* to Bonnier three days after the night he read Poe. Given his fluency and energy, there conceivably was time in the interval, as Hans Lindström suggests, for Poe to have had some influence on the novel. But the evidence that is usually offered is unconvincing and in any case is of no moment. There are, to be sure, cryptic messages—the Indian signs or hieroglyphics carved into a tree—and the feat that Professor Törner performs of writing invisibly with marigold juice, thereby dazzling the gypsy, but these are no more than incidental stage business. When Törner plays detective and takes the cast of a footprint to catch a horse thief, he is no Auguste Dupin quietly assembling abstruse facts for the imaginative reconstruction of a crime; he is merely intent on supplying the police with evidence of the gypsy's guilt.[35] There seems to be no reason for questioning the

33. *Brev* 7: 247–248; 212.
34. *Brev* 7: 273.
35. Lindström, *Hjärnornas kamp*, pp. 194–195, suggests Wilkie Collins' Cuff as Törner's model in *Tschandala*, but Dupin as the model for Herr X in "Paria" and for Borg in *I havsbandet* since his deductions proceed with precision from facts. But this is not Dupin's great distinction, as I have already suggested. Elie Poulenard, *August Strindberg* (Paris, 1962), p. 355, assumes that Strindberg had reference to "the analytic genius" of Dupin in claiming that *Tschandala* was "Poe before Poe." There are no grounds for the assumption, but one can only agree with Poulenard that Poe's influence would be most difficult to prove in this story "trop chargée de petits évenements." Eric O. Johannesson, *The Novels of August Strindberg* (Berkeley, 1968), p. 125, finds the Gothic features of *Tschandala* reminiscent of Poe's fiction: a mysterious setting, exotic

sincerity of Strindberg's regret that he had not read Poe before writing *Tschandala*. The novel owes nothing to Poe. It "is Poe" only in being of the "next epoch," a transitional work that has left behind merely "synthetic" literature (fiction) for increasingly "analytic" (psychological) literature based on scientific studies. Its psychology had been given Strindbergian application in a story of psychic influences and unmaskings, a battle of brains such as Strindberg perceived, as we have seen, to be distinctive also of Poe.

In March 1889 Strindberg wrote a one-acter called "Samum" [Simoom] for his experimental theater in Copenhagen. He announced it to Hansson as "A brilliant Edgar Poe piece . . . in which I have used the desert wind's power to evoke visions of terror that drive French soldiers to suicide."[36] The description is not quite accurate of the play as we have it. The decisive force that drives the Zouave prisoner Guimard to his death is not the simoom but the power of suggestion. The setting is present time in a burial chamber in Algeria. In the first scene the Bedouin girl Biskra's powers are hinted at: if the simoom fails to dry up the brains of her white enemies, she can do what the hot winds cannot, and what she cannot, the sun will, for the sun is with her and her people. In the next scene, Guimard enters, pale, confused, and thirsty. He is seated and given a pile of sand for a pillow. He asks for water and is given sand, which he drinks, believing that it is water. He submits, at Biskra's suggestion, to the illusion that he has been bitten in the calf by a rabid dog. Biskra tells him to drink, but he cannot; she offers to play music for him, but he protests he cannot endure it. She chants, her words echoed by a male companion off stage, so that Guimard is further confused and assents to putting himself in Biskra's power. She evokes visions of deception, loss, and betrayal in his home, and finally, his will destroyed, he asks to die, for life

---

inhabitants, strange events, elements of moral depravity, exaggerated and violent gestures, mysterious signs and symbols, mesmerism and magic.

36. *Brev* 7: 272.

is vile. At Biskra's bidding, he curses his wife in a last testament, and Biskra tells him that now he can die. Soon, tearing off his epaulets, he declares that he is dead, and Biskra assures him he has been dead for a long time. She shows him a skull in the mirror and cruelly taunts him, and at this he falls down, dead indeed. The power of suggestion has been shown to be strong enough to destroy life itself. In the third and last scene, Biskra is praised by her male companion as the strong one, stronger even than the simoom.

The play is in some respects like a primitive ritual—Biskra is evidently ordained to perform a role of tribal salvation—and it is an "Edgar Poe piece" only if regarded as a battle of brains. The terror of the victim of irrational forces is not its substance. Biskra is the foreground figure, priestess, mother, avenger, as she presides over the three scenes. The setting is exotic but relatively bare. Even less authentically Poesque is the management of the motif of fear-by-suggestion that results in death, a phenomenon that had been reported in current psychiatric literature.[37]

Taking a larger view of Poe's influence on the play, Gunnar Brandell cites "Samum" in illustration of the lesson in working up suspense in short, seemingly realistic scenes that he believes Strindberg learned from Poe, and of a second lesson as well, that of using nonfunctional props (like the scarab itself in "The Gold Bug") to lend "romantic luminousness" to his scenes. Certain of Strindberg's details—Brandell's example is Borg's bracelet in *I havsbandet*—are clearly not meant to support some Brandesian or naturalistic illu-

---

37. Lamm, *August Strindberg*, p. 196, names the Nancy school as the source of this and other uses of hypnotism in Strindberg's work of this period. Lindström, *Hjärnornas kamp*, p. 281, notes that Lange's *Om Sindsbevægelser*, which Ola Hansson knew (see chap. 4, n. 33), explicitly states that death can ensue from feelings of fear, and (p. 281) that in a work known to Strindberg, J. Liégeois' *De la suggestion hypnotique* (1884), a situation fairly close to that in the play is reported. Madsen, *Strindberg's Naturalistic Theater*, p. 123, suggests "considerable influences from Edgar Allan Poe" in the "exotic, lugubrious [*sic*] setting" and "fantastic hallucinatory atmosphere" of the play.

sion of reality but "open a window on something beyond the real, though it may not be possible to say what."[38] When Borg's bracelet slips down below his cuff, the girl he has just cured of an hysterical illness sees it and is awakened, Strindberg tells us, to a fear of the unknown. This is a bit of romantic mystification, as Brandell says, of a type that may indeed have had its source in Poe or for that matter in E. T. A. Hoffmann. Yet Borg's bracelet is not only non-functional, its appearance in the tale seems quite gratuitous; more than mystifying, it is suddenly ominous—or if one is not sympathetic, it is merely portentous. The unprepared and undeveloped use of a detail like this is not confined to Strindberg's fiction of the early 1890s; it is one of the most distinctive features of the late plays. There it raises similar but more urgent and even less answerable questions for the critic, though not always for the biographer or historian. And these questions are not those characteristically raised with respect to Poe's stories. With Poe, probably because of his insistence on unity of effect, questions arise having to do not with an isolated, perhaps displaced, detail, but with the network of atmospheric and perhaps symbolic meaning set in motion by a single detail. The most that can be said of Strindberg's possible indebtedness to Poe in the "subjective" use of detail is perhaps that both kinds of questions ultimately owe their existence to the degree of subjectivism we are willing to allow in our reading of Poe and Strindberg. Recent Poe criticism, notably that of Edward H. Davidson, has shown what gains may be had from reading a tale like "The Black Cat" as a projection in every detail of the guilt-ridden or

38. Brandell, *Strindbergs Infernokris*, pp. 205–206. Bjurman, *Edgar Allan Poe*, p. 423, also suggests that the concentrated form of the one-act play became natural to Strindberg after he had read Poe. Torsten Eklund, "Strindbergs I havsbandet," *Edda* 29 (1929): 113–144, regards *I havsbandet* as an example of Strindberg's growing interest in symbolism, the treatment in which of the "night side" of human nature is said to derive from his knowledge of Ola Hansson's work and his acquaintance with Poe, "whose art of rich tonal effects, with its depiction of occult, 'mesmeric' phenomena and abnormally heightened psychic conditions had had a powerful impact on Strindberg" (p. 143).

otherwise disturbed mind of the first-person narrator. It is such a method that becomes increasingly useful and even necessary in reading Strindberg's fiction and drama from the 1890s on. Gunnar Brandell uses Ola Hansson's term "subjective naturalism" from an essay of 1890 to designate the tendency in both Hansson and Strindberg in the following decade away from orthodox naturalism and toward the subjectivism being given new emphasis in French symbolism, in which the reality of the ego is asserted against the dreamlike appearance of the world. Brandell quotes from Hansson's essay: "And the fixed middle point around which all these dreams move like the vapor around an evolving planet is the sovereign personality, which makes of all outer reality merely an instrument on which can be played all the noble melodies slumbering in its own soul."[39] "Subjective naturalism," whether stimulated by the example of Poe or of French symbolism, or of both, is only a step away from the subjectivism of the dream plays and indeed of all modern nonrepresentational art. In it, the processes, already highly developed in Strindberg, of absorption and transformation of material from his own life and from his reading were accelerated; the consequence is that the problems of assigning value to or even of identifying sources for this or that detail have grown apace. They threaten to multiply beyond solution in the work of this writer who as he headed into the psychotic crises of the Inferno period already had begun experiencing difficulty distinguishing between appearance and reality. The artistic legitimacy of a detail like Borg's bracelet, erupting out of who knows what deep well of literary or personal experience (or no experience at all), is scarcely demonstrable: it simply exists, mystifying, luminous, ominous, portentous—in whatever significance a willing reader can discover support for in the novel itself.

It appears then that every attempt to discover specific links between Poe's fiction and Strindberg's work from this time on will

39. Quoted in *Strindbergs Infernokris*, pp. 206–207.

fall victim to the realization that Strindberg's transformations of borrowed ideas or details are so drastic that the question of sources quickly threatens to become not only virtually insoluble but practically irrelevant. This is illustrated in Strindberg's remark to Hansson in July 1889 that he is working on "a modern novel in the footsteps of Nietzsche and Poe."[40] In *I havsbandet*, the novel in question, possible influences from Poe, Nietzsche, and Victor Hugo, and continuing themes and ideas from Strindberg's earlier work merge almost indistinguishably. The leading character, Borg, is a superman but in the decadent style. He is notably erudite; so too are not only Auguste Dupin, Roderick Usher, and other Poe characters, but the Captain in *Fadren* and Professor Törner, to name only two of Strindberg's characters from this period. Borg's learning is not esoteric nor has it been easily acquired, like Dupin's, and it is not put to curious and astonishing uses in the solution of crime. The novel's seaboard setting, its use of dialect to reveal rustic stupidity, its battle of brains, have only limited precedent in "The Gold Bug" and other stories. And if, as it has sometimes been suggested, Borg's love of solitude and his experiments in mind reading and hypnotism are in any way *indebted* to Poe, they have been put to uses not merely different from but so foreign to the original that the conjecture, already tenuous, seems hardly to much purpose.[41]

40. *Brev*, 7: 347.
41. Suggestions of this sort of indebtedness to Poe were made by Johan Mortensen, *Från Röda rummet till sekelskiftet* (Stockholm, 1918), 1: 157, and have been frequently repeated. The most detailed study of *I havsbandet*, which adds Hugo's *Les Travailleurs de la mer* to the list of possible sources for its seaboard setting and titanism motif, is Torsten Eklund, "Strindbergs I havsbandet," *Edda* 29 (1929): 113–144. Eklund, p. 144, suggests that the motif of hidden treasure in the story "Silvertrasket" [The silver marsh, 1898] was borrowed from "The Gold Bug." In the same story, Poulenard, *August Strindberg*, pp. 385–386, finds the use of cipher as well as the general air of mystery reminiscent of Poe, and declares (p. 520) that in *Taklagsöl* [The roofing feast, 1907] Strindberg probably found "dans la lecture de certaines œuvres d'Edgar Poe un exemple, une technique et un encouragement pour l'utilisation difficile des états liminaires de la conscience." This and the discussion of details of the

So too with the tempting speculation that "la réalité intérieure" projected in Strindberg's autobiographical and dream plays may in some aspects be descended either directly from Poe or collaterally through French symbolism: the currents eddying in those plays are deep and were fed by very many streams. The "private tragedy," as Raymond Williams has called it, of Strindberg (and O'Neill and others) has at best only approximate counterparts in Poe—in, for example, the "mesmeric revelation" that "pain [in earthly existence] . . . is the sole basis of the bliss of the ultimate life in Heaven," or in the transcendental teaching of Monos in his colloquy with Una of the necessity of earthly suffering, or more broadly and simply, in the analytical subjectivism of any number of the tales.[42] But this is not the Poe that Strindberg seems to have defined in his correspondence with Ola Hansson. When Hansson's Poe essay appeared in *Vossische Zeitung* in May 1889, Strindberg complimented him, "Your essay on Poe is fine!" then immediately added, "But—poetry without philosophy is nix!"—a reference again to his distaste for "synthetic" literature. Preceding these remarks, however, he had adverted once more to *Tschandala*: "It is strange that all of *Tschandala* was written before I had read Poe."[43] The claim of prior rights to Poe was again reasserted. It was in this context of the battle of brains waged by means of the forces of suggestion that Poe had evidently left the deepest impression on Strindberg.[44]

---

curator's nervous state and physical appearance quite rightly stop short of asserting "influence."

42. Erik Vendelfelt, "Edgar Allan Poe och Strindbergs drömspel," *Meddelanden från Strindbergssällskapet*, no. 26 (April 1960), pp. 7–10, speculates that the dream techniques in the late plays may derive from Poe, and that certain details, most convincingly among them the naming of two characters Edgar and Allan in *Dödsdansen* [The dance of death, 1901], have the same source.

43. *Brev*, 7: 348. The remark evidently harks back to Hansson's cautious praise of less than two months before: "*Tschandala* is good; the ending of course is Poe, but masterful" (*Brevväxling*, p. 53).

44. It is regrettable that the Poe volume that Ola Hansson lent Strindberg

Except for an eccentric and cryptic reference in 1895 to white and black imagery in *The Adventures of Arthur Gordon Pym*, translated into Swedish in 1890 and the only Poe title besides "The Gold Bug" that Strindberg ever named, no further references to Poe appear in the letters or in the works.[45] After the abatement of his psychotic illness, he returned to Sweden and spent some time intermittently in the late 1890s in the university town of Lund. There students and teachers would occasionally meet with him, among them a young graduate student in literature, Johan Mortensen, who had published an essay on Poe in 1894 (see pp. 62–63, above). Mortensen tells in a memoir of Strindberg how impressed he had been by his features, which struck him as being remarkably like Poe's. When at last mutual friends arranged for him to meet Strindberg, the conversation began conventionally enough, but suddenly Strindberg got onto the subject of personal invisibility, remarking to the silent astonishment of the small group of young

---

contained no poems, no criticism, and only eight tales. A writer so troubled by the guilt of an unresolved Oedipus complex as Strindberg has been described as being (Eklund, *Tjänstekvinnans son*, pp. 132–138; Brandell, *Strindbergs Infernokris*, pp. 30–33) could have been expected to respond powerfully to stories like "Ligeia" and "The Oval Portrait" as depictions of an unappeasable hunger for a love too pure to be realized or perhaps of a fear of being consumed and annihilated by sexual passion—the vampire motif that may have constituted Poe's appeal to Edvard Munch and was completely missed by Ola Hansson.

45. *Brev* 11 (Stockholm, 1969): 107–108. The letter was sent from Paris in December 1895 in the midst of the Inferno period. It was addressed to Torsten Hedlund, a Swedish theosophist with whom Strindberg had opened correspondence the previous year to obtain support, if possible, in theosophy for his alchemical experiments. The letter announced Strindberg's break with Hedlund, who he alleged had followed false gods. Then, evidently annoyed by Hedlund's use of theosophical terms in contrasting black and white magic, Strindberg referred him to *Pym*: "It is a book which in a childish form, especially in the last chapter 'The White Giant,' has perhaps foreseen this whole remarkable strife now going on between White and Black, between [Poe's sign for White, as given in the "Note" to *Pym*] and [ditto for Black]. And you will see that the word Tekeli-li which the white birds screamed is my battle cry against Tsalal, where no white object was to be found."

admirers present that he had himself been invisible on several occasions. The conversation lagged, but finishing off his whiskey, Strindberg turned to Mortensen and said, "Let us now talk about something real; let's talk about Poe and ghost stories. You must like Poe; haven't you written about Poe?" They then spoke "long and well" on this new subject. Strindberg had many questions, including one as to the year of Poe's death. Mortensen replied to the question, and someone present added (in jest, he later told Mortensen), "The same year you were born." Mortensen continued:

> "Yes," said Strindberg, casting a serious glance at the speaker and, it seemed to me, looking somewhat embarrassed. Evidently Strindberg had already noted this connection between himself and the mystic American. I started a little, for I guessed where Strindberg's thoughts were taking him. He believed of course in the transmigration of souls and wished to suggest that Poe had been resurrected in him. Absurd though this idea seemed to me, I cannot deny that it made an impression, for I had just said to myself, "Strange how he resembles Poe, to judge by the portraits. The same high forehead with the characteristic breadth across the temples and the same solemnity and dignity of bearing. He is like a burned-out volcano."
>
> "Do you think that Poe himself believed in the supernatural in his stories?" he asked. "He believed in mesmerism and other kinds of mysticism," I replied, "but as a rule there can be found at bottom a natural explanation of the events he depicts. The strange events described in 'Ligeia' are accounted for as the experiences of an opium eater, and in 'The Black Cat' the narrator is a heavy drinker."
>
> "You know," Strindberg continued, "that some years ago Ola Hansson wrote a story about a forger whose unconscious self drove him to copy someone's name. This explanation

seemed unnatural to me at the time, and I rewrote the tale as I thought it should be and made a little play of it."

"I remember," I answered, "not least because I immediately noticed the difference between Ola Hansson's explanation and yours. Particularly for a play your explanation was much more natural."

"Yes, but now," Strindberg replied, "I have just about gone over to the other point of view." And our talk went deeper and deeper into mysticism.[46]

After eight years, "Paria" was still the subject of differences between Strindberg and Ola Hansson and still the focal point, it would appear, of Strindberg's interest in Poe. Now, however, after the ravages of the Inferno period, contention was all in the past, the old battle of brains was largely spent, and Strindberg was resigning himself to "the other point of view"—to pity, as Indra's Daughter was to say in "The Dream Play," to pity for mankind for the pain that it finds itself compelled on this earth to inflict and to endure, and to the mystic's doctrine of the redemptiveness of that suffering.

46. *Strindberg som jag minns honom* (Stockholm, 1931), pp. 15–16.

CHAPTER 6

AFTER THE 1890s

When the Norwegian newspaper editor and critic Carl Nærup, who had been in the United States in the 1880s, took notice in 1909 of the centenary of Poe's birth, he supposed that the readers of *Kringsjaa*, where his five-page-long memorial appeared, would think of Poe merely as "one of the ordinary American authors, whom the world might well dispense with," largely because so little of his work has been made available, and that, "moreover, in dreadful Danish translations." But to pass over Poe in this fashion, Nærup protested, would be an injustice to one of the immortals of literature, the creator of unforgettable lyric poetry and of equally beautiful "prose poems" like "Ligeia," "The Fall of the House of Usher," and "The Masque of the Red Death." Poe is not for ordinary readers; his poetry is made up of feelings of "fear and horror and evil," and these reveal an underlying anguish painted in the colors of "disintegration, decay, and death." Poe's mysticism, Nærup continued, is distinguished by its supremely intellectual qualities; in consequence, he is "the only American poet who belongs to world literature. All the more pity that it was his fate to be born and do his work at a time when the great North American republic was still a half-barbaric society."[1]

---

1. "Edgar Poe," *Kringsjaa* 33 (1909): 274, 275. Having objected in the essay to the Danish translations of Poe that Norwegians had to use, Nærup provided generous samples of his own translations in the essay, and in 1919

These are but faint echoes of Poe criticism from the nineties, popularized for the occasion of the centenary. They are indicative of the total diffusion in the twentieth century of the former focus on Poe as the spirit of poetry or as the prophet of the new age of psychological ("analytical") literature. The interest that Scandinavian writers now took in Poe was seldom intense enough to lead to their drawing on Poe in their own work. Poe became instead a subject much more often for critics and scholars to examine and comment upon. He was no longer even the little he had once been of the writer's writer, one to suggest a tone, an ambiance, or a method. He had slipped almost entirely into literary history, a writer to be read and an important literary force to be studied. A clear sign of the distance that overtook the older view of Poe's significance was the rise of scholarly interest in Poe. In 1916 Gunnar Bjurman wrote at Lund University under the supervision of Johan Mortensen a dissertation that surveyed in thirty chapters Poe's esthetics, poetry, prose, including sources and parallels, and his reputation. The last eight chapters were on Poe's reception in France and his influence on the *symbolistes* and writers of science fiction, and (in the final chapter) on his reception in Sweden. Bjurman's *Edgar Allan Poe* was a prodigious effort that took into account all available American and European materials and scholarship touching on Poe's life and work and the nature of his genius. It was the first and for thoroughness by far the most impressive of the academic studies—dissertations, theses, seminar papers, both published and unpublished —that were to be written in Scandinavian universities in the coming years on the subject of Poe.

Young men who had been schoolboys in the 1890s read Poe for the first time unaware of the enthusiasm with which Ola Hansson and Johannes Jørgensen and others had written about Poe as a seminal figure in contemporary literature. They read Poe chiefly

---

published his translation of "A Descent into the Maelström" [*I malstrømmens dyp*].

and simply because translation and criticism had made his work available. Otto Rung, a Danish writer of psychological fiction, writes in his memoirs of having worked in his boyhood through Fenimore Cooper in English, having then advanced to the novels by Victorian ladies that he borrowed from his sisters, and at last having discovered in the early 1890s the art of such storytellers as Robert Louis Stevenson, Bret Harte, Mark Twain, and "above all, Edgar Allan Poe." He read Poe, he writes, wholly unaware at the time of the new literary developments taking place in Johannes Jørgensen's literary circle. Reading Poe's stories may have encouraged Rung, a lawyer by training and profession, to venture into the writing of fiction, but by his own testimony his first novel, published in 1902, was based entirely on Ribot's theories of double consciousness.[2] Psychological interests of this sort seem also to have been uppermost in Rung's mind when he wrote a collection of tales published in 1908 and sometimes said to show signs of influence from Poe. *Desertører* [Deserters] is very much a period piece with its hints of *décadence* and its stories of strange psychological states, but it scarcely needs to be termed Poesque for that. The young man in the first of the stories, it is true, is the last member of an ancient family, and he has devoured many quaint volumes of lore, some of it recent and none of it, to his great distress, forgotten, including the writings of all the popes and the Church Fathers as well as "Shelley, Swinburne, Poe."[3] And when he disappears, an amateur detective equipped with esoteric knowledge (obtained from the study of footprints in Iceland) goes into action. But these details, should they in fact have derived from Rung's reading of Poe, are no more than incidentals in a badly told story. At best, there is only peripheral indebtedness to Poe.

2. *Fra min klunketid: En hjemlig kavalkade* (Copenhagen, 1942), pp. 134, 142, 209.
3. *Desertører* (Copenhagen, 1908), p. 22.

The Swedish poet, essayist, and aphorist Vilhelm Ekelund had also been a schoolboy in the 1890s. He would very early have had special reasons for feeling some of the attraction of the view taken of Poe's significance in those years. Born in 1880 in Skåne, the same province in which Ola Hansson had his birthplace, Ekelund was regarded early in his career as the most brilliant of the generation of poets next after Hansson in capturing a sense of place distinctive of the Scanian countryside. But under the influence of German and French symbolist poetry and the neoclassicism of Hölderlin and von Platen, Ekelund moved away from nature poetry to finely honed lyrics that are regarded as having finally freed Swedish poetry of the necessity for conventional meter and rhyme. "Then came Nietzsche," as Ola Hansson had said of himself; after 1906 Ekelund took the Nietzschean view of lyric poetry as a stagnant form of art and turned instead to prose. In *Antikt ideal* (Malmö, 1909) he wrote, "I do not know whether Dostoevski ever wrote verse, but I know that Nietzsche did—and the 'best' since Goethe. The raging heart that lived under the highest imperative known to any man burst forth at the presentiment of its undoing in tragic dithyrambs— tragic as the overflow of happiness. The masterful 'will to power' has found no mightier expression in the culture of our time than these three: Dostoevski, Nietzsche, Strindberg." In contrast, "the modern lyric obviously has declined into stagnation. More and more a piteous estheticism prevails. Bagatelles of piquant sentiment have become dominant." Is lyric poetry, then, "a dangerous thing for those in whose soul there burns too bright a flame? Leopardi, Lenau, Poe, Baudelaire, Stagnelius—what dismal phantoms on the massive, flaming horizon of lyricism!"[4]

Yet when Ekelund wrote a centenary essay on Poe several years after these lines were written, he called Poe "one of the richest personalities of romantic poetry":

4. *Antikt ideal* (Malmö, 1909), pp. 74, 79, 80.

He carries to its extreme limit the cult of the spiritually visionary and of the supersensually perceptive. He decrees that suffering and melancholy are the principles of poetry. People who are culturally productive have usually observed, it would seem, that what is most beautiful grows best in the shadow of sorrow. But many of them have also observed that out of the will that takes delight in vigorously keeping this fateful element of beauty in balance, a world of beauty can emerge— admittedly not surpassing, perhaps, the former in splendor, but all the more worthy of the spirit who takes his pride in fearing nothing and hoping for nothing. Edgar Poe is the most brilliant revelation of the realm of suffering out of which poetry most often comes into flower.[5]

This seeming reversal in Ekelund's estimation of Poe is to be understood only within the narrow limitations that he had by this time placed on the competence of "romantic" poetry to express the fullness of human experience. He distinguished, moreover, among romantic poets, harshly declaring that Baudelaire and Leopardi allowed their work to descend principally into invective and vituperation, whereas nothing—"neither alcohol, poverty, nor death"— had the power to destroy what was fine in Poe.

Something there was in Poe which the harsh telluric climate could not *bite* into. Everything he does proceeds with a curious ease and cleanness—despite its intellectual solidity. An atmosphere of spirituality [af andligt] surrounds him; the form of his poetry is at the same time both large and simple. He is always inspired, and his life seems to be in mysterious

5. "Till Edgar Poes hundraårsdag," in *Böcker och vandringar* (Malmö, 1923), p. 144. The essay was published first in the newspaper *Arbetet*, 19 January 1909. Ekelund warmly admired some of Ola Hansson's work, but not his journalism, as he called it, presumably including the Poe essay. Yet his reservations are expressed only with respect to work written after Ola Hansson left Skåne. See letter dated 7 September 1906 in *Brev*, ed. Nils Gösta Valdén and Algot Werin (Lund, 1968), pp. 62–63.

correspondence with a good genius, with the good powers of this life in whom he puts his faith with all his heart.[6]

Ekelund took exception to Johan Mortensen's discounting of the significance of erotic experience in Poe's poetry: "Poe is one of the most profoundly erotic persons who have ever lived. His metaphysic is a product of erotic experience—as Plato's teaching stems essentially out of Eros."[7] If Poe's elevation of lyric poetry to the highest place in art must be regretted, Ekelund nevertheless recalls that Poe was not only "a versifier of depth and passion" but also "a master of prose with whom very few can endure comparison. Strindberg, who rightly condemns verse in general as a repugnant, belletristic minor art and handicraft, would find in Poe arguments for verse that he could scarcely refute."[8]

The reference to Strindberg led Ekelund's thoughts to Strindberg's "master in recent years," Swedenborg; immediately a rhapsodic passage followed with Swedenborg's heavenly host now in mind:

Poe has seen the angels of heaven, he has drowned his soul in their eyes, he has felt their hair flowing past his head, and he has listened to a supernatural melody. Few people have had a more inspired belief in a good principle during life. His soul feels itself constantly inundated by mysterious intimations of a distant past; not for a moment has it occurred to him to doubt that this earthly life is merely a station on an endless journey, a fugitive scene from some great mystery. His proper home is Beauty, goodness.[9]

Ekelund deplored the bitter necessity that drives poets into the hackwork of literary criticism, a factor, he surmised, in Poe's al-

6. *Böcker och vandringar*, p. 145.
7. *Böcker och vandringar*, p. 145.
8. *Böcker och vandringar*, p. 146.
9. *Böcker och vandringar*, p. 146.

coholism. "For Poe, the art of the word was holy. His style vibrates with the tautness of his soul. Every line of his writing is charged with life." [10] No wonder, then, the disastrous effects of the banal compromises that Poe had to make in order to please the public. But suffering engendered ecstasy in Poe, whose most memorable work was done in the years when his suffering was greatest. As for the perennial question of what attitude to adopt toward the story of Poe's unhappy life, Ekelund chose the Nietzschean view that Poe's art, like all art, is "necessarily the product of struggle—in the first instance, an inner struggle, but the external one is an analogue to this far from despicable source of inspiration." [11]

After having risen in this fashion to the celebration of Poe's centenary, Ekelund later retired to the opinion that he came more and more firmly to hold, that Poe was relatively negligible, another Tennyson, perhaps, or a Swinburne.[12] The American who became far more congenial than Poe to Ekelund's interests was Ralph Waldo Emerson, whose journals, essays, and correspondence he studied in 1912 and the years following, and about whom he wrote two essays and several newspaper articles. Ekelund placed Emerson in company with Plato, and Poe sank correspondingly in his estimation. Ekelund himself made the comparison, as Sven Lindqvist reports from an unpublished note that Ekelund wrote when he began

10. *Böcker och vandringar*, p. 148.
11. *Böcker och vandringar*, p. 143. Carl-Henning Wijmark, "Symbolistinfluenser hos Vilhelm Ekelund," *Samlaren* 89 (1968): 22–25, finds faint traces of Poe's influence here and there in Ekelund's poetry: the image in the last stanza of "Hafsvik" (*In Candidum*, 1905) of "Och jag låter tanklöst / sand och musslor genom handen rinna" is linked to "And I hold within my hand / Grains of the golden sand—" in Poe's "A Dream within a Dream"; Ekelund's symbolism of the eye and of a glance of the eye for the supersensual is linked to "the divine light in thine eyes" in Poe's "To Helen [Whitman]"; the symbolism of "Cypressallén" for high seriousness or for the powers that rule life is linked to the "alley Titanic / Of cypress" in "Ulalume." But none of this I find convincing.
12. Algot Werin, *Vilhelm Ekelund* 2 (Lund, 1961): 62–63.

reading Emerson: "It is hypocritical to be sentimental about Poe. The case is quite simply that someone like Poe ranks extraordinarily low when compared with Emerson. Emerson had absolutely no call to see him."[13] Although written evidently to correct his own criticism of Emerson's dislike of Poe, the note was definitive and left no room for future revisions of Ekelund's estimation of Poe.

The symbolist call for *poésie pure*, which included in its history Poe's accounts of precisely calculated poetic composition, persisted into the twentieth century both in literature and in painting. Maurice Denis's reminder in 1890 that a picture is essentially "une surface plane recouverte de couleurs en un certain ordre assemblées" and his comparison of the painting of Cézanne and Gauguin with the poetry of Mallarmé were probably the origin of Apollinaire's prediction nearly twenty years later in *The Cubist Painters* that art was moving toward pure painting, more abstract and mathematical than ever before as it aimed at "conceptualized reality."[14] The idea of "constructed" art fired the imagination of Pär Lagerkvist, then at the beginning of his distinguished career as dramatist, poet, and novelist. Curiously enough for someone then engaged in radical journalism and connected with the labor movement in Sweden, Lagerkvist found in cubism what was, in his view, wholly lacking in contemporary literature: esthetic rigor and solidity.[15] He

13. Sven Lindqvist, *Dagbok och diktverk* (Stockholm, 1966), p. 267.
14. Guillaume Apollinaire, *The Cubist Painters*, ed. Robert Motherwell (New York, 1949), pp. 12, 13, 17. The quotation from Denis is taken from "Définition du Neo-traditionnisme," in *Théories 1890–1910 du symbolisme* . . . , 4th ed. (Paris, 1920), p. 1. Lagerkvist's relation to cubism is discussed in Leif Åslund, "Pär Lagerkvists Ordkonst och bildkonst och det nya måleriet," *Ord och Bild* 64 (1955): 35–49. In an article on Cézanne in *Första maj 1915* (Stockholm, 1915), pp. 10–13, Lagerkvist recognized Cézanne as the first cubist, a painter who, despite his alleged mysticism, never indulged in casual speculation, unproductive brooding, or haphazard working habits.
15. Harald Elovson, "Pär Lagerkvists läroår," in Gunnar Tideström, ed., *Synpunkter på Pär Lagerkvist* (Stockholm, 1966), pp. 54–56, 59.

became an outspoken critic of the impressionistic regionalist art that had emerged in the 1890s, and he published a little programmatic book in 1913 titled *Ordkonst och bildkonst* [The art of words and the art of pictures], in which he chose to emphasize the intellectual energy in cubist painting at the expense of its intuitive side, although Apollinaire had said it was of equal importance.[16]

Lagerkvist's review of Apollinaire's book in 1913 reiterated the plea in *Ordkonst och bildkonst* for a literature as "constructed" as cubist painting, "a literature whose separate forces are held together by a unifying idea, a literature that strives for calculated lucidity, monumentality, and artistic meaningfulness," one that is free of mere psychological cleverness but is sturdy and lasting like the Eddas and the sagas.[17] This was the manifesto of a writer who not unexpectedly would bid aspiring writers adopt Poe's conscious artistry as their precept. Vilhelm Ekelund was expressing in these same years a similar scorn of contemporary literature and a demand for artistic seriousness, but not Lagerkvist's emphasis on "construction."[18] Certainly Ekelund's Poe essay of 1909, which Lagerkvist in all likelihood read, showed no interest in Poe's analyses of calculated effects and technique; nor indeed had Strindberg, whom Lagerkvist greatly admired. It is uncertain where Lagerkvist discovered this side of Poe unless it was somehow through his interest in cubism.

Under these circumstances, whatever influences Poe may have had on Lagerkvist's own work will scarcely be definite. It has been suggested, for example, that in the first play in *Den svåra stunden*

16. Gösta Lilja, *Det moderna måleriet i svensk kritik 1905–1914* (Malmö, 1955), pp. 254–255.

17. *Svenska Dagbladet*, 16 August 1913, p. 9.

18. Erik Hörnström, *Pär Lagerkvist: Från Den röda tiden till Det eviga leendet* (Stockholm, 1946), pp. 22–23. Ulf Wittrock, "Pär Lagerkvist och dekadanslitteraturen," *Morgontidningen*, 12 February 1951, notes also the similarity in Ekelund's and Lagerkvist's protest against *décadence*, which in the years 1909–1912 came under heavy fire by many critics.

[The difficult hour, 1918] Poe's influence may be discerned in the obsession of The Man in Tails with his past: "There is something of Poe in the whole of this one-acter, where a memory, an unpleasant detail in one's past gnaws and burrows until the tension at last reaches the breaking point" and one's life is suddenly thrown into full perspective.[19] The macabre tale "Banalt" [Banal, in *Motiv*, 1914], in which a horseman, the chief of the Bloody Riders, exhumes the body of his enemy "the hated one" only to discover his own features on the corpse, has been said to bear vestiges of "William Wilson," or perhaps—it is no less likely—of Ola Hansson's tale with a doppelganger motif, "Husvill."[20] Gunnar Tideström's analysis of the prose poem "Flöjten, en skiss från Paris" [The flute, A sketch from Paris, in *Stormklockan*, Christmas, 1913] suggests that both Baudelaire and Poe lie somewhere in the background of this cubist piece that is so sharp and "mathematical" in its effects yet so full of feeling.[21] And there are hints of Lagerkvist's having perhaps read "The Fall of the House of Usher" in some of the details in the novel *Människor* [People, 1912]: the tarn, the gloom, Gustav Mörk's conviction that he is evil and doomed, his suggestibility and sensitivity, and the superior social station of the Mörks. But other important aspects of the novel, such as the overt eroticism, the lack of learning in the two Mörk brothers, and the attention given to housekeeping, are decidedly un-Poelike. The terror-filled inner world which we enter in this and other early tales and plays by Lagerkvist bears a general resemblance to that of Poe's fiction, but it is as though Lagerkvist's were inhabited by the simple, self-assertive, and joyous people encountered in Whitman's poetry. The healthy and the sick, the evil and the good, combine and coalesce in Lagerkvist's

19. Gösta M. Bergman, "Den svåra stunden I," in *Synpunkter på Pär Lagerkvist*, p. 123.

20. Sven Linnér, *Pär Lagerkvists livstro* (Stockholm, 1961), p. 217. On the Hansson story, see chap. 4, n. 43, above.

21. "Något om Pär Lagerkvists kubism," in *Synpunkter på Pär Lagerkvist*, p. 97.

work, whereas in Poe they flee from each other, the one always lost to the other.

Lagerkvist's slight though perhaps rewarding interest in Poe extended well beyond its years the neoromantic view in the 1890s of Poe as the somewhat uncertain bearer of light for the future of literature. Yet in 1948 he made a curious reappearance in this role in an essay by the Norwegian poet Alf Larsen on "De store dødsdiktere" [The great poets of death].

In Denmark, where he had spent most of his childhood and attended school, Larsen had studied the "new literature" of the nineties, then no longer new. As a young man in France he had then been led to an enthusiastic reading of the *symbolistes* and of Baudelaire, and when he published his first book, a volume of verse, in 1912, he sent Vilhelm Ekelund a copy in acknowledgment of the part the Swedish poet had played in the symbolist movement.[22] In his essay on "the poets of death," a sweeping appraisal of their ultimate significance, Larsen attempted to show that Poe and Baudelaire were indeed the prophets they had once been said to be. It had all begun, he wrote, with the worship of beauty, of "beauty beyond good and evil," of an absolute perfection tantamount to God but secularized, as God has been secularized, into a longing for the remote. This had been the first step toward perdition, the death of the spirit in our time, for the life of the spirit had been made flesh and heaven had been brought down to earth. In reaction, then, to the ugliness of the flesh and the earth, the poets wrote of fleeting things, of antiquity, and of the inner world of their dreams. They turned away from reality and from daylight and yearned for the night and then for the abyss itself:

For it was none other than Death himself that had employed these devious ways to penetrate to the heart of man. It was

22. Werin, *Vilhelm Ekelund*, 2: 93.

he who had elicited the idea of the delectability of sin, the abnormal idea of the pleasures of annihilation and the enticement of disintegration. It was he who had made the day so odious and the evening so desirable, who had filled the artist's palette with colors he himself could not mix, put words in his mouth that had never been in the language before, and sounded notes on his strings that no ear had heard before. It was Death who was the great artist.[23]

What Poe and Baudelaire had written of had become a reality in Russia, hence the apocalyptic character of all Russian literature in the last half of the nineteenth century, composed now by poets not of death but of corruption.

All this, all that had loomed through the mists for the great romantics but came into full consciousness only in Poe, Baudelaire, Leconte de Lisle, Swinburne, Verhaeren and ended in the World War and the Russian revolution—it is this that Oswald Spengler has summed up and synthesized in his magnificent fantasy of death, *The Decline of the West*.[24]

The "endlessness" that Johannes Jørgensen and Nils Kjær and others had spoken of as the exalted state to which true poetry admits us, where Beauty is apprehended as an absolute, was interpreted by Alf Larsen as the endlessness of death. Poe's principle of supernal Beauty was seen to be synonymous with a principle not of goodness but of evil. This was none other than the irony that George E. Woodberry had noted in citing Lauvrière's biography of Poe "that made the worshiper of beauty the poet of the outcast soul":

If it be the office of poetry to intimate the divine, it must be confessed these works of Poe intimate the infernal; they are

23. *Den kongelige kunst*, 3d ed. (Oslo, 1960), pp. 21, 25.
24. *Den kongelige kunst*, p. 33.

variations struck on the chord of evil that vibrates in all life, throbs of the heart of pain, echoes of ruin that float up from the deep within the deep, the legend and pæan and ritual of hopeless death. . . .[25]

This was not the kind of observation expected of Woodberry, who preferred verifiable fact to interpretation. It had as little place in his book as did Alberto Martini's weird Beardsley-like illustrations for "Eleanora" and "Ligeia" and other tales, and it is in fact closely related in spirit to them. Derived from Lauvrière's study of degeneration in Poe, it had struck an alien note in Woodberry's biography. Now, in Alf Larsen's essay, it reappeared in new dress, evidently an invincible idea in the criticism of Poe.

In the year following the publication of Alf Larsen's essay, the Norwegian novelist Egil Rasmussen published two books, one a dissertation making several references to Poe, the other a biography of Poe on the occasion of the centenary of Poe's birth. Both books were deeply concerned with the psychological basis and social function of artistic creativity. Although drawing for some of his facts on Arthur Hobson Quinn's authoritative biography of Poe published in 1942, Rasmussen made fuller use in his biography of several earlier studies. He quotes Quinn, for example, on the worth of Poe's salary in 1842 and on Virginia's death as the emotional source of "Ulalume," but his authority for the suggestion, rejected by Quinn, of Poe's failure to consummate his marriage is Una Pope-Hennessy's *Edgar Allan Poe* (London, 1934), which derives the suggestion from Woodberry's biography of 1909 (1: 85). Rasmussen preserves such apochryphal details as that of Rosalie Poe's having been quieted in infancy by her nurse with bread dipped in gin, and that of Poe's having assumed a pseudonym in order to leave Richmond unnoticed. Rasmussen's other sources included the biographies by Emile Lauvrière, John H. Ingram, and Hervey Allen,

25. George E. Woodberry, *The Life of Edgar Allan Poe* (Boston and New York, 1909), 2: 175.

but chief among them was Joseph Wood Krutch's psychoanalytical study published in 1926. From Krutch's thesis of Poe's disordered sexuality—the lack in his life of "any normal fruition of love" and the absence of "anything like normal human passion"—Rasmussen drew major support for his own thesis, reflected in his title *Angstens dikter* [The poet of anguish], that by strangeness in beauty Poe meant not mere novelty but positive abnormality. Poe created his poetic world as a release from the contradictory currents of his psyche and in consequence became one of the great daydreamers in Western literature.

The source of Poe's psychological difficulties, expressed both in his use of alcohol and drugs and in the kind of prose and poetry he is noted for, was located by Krutch and Rasmussen in Poe's insecurity following upon the death of his parents in his early childhood. From this premise the argument proceeds: lovelessness was compensated for by aristocratism and arrogance; drinking and drug addiction impaired both social and sexual intercourse; this impairment compounded chronic feelings of *Angst* and "a nervous tension that resulted in his being seldom or never able to live fully on an active life level,"[26] a conclusion which becomes thematic in Rasmussen's book. "Ligeia" demonstrates the sublimation of sexuality in spiritual portraits of women. For Rasmussen, the key to Poe's personality and work is his distorted "psychic image of women." In normal love man subdues or "conquers" sexually and in the recurrence of this conquest stabilizes his "active life level" in relation to society at large. The "psychic image of women" was not thus mediated in Poe's life and therefore assumed abnormal proportions. This failure led to social insecurity and a variety of compensations.

Given Rasmussen's use of Krutch's biography, it is strange to read his protest that the worst form of slander that Poe has had to endure is the effort of psychoanalysts to interpret his life; the effort, he wrote, has only succeeded in confining the "free and responsible"

26. *Angstens dikter* (Oslo, 1949), p. 60.

personality of an artist in the straitjacket of neurosis. Rasmussen, however, was nonetheless convinced of the validity of his theory of sexual disharmony in Poe as the cause of his *Angst* and the source therefore of his dreams and his poetic fantasies.

> Woman was always for Poe the unattainable, a dreamer's dream, the very mystery of life. This of course did not prevent the normal functioning of his sexual life. But he either could not or would not bring his psychic dream-image of woman into his normal sexual life-situation. Therefore this psychic dream-image was always in near danger of death and dissolution. . . . Poe not only needed devotion and affection in the woman whom he tried to bind himself to; he sought to desexualize her by turning her psychic dream-image into the *entire* reality. And such a fervent union of souls he could not discover in life's climactic moment, the copulative act, but in its opposite—death.[27]

In his doctoral dissertation, *Kunstneren og samfunnsbildet* [The artist and the image of society], also published in Oslo in 1949, Rasmussen found the example of Poe useful in his discussion of the conflict between the irrational elements in artistic expression and the strong tendencies in social life toward the rational and normal. Poe's praise in "Marginalia" of Mrs. Browning's poem on "the Divine impulsion" that "cleaves / In dim movements to the leaves" served to introduce a contrast between literature that is readily understood by large numbers of readers because it touches upon the social and psychological dynamics of their lives, and Mrs. Browning's esoteric poem, which meets no apparent social need and appeals only to a few readers who have need of "cosmic contact."[28] The problem presented here is said to have been one that

27. *Angstens dikter*, pp. 142–143.
28. *Kunstneren og samfunnsbildet* (Oslo, 1949), p. 77.

Poe was keenly aware of, the problem of translating a purely esthetic experience into rational terms.

Poe was also the example cited in a supplement to Rasmussen's final chapter on the conflict of the personality of the artist with social ideals. Rasmussen qualified Lauvrière's diagnosis in 1904 of Poe as a *dégénéré supérieur* with a disposition for dipsomaniacal episodes, and maintained that it is not hereditary dipsomania that accounts for the content and the direction of his art and life. Poe, after all, was not psychically ill:

> From Ibsen to Poe is a big jump. And yet the distance is far greater between Poe and a true psychopath than between the Norwegian and the American writer. If it is possible at all to release art from the grasp of psychopathological formulations, we must insist: The will and power of the artist develop *in spite of* psychopathic tendencies, are restrained and colored by them, but are in essence free, so that the artist, if only he is able to find a continuous and progressive expression of his art, is a free and fully responsible personality even though his way of life is more or less marked by the destructive activity of psychopathological tendencies.[29]

The point had been made in Rasmussen's Poe biography. It was now illustrated by the telling difference between Poe's highly alliterative verse and that of a true psychopath quoted in Kraepelin's *Psychiatrie*. No better subject than Poe exists, Rasmussen concluded, to demonstrate the divergent possibilities in biographical interpretation. On the one hand there is Ingram's detailed, insistent defense of Poe as a "normal" personality, a writer who despite eccentricities in his character and the accidents of life ruled over his materials; on the other hand there is Lauvrière's "medico-psychological" study, centered on a clearly defined illness at the heart of

29. *Kunstneren og samfunnsbildet*, pp. 140–141.

the artist's psychic structure. In the latter, the artist is deprived of his ethical features and is automatically divorced from the community. Supported in this view especially by Lange-Eichbaum's studies of genius and madness (*Genie—Irrsinn—Ruhm*), Rasmussen conceived finally of the artist, even the "mad" artist (Poe and Strindberg, for example), as the releaser of the universally human stuff of reverie in a form suited to his times.

Poe's usefulness in broad studies of modern cultural problems was additionally demonstrated in an essay published in 1959 by the Danish poet and essayist Thorkild Bjørnvig.[30] The title of the essay, "Den æstetiske Idiosynkrasi" [The esthetic idiosyncrasy], is the term adopted by Bjørnvig from hints in "The Mystery of Marie Rogêt" to designate the problem of the dissociation of sensibility that is especially acute in modern urbanized society. The esthetic disgust felt by the narrator in "The Tell-Tale Heart" for the old man's eye is the leading example in Bjørnvig's definition of his term. It is a sudden and profound aversion to someone's appearance or manner or associations that has, as Ola Hansson would have described it, no *ratio sufficiens*. Bjørnvig finds a contemporary example in the sensational murders committed in Brooklyn in 1954 by two teenagers, one of whom, Jack Koslow, told a detective that he had killed a bum, a total stranger to himself, out of "an abstract hatred for bums and vagrants." Whereas Koslow offered additional "reasons" to justify his crime, Poe keeps the irrationality of the murderous act uncluttered by extraneous matters. The urge to perform a criminal act of this kind arises from abnormal sensitivity coupled with an equally abnormal deficiency in one's emotional life: "sensitivity without emotion, feeling without passion," and reality is rendered intolerable and hateful. At its worst, when aggravated by inimical social circumstances, for example, it leads to criminality; at

30. "Den æstetiske Idiosynkrasi," *Vindrosen* 6 (1959): 525–550; repr. in *Begyndelsen, Essays* (Copenhagen, 1960), pp. 183–237.

its most innocuous, it produces estheticism, a characteristic malady of our times. Bjørnvig's long essay then cites further examples in the work of H. C. Branner and Graham Greene, in T. E. Lawrence (who declared that very early in life he felt that man is ugly), and in abstract art, in which hypersensitivity runs to extremes.

Bjørnvig allowed Poe to serve alone as a "critic of the times" in an essay with that title published in 1963.[31] Here some of Poe's lesser known tales were cited and analyzed as "laboratories" in which human characteristics are tested and self-knowledge is achieved, though at a fearsome expense of the spirit. These tales, Bjørnvig wrote, foreshadow alarmingly the "psychovivisections" that mark our present scientific age. The psyche is exposed to a condition of horror that its organism cannot assimilate and that it will, if it does not succeed in rejecting it, constantly and mechanically recall and rehearse. As examples in this century of the condition of horror that Poe and Baudelaire were the first to discover Bjørnvig names urban ghettoes, concentration camps, war. His principal example from Poe's fiction is "The Man of the Crowd," an essay-like tale that comes to no ordinary conclusion but ends in astonishment—for Poe as much as for the reader—over the realization that the old man in the story wished for nothing more than to be one of the crowd: "he refused to be alone," in a reversal of the modern idea of community yet typical of modern life, especially as it is lived in the cities. It is this paradox of the lonely crowd that Bjørnvig then examines: the urgent need of the man who is involuntarily alone to be with other people no matter what the price. In a similar analysis, Bjørnvig finds in "The Man That Was Used Up" not mockery of the pretensions of the great but satire of the modern delight in artificial substitutes—"ersatzmania." "Berenice" serves Bjørnvig in the essay to illustrate what he had called "the esthetic idiosyncrasy" in his previous essay, for the story depicts a morbid preoccupation with a single object taken from the dream of a hyper-

31. "Edgar Allan Poe som tidskritiker," *Vindrosen* 10 (1963): 590–607.

sensitive dreamer—the "morbid irritability" of the "attentive" prop-
erties of the mind that Poe speaks of in "Berenice." The story also
exemplifies in the business of Berenice's teeth the *concretizing* (a
term almost synonymous, in the sense of "displacing," with Alf
Larsen's *secularizing*) in our time of ideas formerly sublime, exalted,
and platonic. Now, ideas become things; hence the hypersensitivity
in modern art toward things—pieces of half-burned burlap canvas,
twisted pieces of wood, and so on—as the artist attempts, like the
narrator in "Berenice," to possess an idea but instead wrenches a
thing out of its proper context. Bjørnvig's essay concludes in commentary on another essay-like tale, "The Imp of the Perverse." It is
one of Poe's most profound tales, giving once again an extremely
precise account of paradoxical cross-currents in the psyche. It, too,
superbly illustrates the demonic need to know fear and to acquire
self-knowledge in the agony of a moral condition reminiscent of that
described by Kierkegaard and Kafka. In a poem from this time,
"Poes død" [Poe's death], Bjørnvig again cast Poe in the role of
diagnostician of modern life. He becomes here the suffering self
whose visions of love explode in the arctic chill of the abyss of death
and spiritual emptiness and leave behind a world of "blinds, chim-
ney pots, and trademarks." [32]

Poe's usefulness in analyses like Alf Larsen's, Egil Rasmussen's,
and Thorkild Bjørnvig's of contemporary literature and contemporary civilization will no doubt flourish as long as the diseases of
modern life which they describe flourish. It is a use to which the
work of any author might be legitimately put, with benefits accruing

32. "Poes død," in *Figur og Ild* (Copenhagen, 1960), pp. 46–47. Two
recent Danish essays make brief reference to Poe, the first on the concept of
"perverseness," the second on Poe's detective tales: Erik Carstens, "Trangen
til at gøre det man ikke skulle," in *Tvesind og neurose* (Copenhagen, 1949),
pp. 106–110; and Tage la Cour, "Detektiven Edgar Allan Poe," in *Rejsen til
månen og andre indflugter i den lettere bogverden* (Copenhagen, 1965), pp.
71–79.

perhaps on both sides. Such an analysis when based on a demonstrated reading of the literary text, as Bjørnvig provides for example in his commentary on "The Man of the Crowd," can bring fresh insights to the literary work at hand and reaffirm its viability. The danger that has never been wholly avoided, however, is that the literary work, being used principally for illustrative purposes, is left undefined—that is, it is not read anew. In Scandinavia it would appear that the legend of Poe that took shape in the 1890s and made Poe into the type of suffering poet, poetic genius, poetic madman, intuitive psychologist, psychological superman, or seer of death and cultural decay, still answers certain present needs. Because the legend has been refined and has become much more sophisticated than it was to begin with, it has become in application so much the more useful and illuminating. But the need is accordingly even greater than before for modern translations into the three Scandinavian languages of at least the main body of Poe's fiction, poetry, and criticism, and for a modern critical introduction that will supplant old images of Poe with the salient facts and judgments of recent Poe studies now available for the most part only in the academies and in large libraries.

OLA HANSSON'S
"EDGAR ALLAN POE"

HISTORY OF PUBLICATION

Sonntags-Beilagen to *Vossische Zeitung* (Berlin), 12, 19 May 1889 (much abbreviated German translation); reprinted in *St. Petersburger Zeitung*, 23, 24, 25 July (4, 5, 6 August) 1889.

Litteratur og Kritik (Copenhagen), 4 (1890): 385–424 (complete version in Danish translation).

Ola Hansson, *Tolke og Seere* (Kristiania, 1893), pp. 1–71 (slightly cut version in Norwegian translation).

Ola Hansson, *Seher und Deuter* (Berlin, 1894; 2d ed., 1895), pp. 1–61 (another German version, with many omissions and a few additions).

Ola Hansson, *Jasnowidze i Wróżbici* (Warsaw, 1905), pp. 7–58 (Polish translation of the Norwegian, above).

Ola Hansson, *Tolkare och siare*, vol. 10 of *Samlade skrifter* (Stockholm, 1921), pp. 13–87 (complete version in the original Swedish).

NOTE ON THE ENGLISH TRANSLATION

The translation is based on the Swedish printing of the essay in *Samlade skrifter* (Stockholm, 1921), 10: 13–87. A typographically garbled sentence (p. 66, lines 9–10) has been repaired by reference to the Norwegian and German versions. Quotations by Hansson from Ingram's "Memoir" and Poe's works, which he regularly translated into Swedish, are given in the English original. Hansson's omissions in these quotations are indicated within square brackets; where he failed to indicate quotation, quotation marks have been supplied in square brackets, but not around single words or short phrases that I have restored from Poe's text in passages that Hansson sometimes very closely paraphrased. A phrase added by Baudelaire to Willis's story of Mrs. Clemm's search for work for her dear Edgar has been retained and placed in square brackets. Hansson himself twice used square brackets, however, in indicating the sources of his psychological information in part 5 of the essay, and these have been made into pointed brackets. Besides the tales that he cites, Hansson's chief sources for the discussion of Poe's theory of art were the two essays, "[Longfellow's] Ballads and Other Poems" and "The Poetic Principle," and a passage from the *Marginalia* (*Works*, ed. James A. Harrison [New York, 1902], 16: 156).

Two key words in Hansson's essay, *själ* and *sjuk* (and their compounds), are semantically incommensurable with any one of their counterparts in English. As the immediate context at each appearance seemed to require, *själ* has been rendered as "soul," "mind," "psyche," or "spirit," and *sjuk* as "sick" or "morbid" (following in reverse Hansson's own practice in translating from Ingram). The substantive forms *den sjuke* and *de sjuka* have usually been rendered as "the sick one(s)," but occasionally (following Hansson's French psychiatric sources) as "the *malade(s)*." Hansson left in English the term *moral insanity*, current in that form in the literature (see Maudsley's *The Pathology of Mind*); to suggest the emphasis it thus had in the Swedish text of Hansson's essay, I have placed it in quotation marks.

"EDGAR ALLAN POE"

OLA HANSSON

Far to our rear, where *die blaue Blume* of romanticism shimmers on distant horizons, grows the poetry of Edgar Poe. Like some gigantic imaginary plant with flowers like fire and night, like phosphorescence on water, it climbs up into the firmament, and we who live in the twilight of the century see it blooming high over our heads, its tendrils reaching far out into the deep night that lies before us.

Poe is one of the lonely ones, one of the anointed in spirit and in sorrow, one of the prophets whom the world stones. He is one of those in whom the human race has been differentiated toward a higher form, one of the links in the chain which stretches from the simplest cell all the way to man and now continues its organic growth toward an unknown future form of existence. He is one of those in whom the unconscious processes of the soul become aware of their nature,—an eye that opens, the landscape mirrored in a lake as day breaks, the first quickening of the foetus in the womb. He is one of the mystic seers of the world who arrive at new truths not through thought but through vision. The soul of man is a microcosm, just as his body, by virtue of its embryonic development, reaches deep down to the very roots of organic life. The deepest knowledge, the widest prospect, the brightest rays of light behind and ahead are attained not through the methodical use of the intellect but through the unregulated free play of all the powers of the soul. When thought travels along the main highways, man can secure at best a more highly detailed knowledge of things already known, whereas he garners new stores of knowledge by ranging at random through the dark forest of the soul. However much ideas may, through reflection, be interconnected and categorized, they will never be other than a mechanical blending in which each separate subject will forever remain what it had been before; but when they may freely obey their own secret laws and freely pursue their own secret course, it may sometime happen that they will combine chemically to produce something positively new. Surely we have each of us had in some measure the experience of a sudden dawning in the mind, as though a veil had been drawn aside to reveal a world new and bright. What took place then in a mere fraction of a second, and was so fugitive that it vanished before thought could seize upon it, or was so gossamer-like in fragility as to be sundered by its rude fingers—this it is that the mystic seer apprehends and arrests for the purpose of analysis.

But Poe is, in addition, one of the great *malades* of mankind. His sickness is the sickness of beauty at its most sublime and the sickness of nobility of character at its most refined. His sickness extends to his ideal of art; *six* times in his works he quotes Bacon's words: "There is no exquisite beauty without some *Strangeness* in the proportions." All his women are of one and the same kind: half consumptive, half madonna-like, with a glow in their eyes like the luminescence of decay. In the very heart of his being, in his soul and his blood, he is assailed by the pestilent atmosphere that hangs heavy and dead over the center of existence where the great spirits dwell. He is one of the martyrs who are worshiped as saints by the disciples of the great pessimism. Like most princes of culture, he is in *one* person the cloven trunk of madness and genius.

I

Romanticism in Germany was the revolt of germanicism against gallicism. It opposed *Gemüth* to reason, the beauty of poetry to the utility of prose. It represented a polar opposition to the philosophy of the French Enlightenment as to the nature of man, a radical *Umwerthung aller Werthe*. The writers of the eighteenth century had constructed their psychology, and by extension, their idea of society, by means of a mathematical and abstract train of thought analogous to that employed in our time by socialism: they had divided up the sum total of mankind into a large number of equal units, internally as alike as cupboards constructed to one pattern, and the manipulation of these abstract numerical quantities flushed away, like dregs, the absurdly unnatural and nonsensical principles of egalitarianism. The poets of French classicism as well as the philosophers of the Enlightenment pictured man as a not particularly complicated piece of machinery which they placed on display before an eager public in their plays, stories, and essays, as though in glass cabinets. What they saw, they saw clearly and sharply, but it amounted to very little, being only life on the surface. The German romantics dived down to the depths, where they found a rare, profuse vegetation; they forced out into the open the night side of human nature with all its enigmas and abnormalities; they exposed the umbilical cord which binds man to nature, the great mother of us all; they tied the individual to what is past and what is to come, to what lies beyond his earthly existence—they traced him back to before his birth and ahead beyond his death; they demonstrated, at the opposite extreme, that the ego is by no means a seamless whole: they split it, they doubled it; they delineated, in short, what is pathological and abnormal in the nature of man, the essence of good and evil, the mysterious and the magnificent, the great criminal and the great artist, the madman and the man of genius. This romantic image of man was just as one-sided as the wooden stock character of

French classicism, but deep within the fancifulness and the gaudy splendor lay hidden, like writing in ink that turns visible only under the influence of the sun's warmth, the riddle of human nature with which the poets and scholars of our time especially concern themselves. And it is precisely in the solar warmth of Poe's mind that this invisible writing had begun to reveal itself on paper, some of it so clearly that we have only to read.

It was this German romanticism which formed the intellectual milieu the world over in Poe's time. Certainly Poe owes his beginnings to it; his mind was fertilized by it, as may be seen in his literary likes and dislikes, in the parallels and analogies that may be found between his work and that of the German romantics, and in many of the principles of criticism that he incorporated in a perfected system of esthetics.

Its main points are the following:

The mind of man comprises three faculties: pure intellect, taste, and the moral sense. These three faculties function within separate spheres, with different materials and in different ways: through the intellect we are led to truth, through taste to beauty, through the moral sense to duty.

Taste, the sense of the Beautiful, the poetic sentiment, is thus an organic part of the human soul, a definitely circumscribed area within it with a function entirely its own. It is the organ by means of which man transforms into objects of pleasure the multiplicity of forms, sounds, smells, and feelings all about him. But its work does not cease at that point; there is another and higher need which seeks gratification. There is within all these transformed physical phenomena, beneath them and beyond them, something which man has not attained in this imitation, this transformation of reality, but for which he feels an unquenchable thirst by virtue of what is eternal and immortal within him. It is not the beauty that is all about him, for he already has that in his grasp, but a higher form of beauty which he cannot attain.

The functioning of the sense of beauty is thus essentially different, both in kind and in purpose, from that of the intellect and of the moral sense. It functions, in turn, in a variety of ways and in different media—such as painting, sculpture, architecture, dancing, horticulture, music, poetry. Music is its highest form, since in it the soul approaches most nearly the great goal toward which, at the behest of the sense of beauty, it struggles: the creation of beauty over and above the commonplace, a supra- and extra-terrestrial beauty, if you will. This effort is actually realized in music, if only partly and imperfectly. When at the sound of music our eyes irresistibly fill with tears, it is not through an excess of happiness and pleasure, but through sorrow at not being able, here and now, on this earth, at once and for always, to grasp this higher happiness, this higher pleasure of which, through music, we have received but brief and indeterminate glimpses. In accordance with this analysis of the soul's capacity to enjoy art, Poe must consequently conclude that a certain melancholy is inseparable from all perfect manifestations of the beautiful.

Poetry is defined by Poe as "the rhythmical creation of beauty." In poetry the sense of beauty operates with language as its material. From the premises already stated, Poe draws two conclusions, which he erects as the main pillars of his poetics: that that poetry most nearly reaches perfection which is most intimately connected with music, either in union with it or by becoming music itself, and that the sole content and sole aim of poetry is beauty; further, that all other tendencies are foreign to its nature. In other words, Poe honors the theory of *l'art pour l'art*; truth and morality have their place elsewhere in the realms of the spirit and cannot be intermingled in the creations of the sense of the Beautiful except as subordinate elements in the service of the search for beauty.

That the poet creates is therefore tantamount to saying that, with language as his material, he creates beauty. But this act of creation consists only in an act of combination: "all novel conceptions are merely unusual combinations." Originality, the power of the imagination, the faculty for creating beauty, and so forth, are synonyms, different words for the same thing, the quintessence of all poetry: the ability to bring new combinations into existence. The choice of subjects to be combined need not be restricted to the world of beauty; the ugly can also be used. It often happens in intellectual matters, Poe says, as it does in physical chemistry, that the admixture of two elements results in a third that has nothing of the qualities of either of them. Apparently he believes that just as amyl alcohol and butyric acid, each with an intolerable odor, combine chemically to make the choicest of perfumes, several ugly things can be combined into a beautiful whole.

It follows that with such a concept of the nature of the creation of poetry, Poe would naturally place great stress upon the techniques of composition. To reduce creativity to acts of combination amounts indeed to reducing the poet's work to a question of dexterity, to something that can be formulated like a problem in mathematics. There is no greater error, he says, than to believe that true originality consists in inspiration; it is nothing other than a combining, persistent and painstaking. And it is just as great an error, he says somewhere else, to suppose that the mathematical faculty in man is inimical to the ideal; on the contrary, the imaginative intelligence when most potent is always decidedly mathematical.

The worth of a poetic work lies in its power to leave an impression upon the reader. Every true poem aims at making a certain definite kind of effect, at evoking a certain definite kind of response; the art of the poet consists in combining all the means which will lead to the production of this effect and in combining them so that it will be as powerful as possible. But since such a stimulation of the senses, such an exertion of the mind is by its very nature short-lived, the poem cannot go beyond a certain length, for after a given period of time a psychologically necessary slackening occurs. For

Poe, the epic poem is an artistic anomaly; the impression made by such a poem as "Paradise Lost" is not one great whole impression, but a series divided by pauses, evoked therefore not by the poetic work as a whole but as though by a collection of many good, short poems. The literary genres for which Poe has the highest regard are, of course, the purely lyrical poem and the short story.

Given this ideal in art, Poe's literary likes and dislikes, such as they have found expression in his critical essays, require no commentary. Of the poets of the mother country, England, he likes Shelley and Keats best: Keats, the most artistic of the young poets, whose work is sustained solely by the power of his imagination and for whom every impression and mood is put into sensuous form; Shelley, *cor cordium,* whose heart was like the heart of Cosmos, whose imagination was of nature and whose music was of the spheres. Tennyson receives honorable mention as being the least "earthy," while on the other hand he takes every opportunity to lash out at the Lake School for the didactic and moralistic ballast in its poetry. For the "old school," that is, English classicism, he has little liking—Johnson is dismissed with such epithets as "the huge bulk" and "the Elephant"; and what Poe *most* admires in Shakespeare are the romantic plays, "Midsummer Night's Dream." He elevates the old minstrels and minnesingers high above the epic poets; and Thomas Moore, who sings his own verses, is for him the ideal poet. A poetic work to which he constantly reverts is Fouqué's "Undine." "For one Fouqué there are fifty Molières. For one Angelo there are five hundred Jan Steens. For one Dickens there are five million Smolletts, Fieldings, Marryats, Arthurs, Cocktons, Bogtons and Frogtons."

Poe's kinship with the German romantics becomes even more striking in numerous parallels between his and their work. Schelling's theory of intellectual intuition, the cardinal doctrine of romantic metaphysics, reappears in Poe's conception of intuition as a

source of knowledge above and beyond deductive and inductive reasoning. There are no sharply defined boundaries for Poe between
the realm of dreams and that of reality; they intertwine in the life
of the individual, they infiltrate each other so intimately that the
one cannot be separated from the other; the real world is turned into
a sagaland, and the subjective imagination is brought down to earth
to become a factor in objective reality—all in complete accord with
these words of Novalis: "Die Welt wird Traum, der Traum wird
Welt." Between the abstract and the concrete there is essentially
no difference. In "The Power of Words" Poe writes a fantasy in a
scientific vein on the same theme as the Biblical text in Genesis:
"And God said: Let there be light! And there was light." Heavenly
bodies, he says, are no more than words; the word is a creative force
in the purely physical world; for the word is sound, sound is a vibration of air, and such a vibration makes itself felt through never-
ending spheres, forward through endless time, by stimulating other
vibrations, which, in turn, by virtue of their complexity, create a
world. This conception of the cosmic significance of the individual
is not alien to Poe's kindred spirits in Germany. There is no state of
the soul which Poe describes with greater fondness than that lying
between life and death, gleams from the former and shadows from
the latter in changeful play; and one has only to read a fantasy like
"Monos and Una," a dialogue between two lovers after death, to
find once more Novalis's view of life and death as being merely relative concepts, death being a special form of life, the leading characteristic of which is an extraordinary heightening of the senses,
analogous to that which opium induces. Here, as in all areas, Poe
and the German romantics come into agreement on the destruction
of all boundary markers—between dream and reality, between fantasy and thought, between life and death, between abstract and
concrete.

They agree also in their psychology and in their criticism of art.

"The System of Doctor Tarr and Professor Fether"—the story of a visit to a madhouse, the former director of which, himself gone mad, has mutinied against the nurses in league with his unfortunate comrades, has confined them to the cells, treats them according to his own "system," and is the most obliging of hosts to visitors—is composed on the pattern of Chinese boxes which, as is well-known, were especially prized, for example, by Tieck. And when Poe gives a detailed account in "The Philosophy of Composition" of how he composed his immortal poem "The Raven," showing why he used the vowel *o* throughout and why he decided upon the raven as the more appropriate bird than the parrot, and pulverizes his readers' illusions by means of a cold-blooded dissection of the mechanism of the work of art, all in the most calculating sort of prose—is this not perhaps an obvious pendant to romantic irony? "The Bells," verse in which nothing less is attempted than to reproduce as convincingly as possible, by means of certain associations of sound, the distinctive notes of silver, gold, bronze, and iron bells, has many counterparts in the romantic poetry of Germany.

I have already characterized the psychology of this poetry. Poe, too, depicts exclusively the night side of the human soul, the pathological, the divided and the split, the abnormalities, the anomalies. His doppelganger, William Wilson, is essentially a twin to Bruder Medardus in Hoffmann's *Die Elixiere des Teufels*. Chamisso's *Peter Schlemihl*, in which a man loses his shadow, Hoffmann's "Vom verlorenen Spiegelbilde," in which the hero leaves his mirror image behind at a certain place, Poe's "Loss of Breath," in which a man, humorously to be sure, tells how he lost his breath—are shoots from the same subterranean root. Poe is the apprentice here, but an apprentice who leaves his masters far behind. It is, as I will explain later, in these deep pits of the spirit that Poe has broken away pieces in the ore of the great mystery; it is in this respect that his intuition has stretched out its tentacles into our own time and even beyond.

II

One day in 1833 a publication in the city of Baltimore issued an invitation to a literary competition. Two prizes were offered, one for the best poem and one for the best story. Among the lucubrations, presumably not altogether insignificant, which subsequently inundated the editorial offices, there was one manuscript, written in a remarkably distinct and neat hand, to which the appointed committee unanimously awarded both prizes. When the sealed paper bearing the author's name was opened, it was found to contain the name of E. A. Poe.

It was a name unknown to the members of the committee. However, the strange character, the wild fantasy and rare beauty, of the prize-winning pieces had aroused their desire to become acquainted with the author, and one of them, Mr. Kennedy, sent an invitation to the poet. Whereupon he received the following answer: "Your invitation to dinner has wounded me to the quick. I cannot come for reasons of the most humiliating nature—my personal appearance. You may imagine my mortification in making this disclosure to you, but it is necessary." When Mr. Kennedy hastened to seek out his unfortunate correspondent, he found a young man on the point of starvation.

The young man, however, had already formed a varied and intense acquaintanceship with life. Edgar Allan Poe was born January 13, 1809, in Boston. He was descended from ancient Norman nobility who had settled in Ireland in the reign of Henry II. The family's original name was Le Poer or de la Poer; in the course of time, according as the family branched out, this name came to be spelled in various ways. Of the founder himself it was said by an early chronicler that "there was no braver man than Roger la Poer"; and the memorials which have been preserved in Ireland's history of his descendants tell the same tale. It was a race that distinguished itself for its daring and courage, its heroic deeds and romantic adventures. It was of a temperament that could never feel at ease with the complacent wisdom of this world. It was marked out from the great mass of mankind, surpassing it in evil and virtue, in crime and in glorious exploits, in its nobleness of character whetted by madness as well as in its strange excesses. It is an eccentric race; and the fearful mystery that darkens its last and most renowned name moves through the chronicle like a dark, secretive figure with its face concealed, a shadow without a body, looming disproportionately large as on a moonlit night.

The poet's grandfather emigrated to America. He took an active part in the Revolutionary War and attained the rank of Quartermaster General. His eldest son, David, the father of the poet, eloped as an eighteen-year-old student with Elizabeth Arnold, an actress renowned for her talent and beauty, and married her. Rejected by his family, he tried his hand at his wife's profession but with slight success. Evidently a reconciliation took place, and the young couple made their home with the Poes; but shortly thereafter they both died, leaving three little ones unprovided for.

The middle child was named Edgar; he acquired his second name from an intimate friend of the family, Mr. Allan, who, himself childless, took the orphan into his care as a foster child. The child was noted at an early age for his precocity and rare beauty, was shown before guests as a prodigy, and reigned in the house as a little tyrant whose wishes were law. But equally soon, symptoms also were evinced of the child's morbidly nervous temperament.

The Allans traveled in 1816 to England, where they placed their foster son in one of the country's most famous schools. He spent four or five quiet, uneventful years at the school, which he later described in "William Wilson." Here he laid the foundations for his rather unusual knowledge of the classics.

In 1821 he returned to America. He studied for some time first at the university in Richmond. In the accounts we have of him from this time, attention is called to the wealth of his knowledge, to his energy, to his beauty; but above all the trait of morbid sensitivity in the young man's nature is thrown into high relief. His relationship with his foster father seems not to have been based on genuine affection, and the youth turned elsewhere to satisfy his fervent, abnormal longing for sympathy and love. When he aroused the ridicule of his more coarsely constituted fellows, he took refuge with our dumb friends. Thus he became the friend of animals that he continued to be for the rest of his life. Mrs. Whitman, the authoress who was his friend in the latter part of his life, tells a little anecdote about Poe from these years which throws a bright light on his sensibility. "He one day accompanied a schoolmate to his home, where he saw for the first time Mrs. H—— S——, the mother of his young friend. This lady, on entering the room, took his hand and spoke some gentle and gracious words of welcome, which so penetrated the sensitive heart of the orphan boy as to deprive him of the power of speech, and for a time almost of consciousness itself. He returned home in a dream, with but one thought, one hope in life—to hear again the sweet and gracious words that had made the desolate world so beautiful to him, and filled his lonely heart with the oppression of a new joy." Mrs. Whitman states that the memory of this lady played a decisive role in the rest of Poe's life and work.

When Byron journeyed to Greece to fight in the ranks of an oppressed people, his example awakened enthusiasm in many young hearts in both the Old and the New World. Poe was one of those for whom Byron's action shone like a pillar of fire in the desert. In 1827 he left America, not to return until two years later. Whether he ever reached Greece, where he lived during this period, what occupation he may have had, what vicissitudes he suffered—no one knows. Of this, Poe himself would never provide any information.

After his return home, he was enrolled by his foster father in a military school. The result of this experiment can be easily imagined. Military discipline and the artist's volatility got along together about as well as fire and water. It is therefore not the least astonishing to learn that as early as the beginning of 1831 he was tried "for various neglects of duty and disobedience of orders" and was sentenced to be "dismissed the service of the United States."

He now returned home, where, however, great changes had taken place. His foster mother had died and Mr. Allan had remarried. A rupture in their relationship occurred, and Poe once more ventured forth into the world. He contemplated for some time returning once more to Europe to help the Polish insurgents, but this plan came to nothing. The next years in his life are a blank; presumably he passed them in obscurity as a journalist, as he had already made his debut with a collection of poems. Nothing is known of him with certainty before his winning the literary competition in Baltimore; and the condition in which Mr. Kennedy then found him is eloquent witness of the "struggle for life" which probably occupied the two blank years.

But Poe was now and for always closely tied to literature as a profession and as a means of livelihood. At first he held a post as coeditor of a magazine in Richmond; and his financial situation now became so much improved that he was at least provided with his daily bread. But the extent of Poe's innate melancholy is revealed in the following lines which he wrote to his sponsor Mr. Kennedy at the time this financial dawn was breaking: "My feelings at this moment are pitiable indeed. I am suffering under a depression of spirits such as I have never felt before. I have struggled in vain against the influence of this melancholy; *you will believe me* when I say that I am still miserable in spite of the great improvement in my circumstances. I say you will believe me, and for this simple reason, that a man who is writing for *effect* does not write thus. My heart is open before you; if it be worth reading, read it, I am wretched and know not why. Console me—for you can. But let it be quickly, or it will be too late. Write me immediately; convince me that it is worth one's while—that it is at all necessary to live, and you will prove yourself indeed my friend. Persuade me to do what is right. I do mean this. I do not mean that you should consider what I now write you a jest. Oh, pity me! for I feel that my words are incoherent; but I will recover myself. You will not fail to see that I am suffering under a depression of spirits which will ruin me should it be long continued. Write me then and quickly; urge me to do what is right. Your words will have more weight with me than the words of others, for you were my friend when no one else was. Fail not, as you value your peace of mind hereafter."

It was during his stay in Richmond that Poe was married to his cousin, Virginia Clemm. She was very young, but already afflicted with the family illness, tuberculosis; and her beauty was the loveliness of the consumptive woman that seems to belong more to heaven than to earth, with its transparent, white skin and its deep, radiant madonna-eyes. The young couple lived with Mrs. Clemm in a household that was short in everything but love. How deep Poe's love for his mother-in-law was has been given unforgettable expression in the sonnet "To My Mother." And his friend Graham says, "His love for his wife was a sort of rapturous worship of the spirit of beauty which he felt was fading before his eyes. I have seen him hovering around her when she was ill, with all the fond fear and tender anxiety of a mother for her first-born—her slightest cough causing in him a shudder, a heart-chill that was visible. I rode out one summer evening with them, and the remembrance of his watchful eyes eagerly bent upon the slightest change of hue in that loved face, haunts me yet as the memory of a sad strain. It was this hourly *anticipation* of her loss, that made him a sad and thoughtful man, and lent a mournful melody to his undying song." For their part, both women idolized this grown-up child who found the world so puzzling, and they fussed over him as though they were his mothers. "One day," Baudelaire relates in a study of Poe prefacing his French translation of the tales, "Willis saw a woman, old, sweet, serious, enter his office. It was Mrs. Clemm. She was *looking for work* for her dear Edgar. The biographer says that he was deeply moved, not only by her well grounded appreciation and proper appraisal of her son's talents, but also by her whole appearance—by her sweet and sad voice, her slightly old-fashioned but fine, noble bearing. And for many years, he adds, we saw this indefatigable servant of genius, poorly and inadequately clothed, going from paper to paper to sell now a poem now an article, sometimes explaining that *he* was ill— the sole explanation, the sole reason, the invariable excuse that she gave when her son was in one of those periods of sterility which high-strung writers are acquainted with—and without once letting a syllable fall from her lips which could be interpreted as doubt, as a decline in her faith in the genius and good will of her darling. When her daughter died, she attached herself to the survivor [de la désastreuse bataille] with an increase in maternal warmth; she lived with him, took care of him, protected him against life and against himself." And when she is given the news of his own death, she writes an anguished letter to Willis in which she begs him to speak well of the dead man and above all to say what a devoted son he has been to her.

The little household was almost constantly on the move inasmuch as the master's migratory nature precluded long-term residence in any one place. During the next ten years Poe held posts with one publication or another, in Richmond, in New York, in Philadelphia. Wherever he appeared, it seems that his magical pen put the magazines in a position to make a mint of money. At one place he raises the number of subscribers from 700 to about 5000, at another from 5000 to more than 50,000. But he himself remained as poor as ever, so poor that he had to submerge his genius in the drudgery of literary hackwork. And wherever he appeared, enemies arose and swarmed about him—the unknown, unseen enemies, the literary vermin, the mediocrities and plebeians, the hucksters and publicity hounds, all of those whom he chastised with the rod of wit and the whip of ridicule. Poe was too much the aristocrat and too much the genuine artist to accept compromises or to be ruled by practical considerations. "Literature," says Graham, "with him was religion; and he, its high-priest, with a whip of scorpions scourged the money-changers from the temple." The petty took revenge as they have in all times: they laid mines and snares, snares for his domestic tranquility, mines for his reputation. His wife received on her deathbed anonymous letters containing imputations against her spouse, letters which hastened her death; and when he was himself rendered harmless by death, one of this rabble hastened to heap all the filth upon his name which it yet bears—or has borne, at least, until very recent years—in the eyes of the world.

There are various descriptions of his outer person and of the impressions he left on those with whom he came in touch. He appears in all of them as the morbidly sensitive nature and the perfect gentleman that he was, as the aristocrat and the genius. All the magazine people with whom he had literary and financial dealings testified unanimously to his scrupulousness, which, like his feelings of gratitude and everything else about him, was morbidly overdeveloped. His person fascinated his contemporaries, just as his poetry still fascinates us; there was and there is in both a certain hidden magnetic power. "Everything about him," says Mrs. Whitman, "distinguished him as a man of mark; his countenance, person, and gait, were alike characteristic. His features were regular, and decidedly handsome. His complexion was clear and dark; the colour of his fine eyes seemingly a dark grey, but on closer inspection they were seen to be of that neutral violet tint which is so difficult to define. His forehead was, without exception, the finest in proportion and expression that we have ever seen." Another lady in Poe's literary circle, Mrs. Osgood, completes this portrait. Poe had sent her his poem "The Raven," which he had just written, and requested her opinion and at the same time applied for permission to visit her. Mrs. Osgood says she will never forget the morning she met Poe for the first time. "With his proud and beautiful head erect, his dark eyes flashing with the electric light of feeling and thought, a peculiar, an inimitable blending of sweetness and of hauteur in his expression and manner, he greeted me calmly, gravely, almost coldly, yet with so marked an earnestness that I could not help being deeply impressed by it." And she adds, "To a sensitive and delicately-nurtured woman there was a peculiar and irresistible charm in the chivalric, graceful, and almost tender reverence with which he invariably approached all women who won his respect."

In the summer of 1846 Poe moved with his family out into the country where he took up residence in a little cottage in Fordham, in the vicinity of New York. He wished his wife to be able to die here in repose. One of his brother authors—I do not know who— has left a description of life at Fordham so deeply moving and melancholy that I cannot refrain from quoting it. He writes of his first visit:

"We found him and his wife and his wife's mother, who was his aunt, living in a little cottage at the top of a hill. There was an acre or two of greensward, fenced in about the house, as smooth as velvet, and as clean as the best kept carpet. There were some grand old cherry-trees in the yard that threw a massive shade around them.

"Poe had somehow caught a full-grown bob-o'-link. He had put him in a cage, which he had hung on a nail driven into the trunk of a cherry-tree. The poor bird was as unfit to live in a cage as his captor was to live in the world. He was as restless as his jailer, and sprang continually in a fierce, frightened way from one side of the cage to the other. I pitied him, but Poe was bent on training him. There he stood with his arms crossed before the tormented bird, his sublime trust in attaining the impossible apparent in his whole self. So handsome, so impassive in his wonderful, intellectual beauty, so proud and reserved, and yet so confidentially communicative, so entirely a gentleman upon all occasions that I ever saw him; so tasteful, so good a talker was Poe, that he impressed himself and his wishes, even without words, upon those with whom he spoke. Poe's voice was melody itself. He always spoke low, even in a violent discussion, compelling his hearers to listen if they would know his opinion, his facts, fancies, philosophy, or his weird imaginings. These last usually flowed from his pen, seldom from his tongue.

"On this occasion I was introduced to the young wife of the poet, and to the mother, then more than sixty years of age. She was a tall, dignified old lady, with a most ladylike manner, and her black dress, though old and much worn, looked really elegant on her. . . . Mrs. Poe looked very young; she had large black eyes, and a pearly whiteness of complexion, which was a perfect pallor. Her pale face, her brilliant eyes, and her raven hair, gave her an unearthly look. One felt that she was almost a spirit, and when she coughed it was made certain that she was rapidly passing away. The mother seemed hale and strong, and appeared to be a sort of universal Providence for her strange children.

"The cottage had an air of taste and gentility that must have been lent to it by the presence of its inmates. So neat, so poor, so unfurnished, and yet so charming, a dwelling I never saw . . . . The sitting-room floor was laid with check matting; four chairs, a light stand, and a hanging book-shelf completed its furniture. There were pretty presentation copies of books on the little shelves, and the Brownings had posts of honour on the stand. With quiet exultation Poe drew from his side-pocket a letter that he had recently received from Elizabeth Barrett Browning. He read it to us. It was very flattering. She told Poe that his 'poem of "The Raven" had awakened a fit of horror in England.' . . . He was at this time greatly depressed. Their extreme poverty, the sickness of his wife, and his own inability to write, sufficiently accounted for this. . . . We strolled away into the woods, and had a very cheerful time, till some one proposed a game at leaping. I think it must have been Poe, as he was expert in the exercise. Two or three gentlemen agreed to leap with him, and though one of them was tall, and had been a hunter in times past, Poe still distanced them all. But alas! his gaiters, long worn and carefully kept, were both burst in the grand leap that made him victor . . . . I was certain he had no other shoes, boots, or gaiters . . . . if any one had money, who had the effrontery to offer it to the poet?"

Ingram, from whose biography of Poe the above quotation is taken, tells of the same writer's growing intimacy with Poe and of his several visits to Fordham, which he describes: "The autumn came, and Mrs. Poe sank rapidly [. . .], and I saw her in her bedchamber. Everything here was so neat, so purely clean, so scant and poverty stricken. . . . There was no clothing on the bed, which was only straw, but a snow-white spread and sheets. The weather was cold, and the sick lady had the dreadful chills that accompany the hectic fever. [. . .] She lay on the straw bed, wrapped in her husband's greatcoat, with a large [. . .] cat in her bosom. The wonderful cat seemed conscious of her great usefulness. The coat and the cat were the sufferer's only means of warmth, except as her husband held her hands, and her mother her feet. Mrs. Clemm was passionately fond of her daughter, and her distress on account of her illness, and poverty, and misery, was dreadful to see."

One dark and dreary day in January the dead body of the young woman was carried away from Fordham, and Poe was left there alone with the dear departed's mother. He sank into gloomy apathy. He roamed about in the Fordham countryside, himself a thousand times more lonely in his soul than these forests, in which he could wander by the hour without meeting anyone. His favorite spot was a rocky, spruce-covered ledge in the neighborhood which offered a panoramic view of the surrounding country; "here," says Mrs. Whitman, "through long summer days, and through solitary star-lit nights, he loved to sit, dreaming his gorgeous waking dreams." His soul was permeated with a mood of moonlight and churchyard, of the terror of ghostly phantoms and the voluptuousness of melancholy, and he composed "Ulalume":

It was [. . .] in the lonesome October
Of my most immemorial year.

Out in this lonesomeness, without sound, without echo, in the midst of the silence in which nature is not dead but merely seems to be holding her breath, in the midst of the soul's infinitude in which space becomes a word without meaning and time hovers like a tiny, shimmering star high above—his intuitive thought soars, liberated from body and earth, out over the ocean of the universe like a great fantastic bird, and when it turns back and settles on its master's shoulder, it brings with it the wonderful flower of the mystery of life that would bear fruit in Poe's cosmogonic fantasy "Eureka."

It is time to come to the end. In the summer of 1849 Poe was staying in Richmond. "On the 4th of October," Ingram relates, "he left Richmond by train, with the intention, it is supposed, of going to Fordham to fetch Mrs. Clemm. Before his departure he complained to a friend of indisposition, of chilliness and exhaustion, but, notwithstanding, determined to undertake the journey. He left the train at Baltimore, and some hours later was discovered in the street insensible. How he had been taken ill no one really knows, and all the absurd reports circulated about his last moments were absolute inventions. He was dying when found, and, being un-known, was taken at once to the Hospital, where he died on Sunday the 7th of October 1849, of inflammation of the brain, insensible, it is supposed, to the last. The following day he was buried in the burial-ground of Westminster Church, close by the grave of his grandfather, General David Poe. No stone marks the spot where he lies."

But this man's misfortunes were not to end with his death. As long as he lived, his enemies had made life wretched for him and his family; now that he was dead, they had no way of getting at him other than to blacken his reputation. And this they did with thoroughness. No trouble or expense was spared. Naïvely credulous, Poe had appointed as his literary executor a person in whom he had supposed he could put his trust but who actually was his mortal enemy for literary as well as personal reasons. This man—his name is Griswold—wrote a biography of the deceased man in which he demonstrably falsified the facts with the deliberate intention of representing Poe as being, morally, a rogue. His heinous article was greeted with indignation by the American press, but no thoroughgoing refutation of its lies was attempted until that by Ingram, who set for himself in the biography which prefaces his edition of Poe's works the noble task of disproving step by step Griswold's falsifications and has completely achieved what he set out to do.

In his homeland, therefore, Poe's name has been cleared. In Europe, however, Griswold's allegations, having gone unchallenged, have contributed to the view probably taken by the general public of Poe as an incurable alcoholic who died in an attack of delirium tremens. That Poe occasionally drowned his excess of sorrows in drink, he himself freely admits. But what drove him to do so was not the brutish pleasures of the drunkard nor the fatal predisposition and overpowering, morbid instincts of the dipsomaniac. "I have absolutely *no* pleasure in the stimulants in which I sometimes so madly indulge," Poe wrote shortly before his death to a friend. "It has not been in the pursuit of pleasure that I have perilled life and reputation and reason. It has been in the desperate attempt to escape from torturing memories—memories of wrong and injustice and imputed dishonour—from a sense of insupportable loneliness and a dread of some strange impending doom." This is the basic reason for Poe's recourse to drink and at the same time the excuse, if such is needed for the sake of Poe's reputation. But when one reads of the many attestations by persons who knew Poe well, his nature, life and habits—attesting that a single glass, a few drops of firewater were enough to bring to life in this morbid soul the madness that always lay slumbering there—when one reads them, who does not feel then the fury and tears of resentment against this scoundrel who threw stones at the name of an honorable man and at the fame of an indisputable genius?

III

Let us imagine this individuality set down in American society as it was then! What a harsh contrast! A full-blooded aristocrat in an ant hill of plebeians; a romantic fire-worshiper of beauty among hucksters; an ecstatic spokesman for the most ethereal of feelings and the most esoteric of moods standing in the market place of utilitarianism; an apostle of the truths of a distant future and of the quintessence of human intelligence in a community of cultural upstarts who were still learning their ABC's—it was oil and water, an antique vase among Peter Smith's pottery bowls in New Street, Berlioz's dance of the sylphs drowned out by the jingle of ten thousand moneybags. It is no wonder that this man, in loneliness far more terrible than that of the grave, wounded by everything that his soul and senses perceived, shut his ears and eyes to this reality, which seemed to him like a penny engraving in a stationery store and a piece for brass instruments, and lived his life in the strange, wild world of beauty which his imagination spun around him out of the substance of his own soul. Poe reacted against the prosaic materialism of the everyday world just as the German romantics did before him and, in our day, as do the apostles of French *décadence*. As his idealistic yearnings could not transform the woeful reality of a world of whiskers and gluttony to his liking, he created for himself a new world whose secret entrance only he knew and over which he, the impoverished, the despised, the lonely one, was the ruler. Ellison's artificial "landscape-garden" in "The Domain of

Arnheim" and the artistically exquisite furnishings of "Landor's Cottage" are pendants to the artificial milieu and inner life of Des Esseintes in Huysmans's *A Rebours*; and that hero of *décadence* has, moreover, an ancestor of whom he is the direct lineal descendent in Poe's Usher in "The Fall of the House of Usher."

Thus the romantic atmosphere of the time, on the one hand, and the contrast between Poe's individual temperament and the surrounding social milieu, on the other hand, have together exerted a decisive influence on Poe's literary production. I have already indicated what Poe had in common with German romanticism; I will now point out what traces have been left of Poe's personality so that we may see by what adjustments in either direction the final, complete picture emerges of Poe's authorship.

Poe had Gallic traditions and lived in an Anglo-Saxon milieu. The fund of Gallic racial elements stored up in the first generation of the family had perhaps not been completely exhausted in its descent through the generations to the American poet. The air breathed by Poe's ancestors over the centuries was permeated with Anglo-Saxon elements. Whether or not they can be brought into a causal relationship and to what extent, it is certain that the characteristics peculiar to the two races, the lucid thinking of the Gaul and the self-control and moderation of the Anglo-Saxon make up one half of his highly complicated self, just as his animation, his orientally fertile imagination, his carefree, naïve, happy-go-lucky vagabondage, which is ascribed to the Irish Celts as their ancient heritage, form the other half.

The ideal man of the Germans is pure *Gemüth*, introverted reflection, philosophical brooding over profound obscurities, the uninhibited and unlimited primacy of the emotions, the sanctity of the unconscious, the intuition as a source of truth, depths without bottom, ardor in whose warmth the very stones melt. Germanic man clings most closely to the maternal bosom; it is nature itself awakening into self-awareness in what is termed direct intuition. Until the Slav made his appearance in this century, Germanic man was the infant among the races that comprise the family of civilized humanity; he had the trusting eyes of the child and the child's faculty for experiencing life directly. This characteristic of the German race reached its peak in the work of the German romantics. In their hands, it became extreme and paradoxical. It swelled up like one of the abnormal excrescences of the human body.

Let us consider all these various racial characteristics brought together in *one* person, in *one* soul, and raised to their sharpest possible intensity—we shall then obtain a representative outline, an ideal view in cross section of the structure of Poe's soul. It will then become easier to fill in the gradations of light and shadow within, as well as to see the contours without.

What will then appear to be distinctive in Poe's writing is that an imagination for which neither time nor space exists, an imagination limitless and fathomless, is concentrated in a solid mass around which a line is distinctly drawn, as the glowing masses of the planets were originally shaped into spheres and rings. One will then see fantasy and mathematics—that is, oil and water—form a union so close as to be chemical. One will then see the bluish vapors of mysticism hanging in thick velvety ranks, and an analytical instrument, as sharp as a scalpel, slicing through them. But this writing also throngs with exotic blooms, flowers from other worlds, flowers never seen by mortal man. Ghosts stalk by daylight, and ordinary men stand bathed in a phosphorescent glow. A hellish red darts to and fro in the heavenly blue. There is no distinguishing the lamb of innocence from the hyenas of evil. Infinity is confined in a pea, and the spark of a moment sets worlds afire. The incomprehensible is stated in a mathematical formula, and the crystal-clear emerges as the world's great mystery. You light a match with the starlight that took three million years to reach the earth, and the ABC's of your primer become the most indecipherable of hieroglyphics.

IV

It is not unusual that one or another aspect of human nature is especially well developed in one individual. What is peculiar to Poe is that not only are *all* his faculties—the senses, thought, sensitivity to mood—sharpened, but sharpened to that degree that their sharpness is morbid, abnormal. His thought has an edge so fine that it cuts in on itself. His dreams and moods are so intense that they take bodily form and become hallucinatory. His intuition penetrates the darkness and sees what lies enwrapped in the night of the future. His senses perceive what is, according to known physical laws, imperceptible to ordinary mortals.

Poe engages literally in cult-worship of human reason at its highest level, where it no longer knows impediments or difficulties, where it deciphers all riddles and cuts all Gordian knots. A good many of his short stories are really nothing other than the apotheosis of an unnaturally refined perspicacity. What he admires in the structure of the universe is the practical intelligence of the master builder ("The Island of the Fay"). In "The Thousand-and-Second Tale" he gathers together all the strange adventures of the oriental imagination in order to point out in a long series of appended notes how they are all none other than the miracles of nature herself or the masterstrokes of civilization. He writes a thesis on a game of chess which in those days amazed the world as its eighth wonder, and the secret to which all the sharp-witted of the Old and New World tried in vain to discover—a game of chess which directed the moves of the one player and nearly always won against whoever in the audience entered the competition; and he triumphantly presents a solution ("Maelzel's Chess-Player"). He writes a long study of cryptography; he uses as the basis for his famous short story "The Gold Bug" this motif: that an apparently undecipherable code can be deciphered without error; and once while engaged in writing for the papers he declared he would personally undertake to solve all the cryptograms which the esteemed public cared to submit, and when he was subsequently deluged by a whole ocean of them, he solved every one. He assembles under the significant title "Diddling Considered as One of the Exact Sciences" a copious florilegium of the most artful and apparently most complicated dodges which the madcaps of the human race made use of to pull the leg of their less experienced brethren in this noble sport. He collects the autographs of the best known American authors and with this material writes an essay in which he tries to show that reason with its sharp sense of smell can sniff out an individual's character in his handwriting ("Autography"). In "The Man of the Crowd," he claims that by means of certain signs which never err and which he specifies, he can detect at first sight certain kinds of criminals, such as pickpockets and gamblers. The hero in the murder mystery "The Murders in the Rue Morgue" and in "The Mystery of Marie Rogêt" and also in "The Purloined Letter" asserts that no crime can occur, no matter how mysterious it may appear and how inaccessible the truth may seem, which does not leave behind some sort of trace leading to the criminal, and that it is only on account of the undeveloped visionary capacity of detectives that as often as not they lose the trail.

Poe is a visionary. In his waking state he is as we others are in dreams; a relatively weak physical impression, a perception of sound, of light, of cold or of heat, or whatever else it may be, induces a hallucination or a continuous dramatic action which develops into a series of hallucinations. The structure of his mind is such that all his moods take corporeal form, become visions. The dark shadow in the soul, which is sorrow, anguish, fear, death, is released from within him and becomes an external object, a shadow over there across the room, as in "Shadow," a raven on the bust of Athene over the door, as in "The Raven." The *horror* of loneliness, the terror of absolute silence are felt so intensely that they assume the full palpability of the concrete, assume color, form, become a fantastic landscape, a fantastic figure, as in "Silence." The very land-scape with its distinctive character comes alive, the fragrance wafted from it is so strongly sensed by Poe that he sees the flower, its mood congeals into a shape, a living thing. As for example in "The Island of the Fay": The poet is lying one day in June on the grass in a wooded countryside. A river runs through the meadow valley and in the river is an island. It is twilight, when all the colors flame up for a final display, and the woods grow dark and dense. One half of the island gleams in the gold and scarlet of the sunset, butterflies hover like tulips with wings; it is all one great splendor of bloom, a life of joy. But the eastern half of the little island already lies in the blackest shade. The trees stand dark and ghostlike, arousing thoughts of sorrow and untimely death; the grass is the color of the cypress and the leaves droop down like falling drops. "The shade of the trees fell heavily upon the water, and seemed to bury itself therein, impregnating the depths of the element with darkness. I fancied that each shadow, as the sun descended lower and lower, separated itself sullenly from the trunk that gave it birth, and thus became absorbed by the stream; while the other shadows issued momently from the trees, taking the place of their predecessors thus entombed." The poet sinks into revery. He muses whether this place is not the haunt of the creatures that survived the fall of the human race, whether some fays are not still corporeal, wasting away, slowly dying, yielding up their existence layer by layer, like these trees which yield up shadow after shadow, exhausting their substance, emptying it into the water that feeds on it, feeds on darkness. While he thus muses and the sun sinks and the large, dazzling white flakes of the bark of the sycamore eddy in the air, flakes which form strange patterns upon the water, as a quick imagination can make out of anything it pleases—"while I thus mused, it appeared to me that the form of one of [. . .] the Fays [. . .] made its way slowly into the darkness from out the light at the western end of the island. She stood erect in a [. . .] fragile canoe, and urged it with the mere phantom of an oar. While within the influence of the lingering sunbeams, her attitude seemed indicative of joy—but sorrow deformed it as she passed within the shade. Slowly she glided along, and at length rounded the islet and re-entered the region of light. 'The revolution which has just been made by the Fay,' continued I, musingly, 'is the cycle of the brief year of her life. She has floated through her winter and through her summer. She is a year nearer unto death; for I did not fail to see that, as she came into the shade, her shadow fell from her, and was swallowed up in the dark water, making its blackness more black.' [. . .] And again the boat appeared and the Fay; but about the attitude of the latter there was more of care and uncertainty, and less of elastic joy. She floated again from out the light, and into the gloom (which deepened momently), and again her shadow fell from her into the ebony water, and became absorbed into its blackness. And again and again she made the circuit of the island (while the sun rushed down to his slumbers), and at each issuing into the light, there was more sorrow about her person, while it grew feebler, and far fainter, and more indistinct; and at each passage into the gloom, there fell from her a darker shade, which became whelmed in a shadow more black. But at length, when the sun had utterly departed, the Fay, now the mere ghost of her former self, went disconsolately with her boat into the region of the ebony flood—and that she issued thence at all I cannot say, for darkness fell over all things, and I beheld her magical figure no more."

I have quoted this passage chiefly because it so distinctly indicates the connections, the steps between the original impression and the final result, reveals the successive movement of a purely abstract mood over to a concrete view, exposes the entire mechanism, all the wheels and cogs, that allows this process to take place. Even more singular, even more removed from the ordinary is the presence in Poe's work of a general theory, a pure proposition, that can be metamorphosed in a vision. In complete consistency with his concept of the transitional stage between life and death, Poe states that suspended animation and the burial of bodies still alive are far more usual than is believed, indeed perhaps the rule rather than the exception. This assertion, which appears in "The Premature Burial," reappears later in the sketch and takes the following visionary form: "I looked; and the unseen figure, which still grasped me by the wrist, had caused to be thrown open the graves of all mankind; and from each issued the faint phosphoric radiance of decay; so that I could see into the innermost recesses, and there view the shrouded bodies in their sad and solemn slumbers with the worm. But alas! the real sleepers were fewer, by many millions, than those who slumbered not at all; and there was a feeble struggling; and there was a general and sad unrest; and from out the depths of the countless pits there came a melancholy rustling from the garments of the buried. And of those who seemed tranquilly to repose, I saw that a vast number had changed, in a greater or less degree, the rigid and uneasy position in which they had originally been entombed."

It is this lancet-like reasoning and this hallucinatory definiteness of form that circumscribe the fantasies and mark them off. It can be imagined what striking contrasts such writing has to weld together. The majority of Poe's most famous works obtain their effect precisely through this contrast between a hyperfanciful subject and a hyperexact technique. It is this scientific apparatus and tone which lend a semblance of concreteness to the most nebulous material. We can have no defense against the illusion. When in "The Adventure of One Hans Phaall" Poe takes as his subject a journey by balloon to the moon, the antidote he uses is the plain style of a diary crammed with figures and technical terms. When in "Narrative of A. Gordon Pym" he writes of Antarctica, he does so with the same detailed, circumstantial authenticity of a modern African explorer; the imaginary is so firmly embedded in trustworthy facts and its emergence from these wrappings occurs so imperceptibly—we can no more detect this process than we can see grass growing—that we feel as though we have awakened from a hypnotic sleep when we at last find ourselves in a region of darkness where white ashes rain down and the ocean is like luminous milk and huge white birds wheel across black space and directly before us rises an enshrouded colossus in human shape, its complexion of the whiteness of snow. The sketch "Von Kempelen and His Discovery," which deals with the discovery of the art of making gold, has entirely the character of a scientific paper read before an academy—made serious, *so* "factual" and *so* systematic that the ironic humor gives itself away much as someone would give himself away by a movement of the curtain that conceals him.

We encounter the same phenomenon in Poe's metaphysical cosmogony "Eureka"; but we observe it now from another point of view. For Poe, dreams are truer than reality, intuition is a more reliable road to truth than logical reasoning by induction and deduction. The difference between these latter two methods is for him that between "creep" and "crawl." Because the lizard is sure-footed, the eagle's wings need not be clipped. Poe has as little respect as Nietzsche has in our time for the day laborers and hucksters of science who believe they see things more distinctly the closer they are held to the eye. These specialists, who shrug their shoulders at all comprehensive hypotheses, all efforts at generalization in scholarship, who in short cannot see the woods for the trees—they are for him more ignorant than the least educated field worker, who at least shows that he knows something when he admits he knows nothing. To return to "Eureka": this is a work in which Poe has, so to speak, metaphysicized Newton and Laplace by having recreated intuitively the world whose laws these two scientists have formulated. He makes reference to these and other astronomical and physical facts, not to lend support to his intuitive metaphysics, which he feels contains more primary truth than all the scholarly facts in the world, but to serve as necessary corollaries, fragments of the one great center of metaphysical truth, particles hurled into the universe with the atoms, heavenly bodies, and solar systems spun off from the original single mass. Just as the sun's rays take a long time to reach the earth, these fragmentary truths have required centuries to reach mankind; but the intuitive man stands in the middle of the universe, at the center of which is the very light-source of truth.

V

With this abnormal acuity of the faculties, so remarkable in Poe, he apprehends more than does the ordinary person, more comprehensively and more deeply; he encompasses a broader area, plumbs a deeper bottom. He perceives what the ordinary person cannot perceive: events within the physical and spiritual world that become apparent and can be grasped only by his more finely differentiated organs. Just as his nerves of sight and hearing are so sensitive that they are set into motion by the least movement of air, which produces no sense of sound or light to the ordinary person, the least perceptible and the quietest vibrations of the human soul disclose themselves in the most distinct fashion to his spiritual nerve endings, to his sensibility and disposition. Events of the soul, states of being, which for us are simply one homogeneous mass, he divides into the countless parts of which they are comprised.

It would appear that the highest intelligence and the greatest refinement are indications of sickness. It is only with an acuity that is abnormal and that was Poe's, the opium eater's and the visionary's, that the gaze can pierce the curtain concealing the future. "Folie et génie sont congénères, in radice conveniunt," says a French scientist (Moreau, *Psychologie morbide*); and he adds, "the mental traits which make for a differentiation of one person from other persons through the originality of his thoughts and outlook, through the extremity or the strength of his affective powers, through the superiority of his intellectual powers, emanate from the same organic conditions as the particular moral aberrations most fully characterized in insanity and idiocy." In every period the geniuses have therefore been regarded as madmen by their contemporaries. Their right and proper contemporaries were not those among whom they dwelled bodily, but the coming generations to whom they were bound by spiritual ties. The world which they discerned with organs more highly developed than those of the average person was not the same that the ordinarily equipped lived in; it had other boundaries and other proportions. Therefore the tragedy is eternal that has been enacted from age to age and the hero of which is the sick one, who stands alone with his gospel of the future, the madman who alone can advance the human race. Genius and the martyr's halo are indistinguishable; and the healthy ones will in all ages stone their great sick ones.

Mental pathology of the future will have the last word on this subject. In the meantime it is interesting to see how Poe himself fully understood this lesson, which his poetry was to illustrate so incomparably. "Men have called me mad," says the hero in "Eleonora"; "but the question is not yet settled, whether madness is or is not the loftiest intelligence—whether much that is glorious—whether all that is profound—does not spring from disease of thought—from *moods* of mind exalted at the expense of the general intellect. They who dream by day are cognizant of many things which escape those who dream only by night. In their gray visions they obtain glimpses of eternity, and thrill, in waking, to find that they have been upon the verge of the great secret. In snatches, they learn something of the wisdom which is of good, and more of the mere knowledge which is of evil. They penetrate, however, rudderless or compassless into the vast ocean of the 'light ineffable,' and again, like the adventures of the Nubian geographer, *'agressi sunt mare tenebrarum, quid in eo esset exploraturi.'* " In one of his "Marginalia," Poe says that he sometimes amused himself by speculating on what fate would be in store for a person whose soul raised him above all others; and he shows how this individual necessarily will be regarded as a sick man, will be misunderstood, stoned, be taken for a madman, end as a martyr.

It is this knowledge of things hidden which gives Poe's psychology its value. What he depicts in human nature is its basis in nature and its night side, the secretive and the abnormal, in the darkness of which all proportions are twisted awry, obsessions rise up like the heads of Medusa, anguish stalks like some ghost at midnight, incomprehensible impulses shine like a woman's sea-green eyes which must be pursued wherever they lead, no matter whether it is as revolting as bathing in warm blood and your hair stands on end. As a psychologist, Poe is the mystic and the subtle analyst. Above all he describes the border region between life and death as well as the changeful aspects of degeneration.

There is in the soul a class of phenomena, a distinct group of products of the soul's functioning, which are neither wholly thought nor wholly vision, whose duration is merely a fraction of a second and for which language, that bungling medium, has no words. They traverse the soul like the shadows of cirrus clouds. Poe attempts to define their ethereal nature in the term "psychal impressions." These flowers, whose blossoms are wrought of all that is on earth the most unearthly, the sun's rays and dew and cobwebs, flourish in the border regions between waking and sleep. And kindred to the states of soul that are transitional between waking and dreaming are the states of soul between life and death.

It is one of Poe's favorite tasks to fix and analyze these states of the soul. Hence he depicts many times over in his stories suspended animation, hypnotism, epileptic seizures—each phenomenon in all its phases: inception, growth, reawakening. He unravels skeins of threads like an anatomist unraveling muscle fibers and nerve fibers, and he does not lag behind such modern analysts in this dissection of the soul as the brothers Goncourt, Bourget, Huysmans, Dostoevski. He performs this sort of experiment in "The Premature Burial." In "The Facts in the Case of M. Valdemar," he relates how hypnosis of a dying man can keep him alive; the person hypnotized is meanwhile conscious of the progress of his bodily dissolution, and at the very moment the hypnosis comes to an end, his body stretches out on the bed a stinking mass. He seeks out all possible analogous cases and among them comes upon a heretic, in "The Pit and the Pendulum," who is put to torture until he loses consciousness; Poe devotes several pages to those seconds of the coming and going of unconsciousness, divides and subdivides, separates one element after another, adumbrates a nuance out of which a new rainbow in turn is projected through the prism of his thought—it is like calculating fractions to a dizzying millionth part.

Poe, however, is not only the forerunner in his psychology of the modern psychological novel; he is especially concerned—combining German romanticism with French *décadence*—with subjects that criminal psychology and mental pathology in our day are most preoccupied with. He depicts various forms of disease of the personality and of the will; his characters belong almost exclusively to the class called degenerates; and he enlarges upon the subject of the *criminel-né*, of criminality as a form of sickness, of the absence of *ratio sufficiens*, which surely is to be termed, if anything can, the burning issue of our time. It is astonishing to see by how much he was beforehand in this respect and how deeply he has penetrated to the heart of modern research.

What is the "I", personality, consciousness? According to the metaphysical hypothesis, consciousness is something primary, a first premise, something in and of itself, an abstract entity like a mathematical point, a cause, a starting-point. Again, according to the hypothesis advanced by modern psychophysiologists, consciousness is something that in the beginning did not exist, something that has emerged in the course of the evolution of the organic world, something bound in with a physical substratum to which it exclu-

sively owes its existence, a product of physical processes, itself a
concrete whole, a complex, a terminus. The core of being, the basis
of personality, is our primitive animality, and the first sprouting of
consciousness, out of which all its manifestations come, that which
determines their character and constitutes the center around which
they all are stratified, is the very awareness of the body, the awareness of the body's animal functions. One must go back to an organism low on the scale, whose consciousness includes nothing more
than this awareness, if one would see it at its most conspicuous and
see its mechanism revealed; the lower one goes, the more dominant
is this awareness until at last it comprises the entire psychic individuality. In man, on the other hand, the sound of this basic apparatus is almost wholly drowned out by the noisy world of passions,
perceptions, images, and ideas; it is heard only at brief moments or
like an indistinct, remote rumbling. The soul of man is like a rich
embroidery that has covered over almost the entire surface of the
fabric. When the apparatus is functioning normally, little attention is given to it; for one never notices what has lost through habit
the relief of its design. But when it gets out of order, it is seen to be
that which constitutes the center of personality. When its wheels
cease turning, the entire apparatus comes to a halt; when its speed
increases or decreases, the effects are felt in every nook and cranny
of the personality; when this physical basis of personality is disturbed, the whole superstructure totters. It is through this sense of
organism that man has a sense of his wholeness, of who he is and
what he is. The sense of organism, however, is only one of the two
factors entering into personality; the other is memory, the "subjective" memory, which pools the states of consciousness in which a
part of the organic processes culminates. If for one reason or another
this sense or this memory, partially or wholly, is afflicted by sickness,
the necessary consequence is that the personality itself becomes
sick. All the innumerable incidents in the pathology of personality
form one continuous series, beginning with the first feeble manifes-

tation—which is no more than a raising or lowering of the median tone and median level of the individual life, yet by virtue of which the personality feels different from its ordinary state, in other words an exaltation or a depression—and ending with the total metamorphosis of the personality in the phenomenon of doubling, in which the memory also is paralyzed. Between these two extremes and joining them in imperceptible gradations, a host of the phenomena of sickness range themselves and branch out, principally with their sites in the senses, in the affective organs, or in the intellect, but all indirectly growing from the one seed, the primordial organic fact of human life. There are abcesses which fester, disruptions of the normal functions, partial paralyses, parasites that cling fast. While one man feels split in two, another feels doubled; the one forms a new person, independent and complete, from parts of his proper self, his desires, his voice, his bones; the other feels parts of his body to be enlarged or contracted or disfigured; a man feels like a woman, or a woman like a man; in the one the original personality has entirely disappeared and left room for a new, in the other the two personalities alternate. But all these conditions have one thing in common: they are manifestations of a partial or total metamorphosis of the sense of organism, the firm, granitic foundation on which individuality rests. "Tel organisme, telle personnalité." But *what* are the physical changes *in which* they consist? No one knows (Th. Ribot, *Les Maladies de la personnalité*).

As with consciousness, so with the will. The latter is no more than the former an abstract entity like a mathematical point. Just as consciousness is a series of states of consciousness, the will is a series of volitional acts. The will has a very simple origin, namely the biological property innate in all living material known as irritability, that is, reaction to outside influences, the physiological form of *lex inertiæ*. The type of the volitional act is reflex action. In other words, the volitional act is not the beginning but the conclusion, not cause but result. In every such act there are two distinct elements and phases: willing and acting, a state of consciousness embodying an inclination, and an especially complicated psychophysiological mechanism, in which alone the power later resides to act or to refrain from acting. To act or to refrain, for the volitional act can also take the form of the power to leave undone, although this deviation of the nervous current from its course is not a primitive fact but is of a secondary character, the only result of which is a lower level of action. But how can an idea produce movement? The connection is not to be found between an idea and a movement, but between two states of the same kind, between two physiological states, between two groups of nerves, the one belonging to the area of sensitivity, the other to that of movement. For it is feelings that govern man; ideas as such, in and of themselves, have an extremely weak disposition toward being converted into action, a circumstance in which an explanation may also be sought for the fact that it is *one thing* to feel what is good and *another* to do it, *one thing* to see the absurdity of a doctrine, *another* to liberate oneself from it, *one thing* to censure passion, *another* to renounce it.

The volitional act, however, is not merely a simple transference of a state of consciousness to movement or the power quite simply to refrain: it is at the same time a particular individual's reaction. Volitional acts are adjusted in a way that is highly variable and very complicated, different for different individuals and for the same individual at different times. There is in this respect a choice to be made. Looked at in its formal aspect, a volitional act is admittedly nothing other than a judgment. But in its substance, its nature, it has some relation to the fact that iron is attracted to a magnet and that some insectivorous plants select certain bodies for food to the exclusion of others. Presumably, the resemblance in molecular structure of that which selects to that which is selected is decisive. This affinity holds good for man with respect to virtue and vice, and so forth. Thus the basis for the kind of choice made is precisely that which constitutes the character of the individual, that which differentiates this individual from other individuals. And what constitutes his uniqueness as an individual is his affective structure, the particular way he feels, the persistent tone of his organism.

To will is thus to make a choice in order to act. The anomalies within the world of the will are therefore of two kinds: either the impulse is wanting, so that no act occurs (*aboulie; agoraphobie; Grübelsucht, folie de doute*); or the impulse is so short and intense that it prevents the choice from being made, bypasses it, and is converted into action at once; or finally, the will totally disappears, so that there is neither willing nor acting (ecstasy; somnambulism).

The law for the pathology of the will, on the genesis of which it is based, is this: deterioration proceeds regressively from the more voluntary and the more complex to the less voluntary and the simpler—in other words, to the automatic. The point that comes last in evolution is the first in the process of deterioration. Precisely the same law applies in the pathology of the memory: forgetfulness first affects words, that is, rational discourse, then exclamatory phrases, interjections, what Max Müller calls emotional language, and finally, in certain rare cases, gestures. This law is in fact the same great overriding biological law, according to which the functions that were last to appear are the first to degenerate, in the individual as well as in the species. (Th. Ribot, *Les Maladies de la volonté.*)

There is a numerous class of persons that modern mental pathology classifies under a common heading: degenerates. They are sick people, born with a certain disposition which only awaits favorable circumstances in order to become manifest in abnormal impulses or criminal acts. They betray definite bodily anomalies, possess in general external peculiarities of the skull and face, of the trunk and limbs, the common characteristic of which is their asymmetry. The symptoms are numerous and appear sometimes in isolation, sometimes in greater or smaller combinations, but they are all to be regarded as shoots from one and the same stem; they range all across the whole spectrum of the degenerate temperament. The degenerate type has many variations, yet all the way from the idiot to the individual afflicted with "moral insanity" though with unimpaired and sometimes even superior intellect, the same distinguishing features recur. The degenerate person is a sick person. He is governed in everything by his inherited disposition, he cannot act otherwise, he commits follies and crimes through the same necessity that results for example in his beard being thin or his teeth growing crooked. No treatise in defense of free will can stand up against the anatomical fact that more or less of this or that part of the brain generates more or less of this or that definite amount of reflective thought and instinctive action. In general it can be said that every depraved and unnatural tendency that cannot be explained by some fateful influence from society or the family milieu is an infallible sign of degeneration. The majority of famous criminals are recruited among the degenerate. The morally insane, the sexually perverted, the born criminal (*criminel-né*) are degenerates. Probably the symptoms of degeneration are atavistic relapses. For there is the one and the same prototype for the *criminel-né,* the "morally insane," the epileptic, prehistoric man, and certain half-savage peoples. This type appears in the midst of our civilization like a *revenant* from the days of barbarism, and whoever betrays these traits may be likened to those animals which though born of ancestors long since tamed suddenly relapse into the complete unrestraint of their original wild condition. (H. Saury, *Étude clinique sur la folie héréditaire* ⟨*les dégénérés*⟩; Lombroso, *Der Verbrecher* ⟨*Uomo delinquente*⟩.)

It is against this background of modern research that I wish to place Poe's characters. I must, however, confine myself to a few typical examples.

"William Wilson" is one of Poe's well-known short stories. The main character is a young man whom we first meet while he is attending an English school, where because of his personal superiority he is treated like a king by his comrades. By all but one. Another young man, looking as though he were his twin brother, was enrolled the same day in the school. He resembles him in everything —clothes, gestures, bodily height and figure, the intonation and timbre of the voice—as a good copy resembles the original. He turns out to have been born on the same day and goes by the same name, William Wilson. A most peculiar relationship develops between these two: the first feels hatred for his namesake, who, unlike his other schoolmates, will not bow to his rule—a hatred mixed with a certain fear; and in the other's unruffled superciliousness there is, beneath all his scorn and all his perceptions, a certain concealed affection. Meanwhile they become inseparable companions. Despite everything, the real William Wilson feels irresistibly drawn to his namesake; there is something about the latter that conjures up dim memories from his childhood, memories from a time when the memory was not yet born; it is as though he has known the other from very long ago.

In the meantime he leaves school and goes to the university. Here he gives free rein to the base tendencies that are inherent in his nature and hurls himself into youthful excesses. One night he has arranged a wild party in his rooms which goes on hour after hour. Toward daybreak, just as the host makes ready to propose some sort of blasphemous toast, the door is suddenly thrown open and a servant's shrill voice is heard outside announcing the arrival of a visitor. The host, expecting some new hilarity, arises and staggers out to the vestibule. In the small, low room no light is admitted but for the dim rays entering through a semicircular window. But in the darkness he becomes aware of a young man his own height and dressed just like himself. At the same moment he steps over the threshold, the stranger hurriedly approaches, seizes him by the arm with an impatient gesture and whispers in his ear: "William Wilson!"

Two years pass. A game of cards is arranged in the rooms of a friend of Wilson's, where the latter, who has taken to fleecing wealthy young men by cheating at cards, has determined to empty the purse of a newcomer rolling in wealth. In this he succeeds; the young man sits pale as death, and the others in the party stand mute around the two players. Then the doors are thrown wide open, and the lights go out as though by magic. In the darkness Wilson catches sight of a person his own height; and in a voice that cuts to the quick, a voice he knows well, the voice of his schoolmate and namesake, his own voice, the stranger reveals to those present Wilson's artful dodges, shows them how they may find proof of his guilt in cards concealed among his clothes, and disappears.

Wilson is obliged to leave the university. He roams the world over to flee his mysterious and awful namesake, but in vain. The latter follows him wherever he goes like his own shadow. He turns up whenever the wretched Wilson least expects him.

It is carnival season in Rome. Wilson, half drunk with wine, is planning an amorous adventure with a young married woman, when he feels a hand placed upon his shoulder and hears a whispering in his ear. In a frenzy he seizes hold of his pursuer, drags him into an adjoining room and runs his sword through him. "At that instant some person tried the latch of the door. I hastened to prevent an intrusion, and then immediately returned to my dying antagonist. But what human language can adequately portray *that* astonishment, *that* horror which possessed me at the spectacle then presented to view? The brief moment in which I averted my eyes had been sufficient to produce, apparently, a material change in the arrangements at the upper or farther end of the room. A large mirror, —so at first it seemed to me in my confusion—now stood where none had been perceptible before; and as I stepped up to it in extremity or terror, mine own image, but with features all pale and dabbled in blood, advanced to meet me with a feeble and tottering gait.

"Thus it appeared, I say, but was not. It was my antagonist—it was Wilson, who then stood before me in the agonies of his dissolution. His mask and cloak lay, where he had thrown them, upon the floor. Not a thread in all his raiment—not a line in all the marked and singular lineaments of his face which was not, even in the most absolute identity, *mine own!*

"It was Wilson; but he spoke no longer in a whisper, and I could have fancied that I myself was speaking while he said:

" '*You have conquered, and I yield. Yet henceforward art thou also dead—dead to the World, to Heaven, and to Hope! In me didst thou exist—and, in my death, see by this image, which is thine own, how utterly thou hast murdered thyself.*' "

This is a case of doubling of the personality; analogies in quantity may be found in modern pathology. There are two separate centers of personality in Wilson from which two coexisting persons simultaneously develop. Because of sickness in the physical stratum of the personality, the moral sentiment, the monitory voice of conscience, has been shifted outside the organism and assumes a separate existence at precisely those moments when this sentiment and this voice are made most perceptible through contrast with the excesses of base tendencies. The short story is told in the first person and the narrator asks himself: "Have I not indeed been living in a dream? And am I not now dying a victim to the horror and the mystery of the wildest of all sublunary visions?" It can all be interpreted as an allegory, a personification of two sides of human nature, a conflict of good and evil within the individual; but the psychology is no less profound, the pathological truth is no less clear. But it is in that case a moral allegory for which parallels are constantly provided in reality. And that being so, surely it is not inappropriate to speak of allegories?

In "The Tell-Tale Heart" the narrator describes the murder of an old man which he has committed without knowing why, driven by forces whose nature was unknown to him but which were stronger than his will power. "It is impossible to say how first the idea [of murder] entered my brain; but once conceived, it haunted me day and night. Object there was none. Passion there was none. I loved the old man. He had never wronged me. He had never given me insult. For his gold I had no desire. I think it was his eye! yes, it was this! One of his eyes resembled that of a vulture—a pale blue eye, with a film over it. Whenever it fell upon me, my blood ran cold; and so by degrees—very gradually—I made up my mind to take the life of the old man, and thus rid myself of the eye forever." The intellect of this degenerate, this murderer afflicted with "moral insanity," is fully intact. He sets about his deed with all requisite care. Seven nights in succession he steals at midnight into the old man's chamber and nicely adjusts his lantern so that the light falls on the vulture eye; "but I found the eye always closed; and so it was impossible to do the work; for it was not the old man who vexed me, but his Evil Eye." On the eighth night, just at the hour of midnight, he is standing again with his lantern in the old man's chamber. The old man has awakened and called out, "Who's there?" but the murderer is as quiet as a mouse. Then he hears a groan, not the groan of hunger or of grief, but the groan of deathly fear from the old man lying transfixed, motionless, in paralyzing terror. An hour goes by. Then the murderer decides to open a slit in the lantern, at first only a little, then more and still more, until at last a single dim ray like the thread of a spider falls upon the vulture eye. It is open, wide open. And the murderer hears a strange sound, a low, dull, quick sound like a watch enveloped in cotton. It is the beating of the old man's heart. Quicker and quicker it beats, ever louder and louder. Then the murderer is seized by terror at the night, at the silence, and in a frenzy throws the lantern wide open with a shriek, hurls the old man against the bed, smothers him and buries him under the floor boards. At four o'clock, there is a knocking at the door. Three policemen enter. Neighbors have heard a shriek, and an investigation is under way. The murderer experiences a morbid, wild, triumphant joy at having eradicated all traces of the crime, is excessively courteous to the police, boastful, arrogant, defiantly insolent, as he leads them about the house, invites them to sit down, and so on. But it is a nervous, fitful exhilaration bordering on horror, on madness. Suddenly he hears a sound, faint at first, then more distinct, a low, dull, quick sound as from a watch enveloped in cotton. He paces back and forth in the room, he swings the chair over his head—but the sound grows and grows. The policemen smile, as though they heard, suspected, knew. And the sound grows and grows, louder, louder, louder. " 'Villains,' I shrieked, 'dissemble no more! I admit the deed!—tear up the planks!—here, here!—it is the beating of his hideous heart!' "

It is, as we see, a story of a degenerate who commits murder with no *ratio sufficiens* whatever. He murdered from the same puerile compulsion that makes some people touch some object or other a certain number of times; there is no difference in kind between these phenomena, only in degree. He is one of those individuals who demonstrate by their actions that there is no definite boundary between the sick and the criminal, that the human will is the frailest of all vessels, that it is out of the unknown, ungoverned depths in human nature, from the hazy realm of unconscious impulses that the sibylline words of madness, which are the laws of mankind, come. And when the deed is done, another phenomenon of degeneration follows in its tracks which redounds as little to the moral honor of the sick man as murder redounds to his moral disgrace: the inexplicable and irrepressible need to reveal the crime himself. It is nemesis, if you will; but it is not a question of responsibility, provided that we do not speak of the responsibility of a madman.

What is more, Poe himself has presented this modern theory in "The Imp of the Perverse." "In the consideration of the faculties and impulses—of the *prima mobilia* of the human soul, the phrenologists have failed to make room for a propensity which, although obviously existing as a radical, primitive, irreducible sentiment, has been equally overlooked by all the moralists who have preceded them. In the pure arrogance of the reason, we have all overlooked it. We have suffered its existence to escape our senses, solely through want of belief—of faith;—whether it be faith in Revelation, or faith in the Kabbala. The idea of it has never occurred to us, simply because of its supererogation. We saw no *need* of the impulse—for the propensity. We could not perceive its necessity. We could not understand, that is to say, we could not have understood, had the notion of this *primum mobile* ever obtruded itself;—we could not have understood in what manner it might be made to further the objects of humanity, either temporal or eternal." We should "admit, as an innate and primitive principle of human action, a paradoxical something, which we may call *perverseness*, for want of a more characteristic term. In the sense I intend, it is, in fact, a *mobile* without motive, a motive not *motiviert*. Through its promptings we act without comprehensible object." For purposes of illustration, Poe then refers to some instances to which closely related analogues in the works cited above can be found. In this regard, by means of his lucid intuition the American poet has anticipated modern mental pathology. What he calls perverseness coincides exactly with what is designated in Saury by the term degeneration.

In the area in the psychology of sickness which is Poe's specialty—namely, dread of life and horror of death—he has received the best possible corroboration from the scholar who more than anyone else in our time has devoted himself to this problem. Professor Mosso of Turin says in his extremely fine treatise *La Peur*—I am not acquainted with the original title in Italian—: "Edgar Poe, the unfortunate poet . . . may be considered one of those who have studied the effects of fear. No one has described it in greater detail, no one has known better to analyze and to make us perceive more agonizingly the anguish of feelings which stupefy, the tremors which break the heart and agitate the soul, the anxiety which chokes in the throes of death."

It is this *horror* that we encounter throughout Poe's work like the glazed look of terror in an eye. It may be the dread of being alone, the fear that so grips "The Man of the Crowd" that he roams nightlong the worst slums of the world's greatest city, among the rabble and the vileness only in order to feel the people around him, exactly as it pursues the old poet in Maupassant's "Bel-Ami." It may be anguish at the thought of dying a mock death and of being buried alive, as described in "The Premature Burial"—an *idée fixe* that haunts the unhappy man like a nightmare. It may be fear that is nothing but the fear of fear itself, as in the hero of "The Fall of the House of Usher": " 'I shall perish, . . . I *must* perish in this deplorable folly. Thus, thus, and not otherwise, shall I be lost. I dread the events of the future, not in themselves, but in their results. I shudder at the thought of any, even the most trivial, incident, which may operate upon this intolerable agitation of soul. I have, indeed, no abhorrence of danger, except in its absolute effect—in terror. In this unnerved, in this pitiable, condition I feel that the period will sooner or later arrive when I must abandon life and reason together, in some struggle with the grim phantasm, FEAR.' " It may even at times be the element in horror that is pleasure, the voluptuous shiver in the midst of dread.

VI

No doubt many who have read the foregoing will ask themselves in wonder: but has this poet nothing to say then about just that which has provided all his fellow artists with a profusion of material and has been an inexhaustible mine for all poets: woman and love? I have intentionally saved this subject to the last. For I believe that the feminine ideal of every artist represents the kind of beauty he admires, the same beauty that is to be glimpsed in his ideal of art. I am convinced that a writer's general outlook on life nowhere receives so distinct expression as in his portrayal of the relationship between the sexes. It is in love that human nature most fully reveals itself; and the literature concerning this most intimate of all of life's relationships gives to the delineation of individuality the features of a plaster mask.

Poe applies to woman as well as to art Bacon's words that in all beauty there is an element of strangeness. What appears in nearly all of Poe's women is sorrow and a mysterious expression in the eyes. The relationship between his men and women has a morbid, overstrung, nerve-shattering intensity as well as the horror that turns his people into pillars of stone. His Adam is a degenerate, and his Eve is the personification of the mystery under whose sphinx-like gaze the sick man stares himself to madness. His Venus is not the buxom priestess of sensuality, nor the goddess of wholesome, natural, happy love; she glides through the world as a shadowy figure glides through the night, furtive and ominous as a ghostly vision, or sits white in the moonlight like a musing spirit.

They live in "the Valley of the Many-Colored Grass," by the "River of Silence"—he, his cousin, and her mother. As the two young people roam in the woods, the God Eros awakens in them the hot blood of their ancestors. They love, and all things are transformed. Flowers burst open on trees which never before have borne flowers; the grass acquires a deeper shade of green than before, exotic birds flit through the landscape, and the brook hums a melody excelled in sweetness only by the voice of Eleonora. But she—she soon begins to tell of the fate which hangs over mankind like a veil of sorrows: the mortality of all things; and this theme recurs again and again, like the one and the same image in a poem. It is Death speaking through her, Death that already spreads deep shadows over her soul. She fears that when she is gone he will leave "the Valley of the Many-Colored Grass" and choose a girl from the outer, everyday world; but then he swears to her by her memory and by heaven that he will never love a daughter of Earth. And so she dies, and he leaves the valley, and he loves a woman in the outside world. And one night he hears a familiar, sweet voice whispering in the silence: " 'Sleep in peace! For the Spirit of Love reigneth and ruleth, and, in taking to thy passionate heart her who is Ermengarde, thou art absolved, for reasons which shall be made known to thee in Heaven, of thy vows unto Eleonora.' "

If Eleonora is a phantom on the meadows in summer moonlight, Ligeia resembles a will-o'-the-wisp at black midnight. Her beauty has the radiance of an opium dream, her hair is as black as a crow, her skin has the whiteness of ivory, her profile is like those on Hebrew medallions. But the miracle of all miracles is Ligeia's eyes. In them resides the secret of beauty to which Bacon alludes. In this slender, hysterical woman, they are black, morbidly large gazelle-eyes. Her lover struggles an entire midsummer's night to comprehend their expression, for in that, he feels, lies the secret. He conceives himself to be close to it at times, but the next moment he is once again distant from it. And he ponders and ponders. He sees those eyes everywhere; he encounters them wherever he turns his thoughts and his gaze, wherever he turns his steps; they fill the whole world. He sees them in the clinging tendrils of a vine, in the sight of a butterfly, in running waters. He sees them in the ocean, in a falling meteor, in some of the stars in the sky. He receives from them the same impressions that come from certain notes on string instruments and from certain passages in books, especially this one: "Man doth not yield himself to the angels, nor unto death utterly, save only through the weakness of his feeble will." Herein lies the secret: the passionate will that glows beneath her placid, chilly surface like the fires of Iceland's volcanoes beneath the snow. It is a steely will tempered by the fires within, a will of passion defying death itself. When she is gone, and he whom she has loved loves another, she slips a drop of the essence of her own nature in her rival, a drop which metamorphoses her, kills her personality, inoculates instead her own, until out of the woman's dying body Ligeia ascends like the phoenix out of the ashes. Can the meaning of this symbol be other than the idea that a man who has loved *one* woman with every fiber of his soul shall never love another woman and that

—no matter how much he believes he loves this or that other woman —it is nevertheless only she, the first one, the dead one, whom he loves in the others? But as always in Poe, this truth has been clad in the colors and features of an intense vision.

The third member of the clover leaf is Berenice. The symptom of degeneration from which her lover suffers is that his subtle mind broods over every sort of trifle and that his most burning irresistible desires are directed to the most worthless and meaningless ends. His feelings never arose in the heart, and his passions were all of the reason. She was for him not the Berenice who lived and breathed, but the Berenice of his dreams, not a woman of this earth but a shadowy figure, not a being to love but a thing to analyze. But deeply pitying her desolation and with the thought that she has loved him long, he proposes marriage to her.

Then one day before the day of the wedding, a mild, dead-calm, and misty winter afternoon, he sat in his library. As he lifted up his eyes, Berenice stood before him. "Was it my own excited imagination—or the misty influence of the atmosphere—or the uncertain twilight of the chamber—or the gray draperies which fell around her figure—that caused in it so vacillating and indistinct an outline? I could not tell. She spoke no word; and I—not for worlds could I have uttered a syllable. An icy chill ran through my frame; a sense of insufferable anxiety oppressed me; a consuming curiosity pervaded my soul; and, sinking back upon the chair, I remained for some time breathless and motionless, with my eyes riveted upon her person. Alas! its emaciation was excessive, and not one vestige of the former being lurked in any single line of the contour. My burning glances at length fell upon the face.

"The forehead was high, and very pale, and singularly placid; and the once jetty hair fell partially over it, and overshadowed the hollow temples with innumerable ringlets, now of a vivid yellow, and jarring discordantly, in their fantastic character, with the reigning melancholy of the countenance. The eyes were lifeless, and lustreless, and seemingly pupilless, and I shrank involuntarily from their glassy stare to the contemplation of the thin and shrunken lips. They parted; and in a smile of peculiar meaning, *the teeth* of the changed Berenice disclosed themselves slowly to my view. Would to God that I had never beheld them, or that, having done so, I had died!"

For when she has disappeared, the vision of those teeth remains with him. And it continues to stay with him like a ghost in white. They haunt him with their unbearable whiteness—["]not a speck on their surface, not a shade on their enamel, not an indenture in their edges.["] He sees them a thousand times more clearly in this vision than he saw them in reality, when they were revealed to him for the first time. "The teeth!—the teeth!—they were here, and there, and everywhere, and visibly and palpably before me; long, narrow, and excessively white." They turn him into a full-fledged monomaniac. Nothing exists for him in the world but those teeth. He longs for them in a frenzy. All his other interests are submerged and disappear in the vision of the teeth now surrounding him on all sides like an expanse of sea. They form the core and substance of his psychic life. "I held them in every light. I turned them in every attitude. I surveyed their characteristics. I dwelt upon their peculiarities. I pondered upon their confirmation. I mused upon the alteration in their nature. I shuddered as I assigned to them, in imagination, a sensitive and sentient power, and, even when unassisted by the lips, a capability of moral expression. Of Mademoiselle Salle it has been well said: '*Que tous ses pas étaient des sentiments,*' and of Berenice I more seriously believed *que tous ses dents étaient des idées. Des idées!*—ah, here was the idiotic thought that destroyed me! *Des idées!*—ah, *therefore* it was that I coveted them so madly! I felt that their possession could alone ever restore me to peace, in giving me back to reason."

She dies of epilepsy, and what he has been engaged in since her burial, not even he can say; nothing remains from that event but a memory replete with veiled horror. But in the evening there is a light tap on his door, and ["]pale as the tenant of the tomb, a menial entered upon tiptoe.["] "His looks were wild with terror, and he spoke to me in voice tremulous, husky, and very low. What said he?—some broken sentences I heard. He told of a wild cry disturbing the silence of the night—of the gathering together of the household—of a search in the direction of the sound; and then his tones grew thrillingly distinct as he whispered me of a violated grave—of a disfigured body enshrouded, yet still breathing—still palpitating— *still alive!*

"He pointed to my garments; they were muddy and clotted with gore. I spoke not, and he took me gently by the hand: it was indented with the impress of human nails. He directed my attention to some object against the wall. I looked at it for some minutes: it was a spade. With a shriek I bounded to the table, and grasped the box that lay upon it. But I could not force it open; and, in my tremor, it slipped from my hands, and fell heavily, and burst into pieces; and from it, with a rattling sound, there rolled out some instruments of dental surgery, intermingled with thirty-two small, white, and ivory-looking substances that were scattered to and fro about the floor."

Poe's fiction is as beautiful as this woman, beautiful as hectic fever, beautiful as madness, beautiful as horror, beautiful as doomsday. It sends a shudder of pleasure through our marrow and bones, but a pleasurable shudder of dread as though we saw the universe extending before us beyond measure, without end like a single expanse of sunlight, and out over this expanse there suddenly fell a shadow so inexpressibly, unembraceably great that nothing in heaven or earth can cast such a shadow save for one thing: *Death.*

[The essay concludes with a translation of all of "Shadow—A Parable" less the title and epigraph.]

INDEX

Peripheral references to persons and places have not been included. Poe titles are given under the entries for Poe; all others appear alphabetically. The letters æ and ä have been treated as ae, ø and ö as oe; å has been treated as aa, and ü as ue.

"Æstetiske Idiosynkrasi, Den" [The esthetic idiosyncrasy], 158–159
Allen, Hervey, 154
Andersen, Tryggve, 46–47
Andersen, Vilhelm, 4
"Andliga produktionssätt" [Methods of literary composition], 64, 96–97
Angstens dikter [The poet of anguish], 154–156
Antikt ideal [Ancient ideal], 145
Apollinaire, Guillaume, 149, 150
"Arabesk, En" [An arabesque], 19–20
Aurevilly, Barbey d'. See d'Aurevilly, Barbey

Ballin, Mogens, 38
Balzac, Honoré de, 10, 82
"Banalt" [Banal], 151
Bang, Herman: as author of early décadent novel, 29, 78; interest in Poe, 22–23
Barrès, Maurice, 53
Battle of brains: associated by Strindberg with Poe, 117–121, 123, 127, 129, 132, 133, 137–138; compared with situations in Poe's fiction, 121, 123, 125; defined, 109–111; in "Hjärnornas kamp," 109–110; in I havsbandet, 137; in "Paria," 115–116; in Rosmersholm, 126; in "Sam-

um," 133–134; in Strindberg's personal relationships, 110–117, 118, 121, 127, 128–129, 138, 141; in Tschandala, 113–115
Baudelaire, Charles: cited as Poe authority in Denmark, 5, 15, 40, in Sweden, 5, 54, 62, 70, 71, 72, 78, 80, 81, 91, 165, 180; reputation and influence in Denmark, 5, 15, 27, 31, 39, 159, in France, 5, 7, 24, 25, 66 n. 3, 82, 88, 104, in Norway, 5, 152, 153, in Sweden, 5, 145, 146, 151
Bernheim, Hippolyte, 11, 26, 90, 108, 115
Beyle, Marie Henri. See Stendhal
Bjørnson, Bjørnstjerne, 9, 10, 43
Bjørnvig, Thorkild, 158–160, 161
Bjurman, Gunnar, 143
Bonnier, Karl Otto, 120, 132
Bourget, Paul: as conveyer of Ribot's psychology to Swedish writers, 86–87; as theorist of décadence, 25, 88; conservative in French culture, 53; criticism of, in Norway, 44n; criticism of, in Sweden, 76, 77, 81, 101, 102, 119, 120, 127, 130, 199
Brandell, Gunnar, 111, 134–135, 136
Brandes, Edvard, 9
Brandes, Ernst, 32

Poe (*Continued*)

Hansson, 72, 215–217, by Møller, 40; parallels to, in Jacobsen,
20

"Black Cat, The,": as possible
source for Strindberg, 105n, 124
n. 22; cited by Mortensen, 140;
interpreted by Davidson, 135;
translation of, 14, 15, 54 n. 20

"Cask of Amontillado, The": as
possible source for Strindberg,
105n; interpreted as battle of
brains, 122, 123, 127; translation
of, 14, 33 n. 39, 54 n. 20

"City in the Sea, The," as possible
influence on Fröding, 60

"Coliseum, The," translation of, 62
n. 37

"Colloquy of Monos and Una,
The": cited by Hansson, 174; related to theme in Strindberg's
plays, 138

"Descent into the Maelström, A,"
translation of, 14n, 15, 54 n. 20

"Diddling Considered as One of the
Exact Sciences," cited by Hansson, 192

"Domain of Arnheim, The," cited
by Hansson, 188–189

"Dream within a Dream, A": as
possible influence on Ekelund,
148 n. 11; translation of, 62 n. 37

"Eldorado," translation of, 62 n. 37

"Eleanora": cited by Hansson, 72,
198, 213; illustrated by Martini,
154; parallels to, in Jacobsen, 20;
translation of, 15

"Eureka": cited by Hansson, 186,
196; cited by Kjær, 51; quoted by
Jørgensen, 36–37

"Facts in the Case of M. Valdemar,
The," cited by Hansson, 200;
translation of, 54 n. 20; unmen-
tioned by Strindberg, 122

Poe (*Continued*)

"Fall of the House of Usher, The":
cited by Hansson, 89, 212, by
Kjær, 51, by Nærup, 142; related
to *I havsbandet*, 137; translation
of, 54 n. 20

"Gold Bug, The": cipher in, 129;
cited by Strindberg, 117, 118,
119, 121, 122, 123, 125, 127,
139; cited by Hansson, 191; interpreted as battle of brains, 121,
127, 137; possible influence on
"En Paria," 95, on *I havsbandet*,
134–135, on "Silvertrasket," 137
n. 41; translation of, 14n, 15, 54
n. 20

"Hans Phaall": cited by Hansson,
195; translation of, 54 n. 20

"Imp of the Perverse, The": cited
by Bjørnvig, 160, by Hansson, 71,
210–211; possible influence on
"En Paria," 95; possible parallel
to passage in Strindberg, 108 n.
7; recalled by Jørgensen, 38; referred to, by Hansson to Strindberg, 130

"Island of the Fay, The," cited by
Hansson, 71, 191, 193–194

"Landor's Cottage," cited by Hansson, 189; translation of, 38

"Lenore," translation of, 62 n. 37

"Ligeia": cited by Hansson, 72,
214–215, by Kjær, 51, by Mortensen, 140, by Nærup, 142, by
Rasmussen, 155; echoed in Jacobsen poem, 19; illustrated by Martini, 154; unread by Strindberg,
127, 138 n. 44

"Loss of Breath," cited by Hansson,
175

"Maelzel's Chess-Player," cited by
Hansson, 191

"Man of the Crowd, The," cited